SUSTAINABLE DEVELOPMENT GOALS

CONTEMPORARY STUDIES IN ECONOMIC AND FINANCIAL ANALYSIS

Series Editor: Simon Grima

CONTEMPORARY STUDIES IN ECONOMIC AND
FINANCIAL ANALYSIS   VOLUME 113B

SUSTAINABLE DEVELOPMENT GOALS: THE IMPACT OF SUSTAINABILITY MEASURES ON WELLBEING

EDITED BY

RIDHIMA SHARMA
Vivekananda Institute of Professional Studies, India

INDIRA BHARDWAJ
Vivekananda Institute of Professional Studies, India

SIMON GRIMA
University of Malta, Malta; University of Latvia

TIMCY SACHDEVA
Vivekananda Institute of Professional Studies, India

KIRAN SOOD
*Chitkara Business School, Chitkara University, Punjab, India;
Research Fellow, Women Researchers Council (WRC),
Azerbaijan State University of Economics (UNEC)*

AND

ERCAN ÖZEN
University of Uşak, Türkiye

United Kingdom – North America – Japan
India – Malaysia – China

Emerald Publishing Limited
Emerald Publishing, Floor 5, Northspring, 21-23 Wellington Street, Leeds LS1 4DL.

First edition 2024

Reprints and permissions service
Contact: www.copyright.com

British Library Cataloguing in Publication Data
A catalogue record for this book is available from the British Library
Printed and bound by CPI Group (UK) Ltd, Croydon, CR0 4YY

ISBN: 978-1-83549-461-5 (Print)
ISBN: 978-1-83549-460-8 (Online)
ISBN: 978-1-83549-462-2 (Epub)

ISSN: 1569-3759 (Series)

INVESTOR IN PEOPLE

CONTENTS

ABOUT THE EDITORS

Dr Ridhima Sharma is currently working as an Assistant Professor in Vivekananda Institute of Professional Studies-TC. She graduated from Delhi University and went on to complete her MBA (Hons) from the University School of Management, Kurukshetra University. Later, she earned her MPhil Economics and further obtained her Doctorate degree from Banasthali Vidyapith. Her academic excellence is underscored by her achievements as the University Topper during her Master's programme and being honoured with the University gold medal for securing the highest CGPA in her MPhil. Dr Sharma's scholarly contributions extend beyond the classroom, with several articles published in national and international journals, presentations at both national and international conferences and authorship of notable books too. With a wealth of experience in academia, Dr Sharma holds a rich experience of 12 years. Her professional journey also includes impactful roles in the corporate sector, where she held managerial positions in respected banks and corporate houses. She has acted as a convenor and is a member of the scientific programme committee on some International conferences. Her research focus is on relationship management, sustainability, corporate governance and green marketing.

Dr Indira Bhardwaj, Dean & Director, Vivekananda Institute of Professional Studies-TC, is an academician with more than 24 years of teaching and corporate experience across institutions in India. She has done her FDP from IIM Indore and has also worked at IIM Indore as Academic and Research Associate. Her PhD is from AMU, Aligarh in Understanding Corporate Value Using Intellectual Capital Assets and Reporting. Her research interests include Corporate Valuation, Corporate Finance and Banking. Her other areas of interest include Sustainability Management and Sustainability Reporting. She has been a Lady Cadet at OTA Madras for Commission in the Indian Army Education Core. Her corporate work experience includes being a Knowledge Manager with a Forbes KPO EduMetry engaged in Assessment of Learning using Learning outcomes. She has worked as an Assessment Faculty with a few Universities of US and SE Asia including Butler University, U21Global, UniSIM Singapore, George Washington University, University of Northern Iowa, Sonoma State University and Capella University during her tenure with EduMetry. She has also worked as an Assessment Content Developer for Cengage Publications. Currently, she is a Content Developer with GGSIPU for UG Program Curriculum of Business Studies and Content Reviewer with CBSE for Class XII Textbooks. Her work with CBSE includes competency mapping of content and assessments in textbooks and she has created and mapped course outcomes and program outcomes for UG courses of the IP University curriculum of business studies. Her area of expertise is outcomes based education by measuring and managing outcomes attainment using rubrics for the cognitive domain of higher order thinking skills. She is well versed with development of customised rubrics for assessments of course outcomes. She also develops techniques to assess critical thinking skills in students and designs assessments to entice students to think out of the box. She also takes workshops on critical thinking. She has edited four books, written chapters in international books by Springer and published multiple articles in *ABDC Journal* as a part of her research work. She has been a member of CII Committee on Higher Education, ASSOCHAM Council on Skill Development and PHDCCI Committee on Higher Education.

Prof Simon Grima is the Deputy Dean of the Faculty of Economics, Management and Accountancy, Associate Professor and the Head of the Department of Insurance and Risk Management. Simon is also a Professor at the University of Latvia, Faculty of Business, Management and Economics and a Visiting Professor at UNICATT Milan. He served as the President of the Malta Association of Risk Management (MARM) and President of the Malta Association of Compliance Officers (MACO) between 2013 and 2015 and between 2016 and 2018, respectively. Moreover, he is the chairman of the Scientific Education Committee of the Public Risk Management Organization (PRIMO) and the Federation of European Risk Managers (FERMA). His research focus is on Governance, Regulations and Internal Controls and has over 30 years of experience varying between financial services, academia and public entities. He has acted as co-chair and is a member of the scientific program committee on some international conferences and is a chief editor, editor and review editor of some journals and book series. He has been awarded outstanding reviewer for *Journal of Financial Regulation and Compliance* in the 2017 and 2022 Emerald Literati Awards. Moreover, Simon acts as an Independent Director for Financial Services Firms, sits on Risk, Compliance, Procurement, Investment and Audit Committees and carries out duties as a Compliance Officer, Internal Auditor and Risk Manager.

Dr Timcy Sachdeva holds a Doctorate degree in Management, specialising in finance from Guru Gobind Singh Indraprastha University. With a teaching and research experience of 17 years, she has various publications in international Scopus-indexed and ABDC-listed journals. Dr Sachdeva has participated in many national and international conferences and has chaired sessions as well. She is a sought-after trainer for financial econometrics and financial modelling and has conducted many FDPs for faculty and research scholars across India. Dr Timcy Sachdeva is currently working as an Assistant Professor in Vivekananda Institute of Professional Studies, affiliated to Guru Gobind Singh Indraprastha University.

Dr Kiran Sood, a distinguished academic, serves as a Professor at Chitkara Business School, Chitkara University, Punjab, India; Research Fellow, Women Researchers Council (WRC), Azerbaijan State University of Economics (UNEC) and an Affiliate Professor at the University of Malta. She holds a

Ph.D. in Commerce, specialising in the Product Portfolio Performance of General Insurance Companies. With 19 years of professional experience, she joined Chitkara University in 2019 after a notable tenure in four organisations. Dr Sood's impactful contributions extend to publications in reputable journals, presentations at international conferences and editorial roles for esteemed journals, including the *IJBST International Journal of BioSciences and Technology*, MDPI. Her research focuses on regulations, marketing and finance in the insurance sector, with expertise in insurance management, economics and innovation. She has edited over 15 books with renowned international publishers such as Emerald, CRC, Taylor & Francis and IEEE. Dr Kiran Sood exemplifies excellence in academia and research, contributing significantly to her field.

Dr Ercan Özen received his BSc in Public Finance (1994), MSc in Business-Accounting (1997) and PhD in Business Finance (2008) from the University of Afyonkocatepe. Now, he is Professor of Finance in the Department of Finance and Banking, Faculty of Applied Sciences and University of Uşak, Türkiye (Turkey). His current research interests include different aspects of finance. He served as co-editor for more than 15 books by eminent international publishing houses and have publications of more than 100 and participated many international conferences. He is board member of five International conferences and workshops. Besides, he is co-chair of International Applied Social Sciences Congress and co-editor of two international journals (*Journal of Corporate Governance, Insurance, and Risk Management* (JCGIRM) and *Opportunities and Challenges in Sustainability* (OCS)). He is also the certificated accountant, member of Agean Finance Association and member of TEMA (Türkiye Combating Soil Erosion, for Reforestation and the Protection of Natural Resources Foundation.)

ABOUT THE CONTRIBUTORS

Dr Anuj Aggarwal is currently serving as an Assistant Professor in the School of Business Studies at Vivekananda Institute of Professional Studies (VIPS). He has completed his PhD in Business Economics from the Dept. of Business Economics, University of Delhi. His areas of specialisation include Microeconomics, Macroeconomics, the Indian economy, Strategic management, etc. He has co-authored three textbooks and has contributed numerous research papers to journals of national and international repute. He is an avid blogger, keen observer of international socio-economic & political trends, cinema enthusiast and an agent of change.

Dr Nikita Agrawal is currently working as Assistant Professor in VIPS, GGSIPU. Her area of specialisation is Human Resources and Organisational Behaviour.

Sparsh Agarwal is currently pursuing BCom (Hons) degree from the School of Business Studies, Vivekananda Institute of Professional Studies (VIPS). He is passionate about trying out new things and applying them in real-life scenarios. He has developed a variety of creative hobbies including management, empirical analysis, cooking, video editing, illustrations & content writing. He has developed a keen eye for detail, sincerity towards work and is willing to collaborate.

Dr Yamini Agarwal is the Director at Bharati Vidyapeeth (Deemed to be University) Institute of Management and Research in Delhi. With a PhD in Finance from IIT Delhi, she has extensive experience in teaching and research. She is recognised for her expertise in corporate finance, financial modelling, international finance and public finance. Dr Agarwal has published research papers, authored two books and received prestigious awards in the field. She is a sought-after speaker and has participated in national and international conferences.

Dr Aanchal Aggarwal is an Assistant Professor at the Vivekananda Institute of Professional Studies. She won the MBA Gold Medal (Insurance & Risk Management from Amity University, Noida). In the area of marketing and consumer behaviour, she has earned her PhD. She has a Fellowship diploma in non-life insurance from the Insurance Institute of India. Insurance, marketing and research methodology are her areas of competence. She also has an IRDA Principal Officer qualification. She has expertise in the fields of insurance, marketing and research methods with 9+ years of academic experience. She has written books on the general insurance industry's regulatory structure and practice. She has also written numerous research papers on insurance and marketing that are listed in ABDC (B & C) and Scopus.

Dr Nupur Arora is an Assistant Professor in the Department of School of Business Studies, at Vivekananda Institute of Professional Studies. She has a Doctorate in the domain of Marketing (Consumer behaviour). She is a Gold Medalist in her Master program (MBA-Insurance and Risk Management from Amity University, Noida). She has a rich 12-year experience including industry and academia. Her research interests include Online Consumer Behaviour, E-commerce and Social Media marketing. She has published quality research papers in international journals of repute which have been listed in ABDC and indexed in Scopus. Some of her prominent research works have been published in the *Journal of Promotion Management* (ABDC-B, Scopus), *International Journal of Global Fashion Marketing* (ABDC-B, Scopus), *Journal of Promotion Management* (ABDC-B, Scopus) and *South Asian Journal of Business Studies* (Emerald publications, ABDC-C category).

Prof Ipshita Bansal is presently serving as Dean, Faculty of Commerce and Management at Bhagat Phool Singh Mahila Vishwavidyalaya, Sonipat, Haryana. She has also discharged the duties of Dean Academic Affairs, Registrar (Additional Charge) and Proctor of the University. Her most engaging research interests are Indigenous Management Thought and Practices and Women at work. She has published more than 48 papers in journals of repute and 2 books. She had undertaken 2 major University Grant Commission projects. In 2019, she was selected for Leadership Development Program at the Oxford University.

Kashish Beriwal is pursuing BBA from VIPS affiliated with GGSIPU. Her areas of interest are Human Resource Management and Finance.

Dr Anu Bhardwaj is an Assistant Professor in the Department of Management Studies, JIMS, Vasant Kunj, New Delhi. She in an MBA, M. Phil and Doctorate in Marketing from Aligarh Muslim University. She has 18 years of teaching experience and published various papers in journals of national and international repute. She received a research grant from ICSSR on the Project of WASH attitudes in 2019. She has organised and attended various seminars, conferences, workshops and FDPs. Her research interests are Sustainability, CSR, CRM & Consumer Behaviour.

Prof (Dr) Broto R. Bhardwaj is a highly accomplished academic in the fields of Data Analytics, Marketing, Innovation and Entrepreneurship. She has held the position of Professor at Bharati Vidyapeeth Institute of Management and Research in New Delhi. Previously, she served as a Visiting Professor at North Eastern Illinois University in Chicago and Hennepin County College in Minnesota, USA. In addition to her teaching responsibilities, Prof Broto Rauth Bhardwaj is also the Head of the Research Department at Bharati Vidyapeeth Institute of Management and Research. Her expertise and contributions in research are evident through her active participation in national and international conferences, where she has presented research papers. Her work has been published in reputable journals, highlighting her significant contributions to the field.

Nisha Daga is pursuing BBA from VIPS, GGSIPU, Delhi. Her areas of interest are HR, Strategy and Consulting.

Ankita Dawar is a Student of BBA at Vivekananda Institute of Professional Studies. Through Holistic education at VIPS, she has excellent interpersonal industry skills. This helped her in gaining indispensable knowledge.

Kriti Dhingra is an Assistant Professor at VSBS, VIPS. She has a Bachelor's degree in Computer Science with Honours from the University of Delhi. She has completed her post-graduation in Masters of Computer Applications from GGSIPU. She has been a rank holder throughout her studies. She is UGC NET qualified in Computer Science and Applications. Currently, she is pursuing her PhD in Information Technology. With a deep interest in the field of computer science, she has a penchant for teaching IT subjects. Her core areas of interest lie in Knowledge Management, Learning Analytics and Machine Learning. She has numerous publications in various international and national journals of repute. As an author, she has published books on subjects like E-Commerce and Information System Management.

Prof Meenakshi Gandhi has two decades of experience in teaching, research and academic administration. She has served as Dean Research and Dean of the Business School of VIPS. Prof Gandhi is an Executive Alumni of the Oxford University U.K. and successfully completed the Academic Leadership Development Program (LEAP) sponsored by the Ministry of HRD, Govt. of India. She has been recognised for her achievements with the Indira Parekh 50 Women Leaders in Education Award in 2018 and the 100 Most Dedicated Professors Award in 2019 by the World CSR Foundation. Her research interest covers marketing, entrepreneurship, sustainability and gender.

Ayushi Garg is currently pursuing BCom from Chitkara University, Rajpura, Punjab. She has also enrolled herself for KPMG certification.

Jitender Kumar Goyal is an adaptable teacher with 10 years of experience in education. Currently, an Assistant Professor at Bharati Vidyapeeth Deemed University, New Delhi, he is pursuing a PhD in Finance from the same university. With an MBA in Finance, MCOM, ATC from ICAI, and BCOM degrees, his areas of interest include Accounting, Finance, Taxation, and Portfolio and Investment Management. He has presented papers at national and international conferences and published research articles in reputable journals. Jitender Kumar Goyal's vast knowledge and passion for teaching make him an invaluable asset in his areas of specialisation. His commitment to student success and his research contributions make him a highly respected and sought-after educator.

Nancy Gupta is a Research Scholar in the Department of Management Studies at Bhagat Phool Singh Mahila Vishwavidyalaya, Sonipat, Haryana. Her main research interests are in the areas of consumer behaviour, sustainable consumption and green consumption.

Dr Nidhi Gupta is Post Graduate in International Business and PhD in Commerce. Her expertise and interest are in Human Resources, International Business, Economics and Management subjects. She has rich experience in academia and currently working as Head of Department of Management Studies and Director-IQAC in JIMS VK, Delhi. Dr Nidhi Gupta has received a Research grant from ICSSR on the Project of WASH attitudes in 2019. She has authored more than 30 research papers published in various international and national research journals. She has also presented more than 25 research papers at various national and international conferences and won the best research paper award.

Rashi Jain is a PhD Student in Management at Bharati Vidyapeeth Institute of Management and Research, Pune. She holds a Master's degree from Guru Gobind Singh Indraprastha University, where she ranked first in her class. With previous experience as an associate in talent acquisition at an HR IT company, she now works as an Assistant Professor at Bharati Vidyapeeth Institute of Management and Research in New Delhi. Rashi Jain is also a co-author of the book *Fundamentals of Digital Marketing: A Step-by-Step Guide to 'A Complete Coverage of Syllabus of GGSIPU University'* (Kindle Edition), which focuses on the syllabus of Guru Gobind Singh Indraprastha University. She has actively presented research papers at national and international conferences and published them in reputable journals.

Vedant Jaiswal is a highly motivated and driven individual with a great capacity for leadership and problem-solving. He is currently serving as Placement Coordinator at Placement Cell, VSBS, and is also at the core of Hult Prize, 2023. He is a BBA student at VIPS, New Delhi and is experienced in driving campaigns, events and marketing activities for the college. He is passionate about working with people and helping them reach their goals. He is dedicated to building strong relationships and delivering positive results. He is committed to learning and innovation, and is always eager to take on new challenges.

Baljinder Kaur is currently working as Assistant Professor at Chitkara Business School, Rajpura and pursuing PhD in the field of Forensic Accounting. She had been assigned as an academic coordinator for B.COM (International Finance and Accounting) program for two years from 2017–2018 to 2019–2020. She had been assigned added responsibility as 'Activity In charge' during the year 2016–2017. She has done her M.Com from MCM DAV Chandigarh and UGC Net qualified in commerce. She has a teaching experience of seven years and her areas of expertise are Accounting & Finance. Her credentials include more than 15 research papers published and presented in national and international journals and conferences. She has effectively convened national level faculty development programs in the years 2017 and 2022. Recently, she has completed two consultancy projects in the field of operations research.

Parul Manchanda is an Assistant Professor in the Department of School of Business Studies, at Vivekananda Institute of Professional Studies-TC, GGSIPU, New Delhi. She has done her Ph.D. from the University School of Management Studies, Guru Gobind Singh Indraprastha University, Delhi, India. She has a rich 10 years of experience including industry and academia. Her research interests include sustainability, general management and consumer behaviour. She has published quality research papers in reputed international journals, which have been listed in ABDC and indexed in Scopus. Some of her prominent research works have been published in the Journal of Promotion Management (ABDC-B, Scopus) and International Journal of Global Fashion Marketing (ABDC-B, Scopus). She has also developed a forte in developing cases and has published a case study in the Asian Case Research Journal and World Scientific Publishing (Scopus Indexed, Web of Science Indexed, ESCI.

Dr Isha Narula is a Graduate in Commerce from Delhi University and MBA in Finance and International Business from IP University. She has a Doctorate from Jamia Millia Islamia (Centre for Management Studies) in Finance. Her areas of interest are stock market efficiency, behavioural finance and derivatives. She has more than 10 years of teaching and research experience. She has many research papers in national and international journals of high repute. She has presented research papers at many national and international conferences organised by IIMs and other institutes of high repute. She has authored four books on project management, derivatives, business environment and stock market efficiency.

Adarsh Rajput is currently pursuing a B.Com from Chitkara University, Rajpura, Punjab. He has also enrolled himself for KPMG certification.

Kanika Dhingra Sardana is an Associate Professor at IINTM. She has a Bachelor's degree in Physics with Honours from the University of Delhi. She has completed her post-graduation in Masters of Computer Applications from GGSIPU. She is UGC NET qualified in Computer Science and Applications. Her core areas of interest lie in Knowledge Management, Learning Analytics and Machine Learning. She has numerous publications in various international and national journals of repute.

Khushi Sehgal is a Student of BBA at Vivekananda Institute of Professional Studies motivated towards learning and growing professionally. Her academic coursework has equipped her with a solid foundation in business and management principles, possessing skills like leadership, problem-solving, communication and adaptability to make me more proficient.

Poonam Sethi is currently an Associate Professor at Hindu College in the Department of Commerce, University of Delhi. Her teaching experience includes her expertise in handling diverse subjects like microeconomics, macroeconomics, business mathematics, business statistics, Human Resource Management, Indian Economy, Business Laws, etc. She is an Elected Member of the Academic

Council of Delhi University for a period of two years 2023–2025. She is also on the Business Advisory Council of Delhi University for a period of two years 2023–2025. She has several publications to her credit including research papers and chapters in edited books.

Dr Anita Tanwar is working as an Assistant Professor at Chitkara University. She has done her MBA from Maharishi Dayanand University and MPhil & PhD in the area of banking. She has a corporate experience of two years in The Ambala Central Cooperative Bank and an experience of nine years in teaching. Moreover, she has published many research papers in UGC Care-listed journals and Scopus-indexed journals and has attended many national and international conferences and seminars. She has been awarded NCC 'C' certificate and moreover best cadet ward. Furthermore, she is a reviewer in Scopus-indexed journal.

Dr Jatin Vaid is working as an Assistant Professor at VSBS, VIPS. He has about 15 years of academic experience teaching postgraduate and undergraduate man-agement courses and about 3 years of rich corporate experience in managerial positions with Citibank N.A and HSBC in the areas of Wealth Management and Business Banking. Dr Vaid was presented with the 'Best Teacher's Award' for the year 2016–2017 at VIPS. Dr Vaid is an avid researcher and has published a num-ber of research papers in reputed journals. His areas of research include 'Tourism Marketing' and MICE Tourism.

Dr Seema Wadhawan is an Associate Professor with the Department of Management Studies, Jagannath International Management School, Vasant Kunj. She is a PhD in management, and an MBA in HR. She carries a satiating 20+ years of experience comprising of substantial stints in corporate and academia. After foraying into academia, she has continuously worked as a member of core com-mittee for seminars, workshops & conferences and has contributed immensely to quality research through paper publications in national, and international confer-ences and journals, having indexed in SCOPUS, ABDC & UGC Care.

FOREWORD

The UN World Commission on Environment and Development states that 'sustainable development is development that meets the needs of the present without compromising the ability of future generations to meet their own needs'. Additionally, the UCLA Sustainability Committee defines sustainability as 'the integration of environmental health, social equity and economic vitality in order to create thriving, healthy, diverse and resilient communities for this generation and generations to come. The practice of sustainability recognizes how these issues are interconnected and requires a systems approach and an acknowledgment of complexity.' Moreover, the 2030 Agenda for Sustainable Development, adopted by all United Nations Member States in 2015, provides a shared blueprint for peace and prosperity for people and the planet, now and into the future. Sustainable development goals (SDGs) are an urgent call for action by all countries – developed and developing – in a global partnership.

In this book, sustainability issues in society are explored, discussed and presented. It starts with the influence of sustainability communication on consumer loyalty and brand reputation and continues by exploring sustainability in higher education via perceived employability, university commitment, perceived organisational prestige and student satisfaction. The key for sustainable companies is studied by revealing the difficulties in measuring service quality. A chapter follows examining the impact of Financial Technology (Fintech) on environmental, social and governance (ESG) goals to promote a sustainable financial system. The determinants and consumer preferences of sustainable consumption and production adoption among fast-moving consumer goods (FMCG) manufacturers are investigating along with the impact of personality and demographic factors on the relationship between work-life balance and well-being.

The crucial issues of surveillance and the right to privacy for sustainability of digital economy along with the enhancing banking sustainability are studied and important results are emerged. Achieving SDGs by sustainable marketing practices is explored while the importance of corporate social responsibility and its link to a financial performance metric called net interest margin in the context of banks and non-banking financial companies is discussed using a comprehensive sample. The impact of carbon neutrality pledges on Indian companies' stock performance is explored while the influence of Gandhian values' on sustainable consumption behaviour is evaluated. Next, a study of the role of tourism in delivering sustainable solutions for the planet reveals a strategic roadmap to achieve the SDGs through sustainable tourism practices.

Next, sustainability through human resource management (SHRM) is explained as a concept through an extensive literature review along with the evolutionary stages and multi-lateral perspectives of SHRM. Sustainability and Industry 4.0 have influenced the global economy. With the Industrial Revolution 4.0, there has been a significant focus on digital sustainability in enterprises. Micro, small and medium enterprises (MSMEs) are the most vulnerable sections regarding new transformations. Deterrents to digital sustainability in MSMEs are examined and commented. Moreover, the impact of foreign currencies like US dollar, Euro and Japanese yen on the Bombay Stock Exchange and National Stock Exchange Index is explored under the auspice of sustainability. Finally, a study on self-brand connection and brand loyalty as an outcome of sustainable cause-related marketing aims to explore, integrate and interconnect concepts of customer relationship management (CRM) and self-brand connection to get more insights into the imperative role of CRM strategy in developing self-brand connections that can lead to brand loyalty in the most sustainable way.

Overall, the book covers most of the aspects related to the impact of sustainability measures on well-being and therefore it is a valuable handbook and source for students, researcher and academics.

I wish the readers a great learning ahead full of inspiration for further contribution to academia and markets.

Prof. Maditinos Dimitrios
International Hellenic University
Member of European Educational Programs Committee
Kavala University Campus
Department of Management Science and Technology

PREFACE

This book *Sustainable Development Goals: The Impact of Sustainability Measures on Wellbeing* (CSEF 113) will delve into issues such as Environment, Sustainability, Economic Sustainability, Digital Sustainability, Sustainable Finance & Accounting, Social Responsibility and Impact of COVID-19.

When it comes to sustainability and combating our current climate emergency, we need sustainable solutions that can protect our water, energy and food resources while also aiming for zero waste. It is important to remember that sustainability can also be practiced individually as citizens and consumers in the world. This can mean rethinking how you use energy, where your waste goes or how fast fashion affects the environment. Most people don't have control of their governments, businesses or economic circumstances, but they do have opportunities to live more sustainably on a smaller scale.

The global community is at a critical moment in its pursuit of the Sustainable Development Goals (SDGs). More than a year into the global pandemic, millions of lives have been lost, the human and economic toll has been unprecedented, and recovery efforts so far have been uneven, inequitable and insufficiently geared towards achieving sustainable development. The current crisis is threatening decades of development gains, further delaying the urgent transition to greener, more inclusive economies, and throwing progress on the SDGs even further off track. It is abundantly clear that this is a crisis of monumental proportions, with catastrophic effects on people's lives and livelihoods and on efforts to realise the 2030 Agenda for Sustainable Development.

It will first begin by introducing the subject of sustainable development. It will detail the framework to address these gaps and shortages in different disciplines and sectors. The global drivers of change will be analysed and the opportunities and challenges w.r.t attainment of development goals will be investigated. To this end, the book will be enriched and strengthened with real-life situations providing a practical and industry dimension. It is intended to seek experts in Economics, Finance, Public Policy, Human Resources and Risk management who will contribute to this book on employability, sustainability and skills of the future such as green skills from across the globe.

KIRAN SOOD
Chitkara Business School, Chitkara University, Punjab, India; Research Fellow, Women Researchers Council (WRC), Azerbaijan State University of Economics (UNEC)

SIMON GRIMA
Associate Professor, Department of Insurance and Risk Management, Faculty of Economics Management and Accountancy, University of Malta, Msida, Malta and *Professor of Finance at the Faculty of Business, Management and Economics, University of Latvia, Latvia*

CHAPTER 1

INVESTIGATING THE INFLUENCE OF GANDHIAN VALUES ON SUSTAINABLE CONSUMPTION BEHAVIOUR

Nancy Gupta[a], Meenakshi Gandhi[b] and Ipshita Bansal[a]

[a]Bhagat Phool Singh Mahila Vishwavidyalaya, Sonipat, Haryana, India
[b]Vivekananda Institute of Professional Studies, Guru Gobind Singh Indraprastha University, Delhi, India

ABSTRACT

Purpose: *This chapter aims to evaluate the significant impact of Gandhian values on sustainable consumption behaviour (SCB) by applying the value-attitude-behaviour (VAB) framework. This chapter contributes by incorporating Gandhian values as one influencing factor for SCB.*

Need for the Study: *Values are considered as guiding principles in people's lives. Studies suggest that values and other social and psychological factors can be vital in determining consumers' behaviour towards sustainable consumption. There needs to be more empirical research on consumer behaviour facets of sustainable consumption for markets in India.*

Methodology: *The study uses partial least square structural equation modelling to empirically test proposed hypotheses and the research model of the relationship. The study results are based on data collected by administering a survey through a questionnaire confined to India.*

Sustainable Development Goals: The Impact of Sustainability Measures on Wellbeing
Contemporary Studies in Economic and Financial Analysis, Volume 113B, 1–20
Copyright © 2024 by Nancy Gupta, Meenakshi Gandhi and Ipshita Bansal
Published under exclusive licence by Emerald Publishing Limited
ISSN: 1569-3759/doi:10.1108/S1569-37592024000113B001

Findings: *The results indicated that Gandhian values, attitude, and sustainable consumption intention significantly influence SCB. Intention acts as a mediator between both outward and inward environmental attitudes and behaviour. The study provides directions for further research.*

Practical Implications: *This research study is helpful for researchers, marketers, and policymakers.*

Keywords: Sustainable consumption; attitude; intention; Gandhian values; consumer behaviour; responsible consumption; sustainable development goals

JEL Codes: Q01; D11; M31

INTRODUCTION

Due to climate change, excessive consumption, and the growing population, there is an adverse effect on the environment and sustainable development of the nations concerned. Achieving sustainable living is an urgent and complex challenge that is gaining importance nowadays, requiring new ways of thinking to utilise environmentally friendly products. There is a need to explore how humans can radically transform their daily activities, now and into the future. Consumer choices have more impact on the environment than reducing consumption (Ivanova et al., 2016). People are concerned about environmental issues and want to lead more eco-friendly lives. For this, the concern needs to be translated into action. The development in technologies, infrastructure, and social expectations do not prioritise sustainability.

There is a need to engage everybody in acts of sustainable consumption and to maintain a balance between growth and the environment. The paradigm shift in consumption patterns is not sacrificing wants but using them wisely and smartly. Increasing price is a barrier that impacts green consumption. If people are provided real-time information about the impact of action and allow them to decide, then the acts of control in the action can be observed. Lifestyle significantly impacts sustainable consumption behaviour (SCB; Matharu et al., 2021). Individual action on conservation is equally critical for environmental protection.

Sustainability has become a critical concern for producers and consumers to reduce the adverse environmental impact. Consumers are increasing awareness and are interested in sustainable consumption. A higher level of involvement in sustainability issues was associated with a more positive attitude towards purchasing such items. Sustainable consumption leads to psychological well-being (Carrero et al., 2020).

It has been investigated that the market's consumption decision is related to values (Banerjee, 2008). Values play an essential role in the consumption decision-making process. Values are considered to influence the behaviour intention towards sustainability (Ghazali et al., 2018). Values here refer to the principles, beliefs or standards of behaviour that are important in a person's life. Values influence people's thinking about sustainability issues and their behaviour towards purchasing sustainably produced items. According to Thogersen and Olander (2002), human values are vital in determining SCB. It is believed that consumers' attitudes, subjective norms and perceived behaviour control are affected by human values. Many researchers have shown personal values (Homer & Kahle, 1988), environmental values (Kautish & Sharma, 2020) and social values (Biswas & Roy, 2015; Lee et al., 2016) related to sustainable behaviour.

SCB has been studied in various aspects of organic buying (Testa et al., 2019), green purchasing (Ghazali et al., 2018), electric efficient appliances (Waris & Hameed, 2020), second-hand products, reducing consumption, using only when required (switching off lights), and transport (Yang et al., 2020), and socially responsive consumption behaviour (Gandhi & Kaushik, 2016).

Past researchers have studied the impact of values on SCB (Biswas & Roy, 2015; Dermody et al., 2015, 2018; Minton et al., 2015, 2018; Wang et al., 2014). At the same time, some have focused on values and green purchase intention (Amin & Tarun, 2021; Awuni & Du, 2016; Chekima et al., 2016; Qasim et al., 2019; Sheng et al., 2019; Wang et al., 2014; Waris & Hameed, 2020). To our knowledge, researchers have studied sustainable consumption (Sharma & Jha, 2017), but few have investigated the impact of values on the intention to buy green/sustainable products in the Indian context (Biswas & Roy, 2015; Kautish & Sharma, 2019; Kautish et al., 2020). Sharma and Jha (2017) focused on human values and environmental attitudes as mediator-moderators on values concerning SCB. Many researchers have worked on the value-attitude-behaviour (VAB) hierarchy (Jacobs et al., 2018; Sharma & Jha, 2017), but there needs to be more evidence supporting the influence of sustainable consumption intention on SCB.

It has been noted that many scholars emphasised values, utilising Rokeach's (1973) – Value system (RVS), Lynn R. Kahle's (1983) – List of values (LOV), Arnold Mitchell's (1983) – Values and lifestyle system (VALS), Schwartz (1992, 1994) – Value inventory, Hofstede et al. (2010) – five cultural dimensions. The Western value system may not apply in the Indian context (Sharma & Jha, 2017).

Mohandas Karamchand Gandhi (1869–1948), popularly known as Mahatma Gandhi, was India's political and moral leader. He is known for mobilising the masses in his non-violent resistance against British rule in India. His Satyagraha (protest of Truth) against the colonial rule played an important role in India's independence, because of which, he is regarded as the 'Father of the Nation'. He had a unique way of living. Mahatma Gandhi was a believer and a propagator of the ideologies of Ahimsa (non-violence) and Truth. United Nations has even recognised his ideas of sustainable development. The inauguration of Gandhi solar park at United Nations headquarters is a testament to that. For Mahatma Gandhi, food prepared at home is purer than purchased from the market and carrying it while travelling not only saves from many unnecessary needs but also makes life simple and beautiful. He says one of the greatest struggles is against one's inhumanity. He has adhered the numerous messages to humankind. Satya (Truth), Ahimsa (non-violence), Sarvodaya, morality, simplicity, enunciation, Equanimity, Punctuality, Continuous Learning, Service, Humility and Creativity (Bansal & Bajpai, 2011).

Mahatma Gandhi has emphasised the importance of natural resources and their conservation. Gandhian ideas can be helpful to reduce the greed of the individual and society. Thus, it encompassed all living beings and embodied the eternal values of life in his thoughts and actions. Values can be taught through formal education (Hakan et al., 2016) or the usage of role models, and Mahatma Gandhi can be considered a role model (Mishra et al., 2019).

As identified by Mishra et al. (2019), Gandhian values may significantly impact sustainable consumption. However, the impact of Gandhian values on sustainable consumption has yet to be studied.

Research Questions

Do Gandhian values affect sustainable consumption behaviour?

Does intention play a mediating role in the sustainable consumption relationship?

LITERATURE REVIEW AND HYPOTHESES

This chapter relies on the VAB theory (Homer & Kahle, 1988) for a better understanding of the impact of consumers' Gandhian values on their SCB. The VAB theory is based on the approach in which individuals act according to the values they prefer based on the attitude they expect from particular/specific behaviour.

The VAB model has been extensively utilised in comprehending consumer behaviour in various fields, including sustainability crowdfunding (Kim & Hall, 2020), organic food consumption (Kamboj & Kishor, 2022), sustainable clothing (Jacobs et al., 2018) responsible consumption, green purchase behaviour (Cheung & To, 2019), ethical consumption, pro-environmental behaviour and sustainable consumption (Sharma & Jha, 2017). For example, scholars have investigated that value perceptions have an active and crucial role in forming the intention to sustainable consumption by buying eco-friendly products.

Kautish and Sharma's (2019) research on young consumers in the Indian context is based on VAB theory with Terminal and instrumental values and green behavioural intentions. Values are good predictors of behaviour. Attitude mediates the value-behaviour relationship (Homer & Kahle, 1988; McCarty & Shrum, 2001). Hence, this theory's framework posits that values result in specific behaviour.

Research Hypothesis

Values that consumers hold play a significant role in determining their behaviour. It helps in the determination of the attitude of people towards sustainable consumption. Research has shed light on how values influence people's attitudes to behave in a certain way. Vermeir and Verbeke (2006) found values significantly related to attitudes towards buying sustainable products. Researchers found a significant relationship between values and behaviour (Grunert & Juhl, 1995; Karp, 1996; Schultz & Zelezny, 1999; Stern & Dietz, 1994; Stern et al., 1999). For example, scholars have investigated that value perceptions have an active and crucial role in forming SCB (Clawson & Vinson, 1978; Leiserowitz, 2006; Neuman, 1986). In the Indian context, values and SCB are significantly correlated (Sharma & Jha, 2017). Values play a significantly crucial role in shaping individuals' behaviour. Studies have shed light on how values influence people's behaviour towards sustainable consumption (Sharma & Jha, 2017).

Vermeir and Verbeke (2006) found higher values were associated with more positive attitudes towards buying sustainable food products and values significantly related to attitudes towards buying sustainable products. Homer and Kahle (1988) found personal values related to attitude. Prior studies have focused on environmental, social and emotional values to explain consumption. Individuals with environmental concerns try to consume environmentally friendly products, not damaging the environment, and for the well-being of the future generation. Consumers' values and attitudes are strongly associated (Nguyen & Dang, 2022). Thus, we propose:

H1. Gandhian values impact inward environmental attitude.

H2. Gandhian values impact outward environmental attitude.

Attitude refers to an individual's overall evaluation of an object or idea. It reflects the positive or negative evaluation of conducting a specific behaviour (action). A direct, significant positive relationship exists between the attitude and intention to purchase sustainable products (Vermeir & Verbeke, 2008). Several studies confirmed the significant relationship between attitude and intention. Attitude influences intention, which impacts behaviour (Yadav & Pathak, 2017). Researches reveal attitude to be interpreter of intention of engaging in sustainable consumption (Joshi et al., 2019), locally produced food (Chen, 2020), purchasing eco-friendly products (Han et al., 2020), second-hand products (Borusiak et al., 2020), energy-efficient appliances (Apipuchayakul & Vassanadumrongdee, 2020; Bhutto et al., 2021; Zhang et al., 2019), green products (Patel et al., 2020; Wang et al., 2020), organic clothing (Zhang et al., 2019), electric vehicles (Yang et al., 2020), environmentally sustainable (Kang & Moreno, 2020; Kautish & Sharma, 2019; Mandliya et al., 2020), environmentally responsible (Kumar et al., 2021) and collaborative consumption (Bhalla, 2021). Therefore, the study implies the following hypotheses:

H3. Inward Environmental attitude significantly impacts sustainable consumption intention.

H4. Outward Environmental attitude significantly impacts sustainable consumption intention.

The VAB hierarchy suggests that value impacts attitude, which impacts behaviour. Jacobs et al. (2018) found values to impact attitudes towards sustainable clothing, which impacts sustainable clothing purchase behaviour. Minton et al. (2018) found that attitude towards sustainable consumption leads to self-focused sustainable behaviour. Sharma and Jha (2017) have shown in their study that environmental attitude directly impacts SCB. Thus, this study proposes the following hypothesis:

H5. Inward Environmental attitude significantly impacts SCB.

H6. Outward Environmental attitude significantly impacts SCB.

Intention reflects the motivation and willingness to act on the opinion. It is considered as a leading factor for sustainable consumption. In recent years, the quantity of research to sustainable consumption intention has increased rapidly. Therefore, consumers intend to consume the goods and services based on the relevant values. Several researchers have found a significant direct effect of intention on behaviour to sustainable consumption (Saari et al., 2021), actually consuming organic food products (Testa et al., 2019) and direct/indirect pro-environmental (Alzubaidi et al., 2021). Therefore, the hypothesis is:

H7. Sustainable consumption intention impacts SCB.

THE MEDIATING ROLE OF SUSTAINABLE CONSUMPTION INTENTION

Research suggests that a significant causal relationship exists between attitude and intention behaviour (Bagozzi et al., 1989). However, studies on attitudes with intention for sustainable consumption are available (Joshi et al., 2019). Attitude influences intention, impacting behaviour (Yadav & Pathak, 2017). People's attitudes to environmental concerns impact their engagement in sustainable consumption (Piligrimiene et al., 2020). Yarimoglu and Binboga (2019) found that ecologically conscious consumer behaviour impacts intention and conspicuous behaviour. Moreover, ecologically conscious behaviour directly influences green purchase conspicuous behaviour.

The mediating effects of intention have been investigated in many studies (Goriparthi & Tallapally, 2017).

H8. Sustainable consumption intention acts as a mediator between environmental attitude and SCB.

METHODOLOGY

Sample and Data Collection

All the questionnaire items were scored on a 'seven-point Likert scale' from 1 (strongly disagree) to 7 (strongly agree). Table 1 shows the items used in the questionnaire to measure the variables. A total of 680 filled questionnaires were obtained for data analysis by PLS-SEM in Smart PLS Software version 4.0.8.7. PLS-SEM usage is a preferred method in the present analysis for the following reasons. First, data were not normally distributed ($p < 0.001$). Second, the conceptual model contains SCB, a higher-order construct comprising reflective-formative

Table 1. Measurement Scales Used.

Variable	Statements	References
Gandhian values		
Personal values	Self-control is desirable to self-indulgence.	Mishra et al. (2019)
	Peaceful ways of persuasion should be followed.	
	Values are required in day-to-day life.	
	Tolerance for all religion and races is essential.	
Economic values	No job is too low to be undertaken.	
	Scarce resources of society should not be allocated for the production of goods and services used only by small section of society.	
	Labor should not be exploited to maximise production.	
	Reduction of inequality must be undertaken (we must buy products from companies that employ people with disabilities and other groups).	
Leadership values	Participative decision-making process is advisable.	
	Transparency in decision-making process is essential.	
	Empowerment of subordinates is a must to enable them to work productively.	
Social values	Sensitivity towards well-being of others must be practiced while making consumption decisions.	
	Cleanliness leads to prosperity and environmental protection.	
Environmental values	Production should not be at the cost of damaging the environment.	
	The environment should be protected and preserved for the well-being of the future generations.	
Sustainable consumption behaviour		
Affective	I feel good when I can control my whims for buying unnecessary things.	Quoquab and Mohammad (2020)
	I try not to waste food or beverage.	
	I prefer to buy organic food since it is environmentally friendly.	
	I prefer to pay more to purchase environmentally friendly products.	
	I prefer to use paper/jute bags since they are biodegradable.	
	I like to purchase only what I need.	
	I feel happy to give priority to environmental welfare.	
Cognitive	I believe wasting food and other consumables is unethical.	
	I am aware that excess consumption can cause a shortage of natural resources.	
	I believe that it is important to use eco-friendly products and services.	
	I believe that individuals should care for the future generation.	
	I believe that it is our responsibility to care for the natural environment.	
	I know that the natural resources are decreasing at an alarming rate.	

(Continued)

Table 1. (*Continued*)

Variable	Statements	References
Conative	I reduce the misuse of goods and services (e.g. I switch off the lights and the fan when I am not in the room). I purchase environmentally friendly products even though they are slightly expensive. I avoid consumption activities that can lead to environmental pollution. I use biodegradable packages and engage in recycling of bottles and containers (e.g. use of cloth/jute/paper bag instead of plastic bag). I do not waste my food and beverage. I spend my money wisely in order to avoid wastage and excessive purchases. I keep contributing to environmental welfare in all respects. I do not engage in any purchase that can have negative effects on the environment.	
Inward environmental attitude	I am very concerned about the environment. I would be willing to reduce my consumption to help protect the environment. I would give part of my own money to help protect wild animals. I have asked my family to recycle some of the things we use.	Leonidou et al. (2010)
Outwards environmental attitude	Major political change is necessary to protect the natural environment. Anti-pollution laws should be enforced more strongly. Major social changes are necessary to protect the natural environment. Humans are severely abusing the environment.	Leonidou et al. (2010)
Sustainable consumption intention	In future, I will consider adopting a sustainable consumption lifestyle. In future, I will consider switching to other brands for ecological reasons. In future, I plan to switch to a sustainable version of a product.	Joshi et al. (2019)

Source: Compiled by the authors.

modelling. Smart PLS is widely accepted to handle multivariate analytical methods (Hair et al., 2017, 2022; Ringle et al., 2022).

EMPIRICAL RESULTS

Multivariate Normality Distribution and Common Method Bias

To evaluate the normality of distribution, one-sample Kolmogorov–Smirnov test was conducted. The result showed p-value <0.001. Thus, the data distribution lacks normality, fulfilling the assumption to adopt variance-based partial least square structural equation modelling.

Harman's single-factor test was conducted to examine the common method bias in this study (Podsakoff & Organ, 1986). The result shows a total of 35.298% variance, which is less than the benchmark value of 50% variance, indicating that common method bias does not seriously influence this study (Podsakoff et al., 2003).

Reliability and Validity

Gandhian values were investigated by reflective–reflective and SCB by reflective–formative measurement assessments proposed by Mishra et al. (2019) and Quoquab and Mohammad (2020), respectively. For higher-order constructs, a two-stage assessment was done. Initially, the latent variable scores of all Gandhian values and SCB dimensions were assessed. Then, the first-order constructs were applied to measure the second-order construct.

As shown in Table 2, this study tests the internal reliability and convergent validity – factor loadings, Cronbach's α, rho_A, and composite reliability, which were found to exceed 0.70 (Ali et al., 2018; Hair et al., 2017, 2020). The factor loading ranged from 0.53 to 0.92, showing acceptable structure validity of the measurement. In addition, the AVE ranged from 0.537 to 0.860, which are above the standard limit of 0.50, indicating that the convergent validity is established (Fornell & Larcker, 1981; Hair et al., 2019).

Table 2. Quality Criterion for Reflective Model Assessment.

Construct	Items	Type	Loadings/ weights	Cronbach's α	CR	Rho_A	AVE
Personal values	PV1	Reflective	0.54	0.712	0.820	0.755	0.537
	PV2		0.818				
	PV3		0.807				
	PV4		0.734				
Economic values	ECV1	Reflective	0.800	0.798	0.867	0.814	0.621
	ECV2		0.715				
	ECV3		0.807				
	ECV4		0.824				
Leadership values	LV1	Reflective	0.869	0.867	0.918	0.879	0.789
	LV2		0.891				
	LV3		0.904				
Social values	SV1	Reflective	0.924	0.823	0.919	0.823	0.849
	SV2		0.919				
Environmental values	ENV1	Reflective	0.924	0.837	0.925	0.838	0.860
	ENV2		0.931				
Affective	AFFE1	Reflective	0.777	0.865	0.899	0.867	0.597
	AFFE2		0.784				
	AFFE3		0.744				
	AFFE5		0.779				
	AFFE6		0.746				
	AFFE7		0.802				

(Continued)

Table 2.   (*Continued*)

Construct	Items	Type	Loadings/ weights	Cronbach's α	CR	Rho_A	AVE
Cognitive	COG1	Reflective	0.613	0.864	0.899	0.874	0.600
	COG2		0.783				
	COG3		0.804				
	COG4		0.804				
	COG5		0.806				
	COG6		0.817				
Conative	CON1	Reflective	0.734	0.900	0.920	0.904	0.590
	CON2		0.688				
	CON3		0.799				
	CON4		0.800				
	CON5		0.767				
	CON6		0.735				
	CON7		0.796				
	CON8		0.817				
Inward environmental attitude	IEA1	Reflective	0.818	0.816	0.879	0.818	0.645
	IEA2		0.813				
	IEA3		0.776				
	IEA4		0.805				
Outward environmental attitude	OEA1	Reflective	0.798	0.874	0.914	0.878	0.727
	OEA2		0.888				
	OEA3		0.876				
	OEA4		0.844				
Sustainable consumption intention	SCI1	Reflective	0.870	0.865	0.918	0.865	0.788
	SCI2		0.896				
	SCI3		0.896				
Gandhian values	PV	Reflective	0.844	NA	NA	NA	NA
	ECV		0.841				
	LV		0.903				
	SV		0.881				
	ENV		0.851				
Sustainable consumption behaviour	AFFE	Composite	0.903	NA	NA	NA	NA
	COG		0.896				
	CON		0.917				

Source: Authors' calculations.

Discriminant Validity

Using the criteria proposed by Fornell and Larcker (1981) discriminant validity of the measurement was accessed. Table 3 shows that the square root of AVE for the respective constructs exceed the inter-construct correlation values indicating that the measurement model had discriminant validity.

As suggested by HTMT inference, all HTMT values must be less than 1. Most of the HTMT values of all constructs are below 0.90 (Gold et al., 2001). On the liberal side, the HTMT inference was applied where HTMT values exceed 0.90. However, as shown in Table 4, all the values were within the confidence interval limits.

Table 3. Discriminant Validity Assessments.

Construct	AFFE	COG	CON	ECV	ENV	IEA	LV	OEA	PV	SCI	SV
AFFE	**0.772**										
COG	0.698	**0.774**									
CON	0.749	0.741	**0.768**								
ECV	0.361	0.383	0.348	**0.788**							
ENV	0.369	0.451	0.328	0.593	**0.927**						
IEA	0.575	0.519	0.591	0.355	0.315	**0.803**					
LV	0.368	0.412	0.376	0.691	0.730	0.379	**0.888**				
OEA	0.501	0.534	0.478	0.314	0.368	0.603	0.354	**0.852**			
PV	0.370	0.359	0.343	0.711	0.629	0.355	0.681	0.325	**0.733**		
SCI	0.506	0.532	0.532	0.336	0.326	0.616	0.348	0.507	0.348	**0.888**	
SV	0.357	0.454	0.358	0.650	0.724	0.341	0.784	0.373	0.636	0.350	**0.922**

Source: Authors' calculations, correlation significant at 0.01 level.

Structural Model Assessments

The model was run to complete bootstrapping process 10,000 subsamples (Hair et al., 2022). The results in Table 5 show that the inner VIFs fall within the recommended limits of 3.33, signifying that collinearity was not a concern in the model (Hair et al., 2017).

In the structural model, Gandhian values and SCB were assessed as second-order constructs. The latent variable scores of five constructs (personal values, economic values, leadership values, social values, environmental values) were considered as reflective and three constructs (affective, cognitive, conative) were considered as formative. The outer weights of the second-order composites (affective, cognitive, conative) were significant at 1% confidence level (Henseler et al., 2016). Fig. 1 shows the structural model assessments.

The coefficient of determination R^2 of endogenous construct SCB was found to be significantly moderate to high at 47.9%, which is above 20% (Rasoolimanesh et al., 2017). The SRMR value of 0.044 in the model is below the threshold limit of 0.08, indicating that the model under the study gives excellent explanatory power (Henseler et al., 2015; Hu & Bentler, 1999). Table 6 shows the hypotheses testing.

Hypothesis Testing

Structure equation modelling is widely used to test the research hypotheses in the model. Our study explores the mediating role of sustainable consumption intention between outward and inward environmental attitudes and SCB. In addition to the mediating effect, the framed hypotheses are also tested.

Main Effect

The model has shown a significant positive impact of Gandhian values towards inward environmental attitude ($\beta = 0.404$, $p < 0.001$) and Gandhian values on outward environmental attitude ($\beta = 0.402$, $p < 0.001$). Therefore, the hypothesis

Table 4. HTMT Ratio of Correlation for Discriminant Validity Assessments.

HTMT criterion	AFFE	COG	CON	ECV	ENV	IEA	LV	OEA	PV	SCI
AFFE										
COG	0.8 CI$_{95}$[0.743, 0.852]									
CON	0.85 CI$_{95}$[0.787, 0.895]	0.83 CI$_{95}$[0.777, 0.883]								
ECV	0.43 CI$_{95}$[0.327, 0.53]	0.46 CI$_{95}$[0.365, 0.557]	0.4 CI$_{95}$[0.303, 0.506]							
ENV	0.43 CI$_{95}$[0.325, 0.531]	0.53 CI$_{95}$[0.415, 0.64]	0.38 CI$_{95}$[0.276, 0.486]	0.72 CI$_{95}$[0.618, 0.799]						
IEA	0.68	0.61	0.69	0.43	0.38 CI$_{95}$[0.28, 0.478]					
LV	0.42 CI$_{95}$[0.316, 0.526]	0.47 CI$_{95}$[0.368, 0.566]	0.42 CI$_{95}$[0.308, 0.533]	0.82 CI$_{95}$[0.731, 0.89]	0.86 CI$_{95}$[0.783, 0.914]	0.45 CI$_{95}$[0.344, 0.544]				
OEA	0.57	0.61	0.54	0.36	0.43	0.71	0.4			
PV	0.46 CI$_{95}$[0.351, 0.571]	0.6 CI$_{95}$[0.534, 0.67]	0.42 CI$_{95}$[0.314, 0.535]	0.94 CI$_{95}$[0.873, 0.994]	0.77 CI$_{95}$[0.668, 0.848]	0.46 CI$_{95}$[0.35, 0.559]	0.84 CI$_{95}$[0.744, 0.908]	0.38 CI$_{95}$[0.295, 0.471]		
SCI	0.58 CI$_{95}$[0.497, 0.656]	0.62 CI$_{95}$[0.539, 0.688]	0.6 CI$_{95}$[0.523, 0.67]	0.4 CI$_{95}$[0.306, 0.498]	0.38 CI$_{95}$[0.277, 0.486]	0.73 CI$_{95}$[0.658, 0.795]	0.4 CI$_{95}$[0.307, 0.491]	0.58 CI$_{95}$[0.5, 0.66]	0.44 CI$_{95}$[0.335, 0.528]	
SV	0.42 CI$_{95}$[0.317, 0.521]	0.54 CI$_{95}$[0.435, 0.634]	0.41 CI$_{95}$[0.308, 0.515]	0.79 CI$_{95}$[0.694, 0.865]	0.87 CI$_{95}$[0.766, 0.951]	0.41 CI$_{95}$[0.307, 0.519]	0.93 CI$_{95}$[0.835, 0.989]	0.44 CI$_{95}$[0.34, 0.53]	0.8 CI$_{95}$[0.691, 0.887]	0.41 CI$_{95}$[0.311, 0.515]

Source: Authors' calculations.

Table 5. Collinearity Statistics.

Construct	IEA	OEA	SCB	SCI
GV	1.000	1.000		
IEA			1.973	1.571
OEA			1.648	1.571
SCI			1.690	

Source: Authors' calculations.

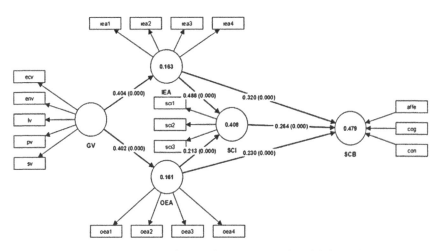

Fig. 1 Structural Model Results. *Source*: Authors' Calculations.

Table 6. Hypotheses Testing.

Hypothesis	Path Relationship	Beta	Sample mean	t-Statistics	CI Lower 2.5%	CI Upper 97.5%	Decision
H1	GV → IEA	0.404	0.408	9.598	0.323	0.487	SUPPORTED
H2	GV → OEA	0.402	0.406	10.508	0.330	0.481	SUPPORTED
H3	IEA → SCI	0.488	0.490	10.778	0.399	0.579	SUPPORTED
H4	OEA → SCI	0.213	0.213	4.098	0.110	0.314	SUPPORTED
H5	IEA → SCB	0.320	0.321	6.732	0.228	0.413	SUPPORTED
H6	OEA → SCB	0.230	0.231	5.569	0.149	0.311	SUPPORTED
H7	SCI → SCB	0.264	0.264	6.219	0.179	0.346	SUPPORTED

Source: Authors' calculations; path coefficient ($p < 0.05$).

is supported. A significant positive impact of outward environmental attitude exists on sustainable consumption intention ($\beta = 0.213, p < 0.001$). Therefore, the hypothesis is supported. The result indicates that inward environmental attitude is the most prominent feature which significantly positively influences sustainable consumption intention ($\beta = 0.488, p < 0.001$). So, the hypothesis is supported. The direct predictors of SCB in terms of outward environmental attitude, inward environmental attitude and sustainable consumption intention were analysed. So, the hypothesis is supported.

In this study, inward environment attitude ($f^2 = 0.1$) discloses a weak effect size, outward environment attitude ($f^2 = 0.62$) discloses a weak effect size and sustainable consumption intention ($f^2 = 0.079$) discloses a weak effect size on SCB. Stone-Geisser's Q^2 investigated the predictive relevance. It was found to be 0.192 (strong) for SCB, 0.155 (strong) for inward environmental attitude, 0.152 (strong) for outward environmental attitude, 0.139 (moderate) for sustainable consumption intention, showing respective relevance of model (Geisser, 1975; Stone, 1974) and generalisability of the results in different contexts in future ahead.

Mediating Effect

The mediation effect is investigated by calculating both the direct and indirect effect (Baron & Kenny, 1986). The bootstrap was run at 10,000 at 95% level of confidence. Table 7 shows the results of the mediation analysis. Both the direct and indirect relationships were significant. Sustainable consumption intention partially mediates the relationship between inward environmental attitude and SCB (indirect effect = 0.129, $p < 0.001$) and even between outward environmental attitude and SCB (indirect effect = 0.056, $p < 0.001$).

DISCUSSION

This study has attempted to predict individuals' SCB in India. Previous researchers have recommended that values play a significant role in predicting SCB, but there needs to be more studies incorporating consumers' Gandhian values to investigate the process. The following findings are generated by considering the impact of Gandhian values, environmental attitude, intention and SCB.

First, Gandhian values significantly influence environmental attitude, which is in line with the findings from where values impact attitude. Environmental attitude is significantly positively influencing sustainable consumption, which is consistent with the findings from Lee et al. (2016). This means that people who have positive feelings about the inward/outward environment value having a clean environment around them and develop a substantial initiative towards sustainability, like reducing waste using renewable resources. Environmental attitude is significantly positively related to sustainable consumption intention, consistent

Table 7. Direct, Indirect, and Total Effects.

Predecessor Construct	Direct Effect on SCB	Indirect Effect on SCB	Total Effect on SCB	VAF	Mediation Type	Significance of Total Effects
SCI	0.264	–	0.264			Yes
IEA	0.320	0.129	0.449	0.287	Partial mediation	Yes
OEA	0.230	0.056	0.286	0.243	Partial mediation	Yes

Source: Authors' calculations.

with the findings from the following authors (Alam et al. 2020; Chen, 2020; Joshi et al., 2019; Lee, 2014; Vermeir & Verbeke, 2008). Moreover, inward environmental attitudes have a substantial effect in comparison to outward environmental attitudes when it comes to shaping the intention of consumers in sustainable consumption. Environmental attitude is significantly positively related to SCB, which aligns with the findings from Jacobs et al. (2018). Sustainable consumption intention is significantly positively related to SCB, which is consistent with the findings from (Alam et al., 2020; Matharu et al., 2021; Saari et al., 2021; Wang et al., 2014). Intention mediates the attitude-behaviour relationship and is in line with the research of Goriparthi and Tallapally (2017) in the context of green purchasing.

CONCLUSIONS

The present study investigated the influence mechanism (based on the VAB theory) of Gandhian values on SCB, considering the mediating role of intention between environmental attitude and SCB. Based on the data analysis of 680 questionnaires from Indian consumers, we find that Gandhian values are significantly positively correlated and help predict SCB, as suggested by Mishra et al. (2019). Intention mediates the relationship between attitude and behaviour. The findings show that the model has good explanatory power. Gandhian philosophies are considered to be relevant in providing the solution to the complex problems that humans, not only in India but also across the globe, are facing today. The model in this study can provide a reference for further study.

Implications

The findings imply that increasing Gandhian values can increase individuals' SCB. Previous research in India paid emphasis on human values (Sharma & Jha, 2017), instrumental and terminal values (Kautish & Sharma, 2019), consumption values (Biswas & Roy, 2015) and many more. Thus, the present study's findings contribute to existing knowledge by predicting that Gandhian values are a predictor of SCB.

The model in the study explains 47.9% of the SCB, which is nearly 50%, indicating good explanatory power. The mediating role of sustainable consumption intention between inward/outward environmental attitude and SCB extends the model and increases the variance in explaining SCB. The model of VAB is extended as value-attitude-intention-behaviour. This extended model can be utilised by future researchers who can test it in other contexts.

The marketers, in order to convince the Indian consumers, can promote locally produced goods, reducing carbon emissions, and even that are safe for society and the environment. Marketers, while advertising the product, can state 'belief in non-violence', 'Labor not exploited for production' and 'sensitive towards the environment'.

Policymakers are advised to focus on reuse, reduce and recycle. The finding found inward environmental attitude to be more prominent in predicting SCB advising to focus on individuals as they are more affected by the inward environment and are concerned about the environment.

Limitations and Future Research

The present study is also subject to limitations that suggest future lines of research. First, though we explore SCB, incorporating Gandhian values, we only studied the mediating role of intention. At the same time, further researchers can check the environmental attitude and other possible mediating variables such as moral norms, frugality, lifestyle and materialism. Second, the study focused on Gandhian values, while in future research, the values of other prominent personalities can be explored to enlarge the scope of the study. Third, this study may be expanded to other nations with similar cultural contexts in future research. Studies can explore the effect of Gandhian values on different groups based on age, income, profession, gender and family size.

REFERENCES

Alam, S. S., Ahmad, M., Ho, Y. H., Omar, N. A., & Lin, C. Y. (2020). Applying an extended theory of planned behavior to sustainable food consumption. *Sustainability*, *12*(20), 8394.

Ali, F., Rasoolimanesh, S. M., Sarstedt, M., Ringle, C. M., & Ryu, K. (2018). An assessment of the use of partial least squares structural equation modeling (PLS-SEM) in hospitality research. *International Journal of Contemporary Hospitality Management*, *30*(1), 514–538.

Alzubaidi, H., Slade, E. L., & Dwivedi, Y. K. (2021). Examining antecedents of consumers' pro-environmental behaviours: TPB extended with materialism and innovativeness. *Journal of Business Research*, *122*, 685–699.

Amin, S., & Tarun, M. T. (2021). Effect of consumption values on customers' green purchase intention: a mediating role of green trust. *Social Responsibility Journal*, *17*(8), 1320–1336.

Apipuchayakul, N., & Vassanadumrongdee, S. (2020). Factors affecting the consumption of energy-efficient lighting products: Exploring purchase behaviors of Thai consumers. *Sustainability (Switzerland)*, *12*(12), 4887.

Awuni, J. A., & Du, J. (2016). Sustainable consumption in Chinese cities: Green purchasing intentions of young adults based on the theory of consumption values. *Sustainable Development*, *24*(2), 124–135.

Bagozzi, R. P., Baumgartner, J., & Yi, Y. (1989). An investigation into the role of intentions as mediators of the attitude-behavior relationship. *Journal of Economic Psychology*, *10*(1), 35–62.

Banerjee, S. (2008). Dimensions of Indian culture, core cultural values and marketing implications. *Cross Cultural Management: An International Journal*, *15*(4), 367–378.

Bansal, I., & Bajpai, N. (2011). Gandhian values: Guidelines for managing organizations. *Journal of Human Values*, *17*(2), 145–160.

Baron, R. M., & Kenny, D. A. (1986). The moderator–mediator variable distinction in social psychological research: Conceptual, strategic, and statistical considerations. *Journal of Personality and Social Psychology*, *51*(6), 1173–1182.

Bhalla, S. (2021). Testing the motivations and constraints of collaborative consumption: An empirical analysis of disruptive innovative business model. *FIIB Business Review*, *10*(2), 146–157.

Bhutto, M. Y., Liu, X., Soomro, Y. A., Ertz, M., & Baeshen, Y. (2021). Adoption of energy-efficient home appliances: Extending the theory of planned behavior. *Sustainability (Switzerland)*, *13*(1), 1–23.

Biswas, A., & Roy, M. (2015). Leveraging factors for sustained green consumption behavior based on consumption value perceptions: Testing the structural model. *Journal of Cleaner Production*, *95*, 332–340.

Borusiak, B., Szymkowiak, A., Horska, E., Raszka, N., & Zelichowska, E. (2020). Towards building sustainable consumption: A study of second-hand buying intentions. *Sustainability (Switzerland)*, *12*(3), 875.

Carrero, I., Valor, C., & Redondo, R. (2020). Do all dimensions of sustainable consumption lead to psychological well-being? Empirical evidence from young consumers. *Journal of Agricultural & Environmental Ethics*, *33*(1), 145–170.

Chekima, B., Chekima, S., Syed Khalid Wafa, S. A. W., Igau, O. A., & Sondoh, S. L. (2016). Sustainable consumption: The effects of knowledge, cultural values, environmental advertising, and demographics. *International Journal of Sustainable Development & World Ecology*, *23*(2), 210–220.

Chen, M. F. (2020). Selecting environmental psychology theories to predict people's consumption intention of locally produced organic foods. *International Journal of Consumer Studies*, *44*(5), 455–468.

Cheung, M. F. Y., & To, W. M. (2019). An extended model of value-attitude-behavior to explain Chinese consumers' green purchase behavior. *Journal of Retailing and Consumer Services*, *50*, 145–153.

Clawson, C. J., & Vinson, D. E. (1978). Human values: A historical and interdisciplinary analysis. *Advances in Consumer Research*, *5*(1), 396–402.

Dermody, J., Hanmer-Lloyd, S., Koenig-Lewis, N., & Zhao, A. L. (2015). Advancing sustainable consumption in the UK and China: The mediating effect of pro-environmental self-identity. *Journal of Marketing Management*, *31*(13–14), 1472–1502.

Dermody, J., Koenig-Lewis, N., Zhao, A. L., & Hanmer-Lloyd, S. (2018). Appraising the influence of pro-environmental self-identity on sustainable consumption buying and curtailment in emerging markets: Evidence from China and Poland. *Journal of Business Research*, *86*, 333–343.

Fornell, C., & Larcker, D. F. (1981). Evaluating structural equation models with unobservable variables and measurement error. *Journal of Marketing Research*, *18*(1), 39.

Gandhi, M., & Kaushik, N. (2016). Socially responsive consumption behaviour – An Indian perspective. *Social Responsibility Journal*, *12*(1), 85–102.

Geisser, S. (1975). A predictive approach to the random effect model. *Biometrika*, *61*(1), 101–107.

Ghazali, E. M., Mutum, D. S., & Ariswibowo, N. (2018). Impact of religious values and habit on an extended green purchase behaviour model. *International Journal of Consumer Studies*, *42*(6), 639–654.

Gold, A. H., Malhotra, A., & Segars, A. H. (2001). Knowledge management: An organizational capabilities perspective. *Journal of Management Information Systems*, *18*(1), 185–214.

Goriparthi, R. K., & Tallapally, M. (2017). Consumers' attitude in green purchasing. *FIIB Business Review*, *6*(1), 34.

Grunert, S. C., & Juhl, H. J. (1995). Values, environmental attitudes, and buying of organic foods. *Journal of Economic Psychology*, *16*(1), 39–62.

Hair, J. F., Hult, G. T., Ringle, C., & Sarstedt, M. (2017). *A primer on partial least squares structural equation modeling (PLS-SEM)* (2nd ed.). Sage Publications.

Hair, J. F., Hult, G. T. M., Ringle, C. M., & Sarstedt, M. (2022). *A primer on partial least squares structural equation modeling (PLS-SEM)* (3rd ed.). Sage Publications.

Hair, J. F., Howard, M. C., & Nitzl, C. (2020). Assessing measurement model quality in PLS-SEM using confirmatory composite analysis. *Journal of Business Research*, *109*, 101–110.

Hair, J. F., Sarstedt, M., & Ringle, C. M. (2019). Rethinking some of the rethinking of partial least squares. *European Journal of Marketing*, *53*(4), 566–584.

Hakan, D., Erdi, E., & Erdem, H. (2016). A role model in light of values: Mahatma Gandhi. *Educational Research and Reviews*, *11*(20), 1889–1895.

Han, H., Chua, B. L., Ariza-Montes, A., & Untaru, E. N. (2020). Effect of environmental corporate social responsibility on green attitude and norm activation process for sustainable consumption: Airline versus restaurant. *Corporate Social Responsibility and Environmental Management*, *27*(4), 1851–1864.

Henseler, J., Hubona, G., & Ray, P. A. (2016). Using PLS path modeling in new technology research: Updated guidelines. *Industrial Management & Data Systems*, *116*(1), 2–20.

Henseler, J., Ringle, C. M., & Sarstedt, M. (2015). A new criterion for assessing discriminant validity in variance-based structural equation modeling. *Journal of the Academy of Marketing Science*, *43*(1), 115–135.

Hofstede, G., Hofstede, G. J., Minkov, M. (2010). *Cultures and Organizations: Software of the Mind. Revised and Expanded*. McGraw-Hill.

Homer, P. M., & Kahle, L. R. (1988). A structural equation test of the value-attitude-behavior hierarchy. *Journal of Personality and Social Psychology, 54*(4), 638–646.

Hu, L., & Bentler, P. M. (1999). Cutoff criteria for fit indexes in covariance structure analysis: Conventional criteria versus new alternatives. *Structural Equation Modeling: A Multidisciplinary Journal, 6*(1), 1–55.

Ivanova, D., Stadler, K., Steen-Olsen, K., Wood, R., Vita, G., Tukker, A., & Hertwich, E. G. (2016). Environmental impact assessment of household consumption. *Journal of Industrial Ecology, 20*(3), 526–536.

Jacobs, K., Petersen, L., Hörisch, J., & Battenfeld, D. (2018). Green thinking but thoughtless buying? An empirical extension of the value-attitude-behaviour hierarchy in sustainable clothing. *Journal of Cleaner Production, 203*, 1155–1169.

Joshi, Y., Sangroya, D., Srivastava, A. P., & Yadav, M. (2019). Modelling the predictors of young consumers' sustainable consumption intention. *International Journal of Nonprofit and Voluntary Sector Marketing, 24*(4), e1663.

Kahle, L. R. (1983). *Social values and social change: Adaptation to life in America.* Praeger.

Kamboj, K., & Kishor, N. (2022). Influence of customer perceived values on organic food consumption behaviour: Mediating role of green purchase intention. *FIIB Business Review*. https://doi.org/10.1177/23197145221125283

Kang, J., & Moreno, F. (2020). Driving values to actions: Predictive modeling for environmentally sustainable product purchases. *Sustainable Production and Consumption, 23*, 224–235.

Karp, D. G. (1996). Values and their effect on pro-environmental behavior. *Environment and Behavior, 28*(1), 111–133.

Kautish, P., Khare, A., & Sharma, R. (2020). Values, sustainability consciousness and intentions for SDG endorsement. *Marketing Intelligence & Planning, 38*(7), 921–939.

Kautish, P., & Sharma, R. (2019). Value orientation, green attitude and green behavioral intentions: An empirical investigation among young consumers. *Young Consumers, 20*(4), 338–358.

Kautish, P., & Sharma, R. (2020). Determinants of pro-environmental behavior and environmentally conscious consumer behavior: An empirical investigation from emerging market. *Business Strategy & Development, 3*(1), 112–127.

Kim, M. J., & Hall, C. M. (2020). Can sustainable restaurant practices enhance customer loyalty? The roles of value theory and environmental concerns. *Journal of Hospitality and Tourism Management, 43*, 127–138.

Kumar, A., Prakash, G., & Kumar, G. (2021). Does environmentally responsible purchase intention matter for consumers? A predictive sustainable model developed through an empirical study. *Journal of Retailing and Consumer Services, 58*, 102270.

Lee, C. K. C., Yap, C. S. F., & Levy, D. S. (2016). Place identity and sustainable consumption: Implications for social marketing. *Journal of Strategic Marketing, 24*(7), 578–593.

Lee, K. (2014). Predictors of sustainable consumption among young educated consumers in Hong Kong. *Journal of International Consumer Marketing, 26*(3), 217–238.

Leiserowitz, A. (2006). Climate change risk perception and policy preferences: The role of affect, imagery, and values. *Climatic Change, 77*(1–2), 45–72.

Leonidou, L. C., Leonidou, C. N., & Kvasova, O. (2010). Antecedents and outcomes of consumer environmentally friendly attitudes and behaviour. *Journal of Marketing Management, 26*(13–14), 1319–1344.

Mandliya, A., Varyani, V., Hassan, Y., Akhouri, A., & Pandey, J. (2020). What influences intention to purchase sustainable products? Impact of advertising and materialism. *International Journal of Productivity and Performance Management, 69*(8), 1647–1669.

Matharu, M., Jain, R., & Kamboj, S. (2021). Understanding the impact of lifestyle on sustainable consumption behavior: A sharing economy perspective. *Management of Environmental Quality, 32*(1), 20–40.

McCarty, J. A., & Shrum, L. J. (2001). The influence of individualism, collectivism, and locus of control on environmental beliefs and behavior. *Journal of Public Policy & Marketing, 20*(1), 93–104.

Minton, E. A., Kahle, L. R., & Kim, C.-H. (2015). Religion and motives for sustainable behaviors: A cross-cultural comparison and contrast. *Journal of Business Research, 68*(9), 1937–1944.

Minton, E. A., Spielmann, N., Kahle, L. R., & Kim, C. H. (2018). The subjective norms of sustainable consumption: A cross-cultural exploration. *Journal of Business Research, 82*, 400–408.

Mishra, A. A., Sharma, S. C., Gautam, V., & Manna, R. (2019). Gandhian values and consumption behavior: Scale development and validation. *Journal of Strategic Marketing, 27*(6), 465–482.

Mitchell, A. (1983). *The nine American life styles.* Warner.

Neuman, K. (1986). Personal values and commitment to energy conservation. *Environment and Behavior, 18*(1), 53–74.

Patel, J. D., Trivedi, R. H., & Yagnik, A. (2020). Self-identity and internal environmental locus of control: Comparing their influences on green purchase intentions in high-context versus low-context cultures. *Journal of Retailing and Consumer Services, 53*, 102003.

Piligrimiene, Ž., Žukauskaite, A., Korzilius, H., Banyte, J., & Dovaliene, A. (2020). Internal and external determinants of consumer engagement in sustainable consumption. *Sustainability (Switzerland), 12*(4), 1379.

Podsakoff, P. M., MacKenzie, S. B., Lee, J.-Y., & Podsakoff, N. P. (2003). Common method biases in behavioral research: A critical review of the literature and recommended remedies. *Journal of Applied Psychology, 88*(5), 879–903.

Podsakoff, P. M., & Organ, D. W. (1986). Self-reports in organizational research: Problems and prospects. *Journal of Management, 12*(4), 531–544.

Qasim, H., Yan, L., Guo, R., Saeed, A., & Ashraf, B. (2019). The defining role of environmental self-identity among consumption values and behavioral intention to consume organic food. *International Journal of Environmental Research and Public Health, 16*(7), 1106.

Quoquab, F., & Mohammad, J. (2020). Cognitive, affective and conative domains of sustainable consumption: Scale development and validation using confirmatory composite analysis. *Sustainability, 12*(18), 7784.

Rasoolimanesh, S. M., Jaafar, M., Kock, N., & Ahmad, A. G. (2017). The effects of community factors on residents' perceptions toward World Heritage Site inscription and sustainable tourism development. *Journal of Sustainable Tourism, 25*(2), 198–216.

Ringle, C. M., Wende, S., & Becker, J.-M. (2022). *SmartPLS 4.* SmartPLS GmbH. http://www.smartpls.com

Rokeach, M. (1973). *The nature of human values.* Free Press.

Saari, U. A., Damberg, S., Frombling, L., & Ringle, C. M. (2021). Sustainable consumption behavior of Europeans: The influence of environmental knowledge and risk perception on environmental concern and behavioral intention. *Ecological Economics, 189*.

Schwartz, S. H. (1992). Universals in the content and structure of values: Theoretical advances and empirical tests in 20 countries. *Advances in experimental social psychology*, 1–65.

Schwartz, S. H. (1994). *Beyond Individualism/collectivism: New Cultural Dimensions of Values.* Sage Publications, Inc.

Schultz, P. W., & Zelezny, L. (1999). Values as predictors of environmental attitudes: Evidence for consistency across 14 countries. *Journal of Environmental Psychology, 19*(3), 255–265.

Sharma, R., & Jha, M. (2017). Values influencing sustainable consumption behaviour: Exploring the contextual relationship. *Journal of Business Research, 76*, 77–88.

Sheng, G., Xie, F., Gong, S., & Pan, H. (2019). The role of cultural values in green purchasing intention: Empirical evidence from Chinese consumers. *International Journal of Consumer Studies, 43*(3), 315–326.

Stern, P. C., & Dietz, T. (1994). The value basis of environmental concern. *Journal of Social Issues, 50*(3), 65–84.

Stern, P. C., Dietz, T., Abel, T., Guagnano, G. A., & Kalof, L. (1999). A value-belief-norm theory of support for social movements: The case of environmentalism. *Human Ecology Review, 6*(2), 81–97.

Stone, M. (1974). Cross-validatory choice and assessment of statistical predictions. *Journal of the Royal Statistical Society. Series B (Methodological), 36*(2), 111–147.

Testa, F., Sarti, S., & Frey, M. (2019). Are green consumers really green? Exploring the factors behind the actual consumption of organic food products. *Business Strategy and the Environment, 28*(2), 327–338.

Nguyen, N. P. T., & Dang, H. D. (2022). Organic food purchase decisions from a context-based behavioral reasoning approach. *Appetite*, *173*, 105975.

Thogersen, J., & Olander, F. (2002). Human values and the emergence of a sustainable consumption pattern: A panel study. *Journal of Economic Psychology*, *23*(5), 605–630.

Vermeir, I., & Verbeke, W. (2006). Sustainable food consumption: Exploring the consumer "attitude – Behavioral intention" gap. *Journal of Agricultural and Environmental Ethics*, *19*(2), 169–194.

Vermeir, I., & Verbeke, W. (2008). Sustainable food consumption among young adults in Belgium: Theory of planned behaviour and the role of confidence and values. *Ecological Economics*, *64*(3), 542–553.

Wang, B., Li, J., Sun, A., Wang, Y., & Wu, D. (2020). Residents' green purchasing intentions in a developing-country context: Integrating PLS-SEM and MGA methods. *Sustainability (Switzerland)*, *12*(1), 1–21.

Wang, P., Liu, Q., & Qi, Y. (2014). Factors influencing sustainable consumption behaviors: A survey of the rural residents in China. *Journal of Cleaner Production*, *63*, 152–165.

Waris, I., & Hameed, I. (2020). Promoting environmentally sustainable consumption behavior: An empirical evaluation of purchase intention of energy-efficient appliances. *Energy Efficiency*, *13*(8), 1653–1664.

Yadav, R., & Pathak, G. S. (2017). Determinants of consumers' green purchase behavior in a developing nation: Applying and extending the theory of planned behavior. *Ecological Economics*, *134*, 114–122.

Yang, C., Tu, J. C., & Jiang, Q. (2020). The influential factors of consumers – sustainable consumption: A case on electric vehicles in China. *Sustainability (Switzerland)*, *12*(8), 3496.

Yarimoglu, E., & Binboga, G. (2019). Understanding sustainable consumption in an emerging country: The antecedents and consequences of the ecologically conscious consumer behavior model. *Business Strategy and the Environment*, *28*(4), 642–651.

Zhang, L., Fan, Y., Zhang, W., & Zhang, S. (2019). Extending the theory of planned behavior to explain the effects of cognitive factors across different kinds of green products. *Sustainability (Switzerland)*, *11*(15), 1–17.

CHAPTER 2

SUSTAINABLE TOURISM: A ROADMAP FOR THE 2030 SUSTAINABLE DEVELOPMENT AGENDA

Jatin Vaid

Vivekananda School of Business Studies, Vivekananda Institute of Professional Studies, New Delhi, India

ABSTRACT

Purpose: *Seventeen sustainable development goals (SDGs) are included in the UN's 2030 agenda of sustainable development that aims to provide a shared blueprint for sustainability and call for urgent action by all member countries. The study aims to study the role of tourism in delivering sustainable solutions for the planet.*

Research Methodology: *The present chapter compiles available studies on sustainable tourism and critically analyses sustainability principles and their relevance to SDGs.*

Findings: *The chapter comprehensively studies the SDGs – 8, 12, and 14 and reveals a strategic roadmap to achieve the SDGs through sustainable tourism practices. The observations may provide deep insights to the government and policymakers to prioritise actions in order to achieve the goals.*

Research Limitations: *Future research studies may be conducted to empirically verify the results from the perspective of different countries.*

Sustainable Development Goals: The Impact of Sustainability Measures on Wellbeing
Contemporary Studies in Economic and Financial Analysis, Volume 113B, 21–26
Copyright © 2024 by Jatin Vaid
Published under exclusive licence by Emerald Publishing Limited
ISSN: 1569-3759/doi:10.1108/S1569-37592024000113B002

Practical Implications: *According to United Nations (2023), 'The tourism sector accounts for approximately 10% of the world's GDP, about 30% of overall service exports across sectors, and provides for 1 out of 10 jobs globally'. Sustainable tourism has particularly been embraced as an important area under the 8th SDG of sustainable economic growth; in the 12th SDG of sustainable production and consumption and in the 14th SDG pertaining to sustainable use of oceans and marine resources, thus highlighting its importance.*

Value: *The chapter is a novel attempt to comprehensively analyse the role of sustainable tourism and the strategic roadmap for achieving the SDGs.*

Keywords: Sustainable tourism; United Nations; sustainability; SDG; economy

INTRODUCTION

The word sustain is derived from the Latin words 'sustinere' and the French word 'soustenir', which means to uphold continuation. The four crucial aspects of sustainability, as noted by (Caradonna, 2018), are the interconnectedness of human society, economy, and natural environment; the need for human societies to function in the realms of ecological boundaries; the belief that humans will strategise sensibly for the future; and finally adopt to the concept of being economical and nationally responsive.

The last few decades have witnessed unprecedented growth in tourism, making it as one of the fastest-growing economic sectors and a crucial driver for socio-economic progress in the world. Specifically, in the case of developing nations, tourism is observed to be a vital source of income. Recent developments in this field of study have led to enhanced activities, making tourism one of the rapid sectors of the global economy (Khalil et al., 2022).

United Nations World Tourism Organization (UNWTO) delves into this very important issue of sustainable tourism by defining it as 'tourism that takes full account of its current and future economic, social and environmental impacts, addressing the needs of visitors, the industry, the environment, and host communities' (UNWTO, 2023). In order to be sustainable in the long run, a delicate balance needs to be maintained amongst the three key dimensions of tourism, viz. Environmental, Economic, and Social dimensions. These are the three vital pillars of sustainable practices, and any tourism organisation intending to incorporate sustainability into its operations should focus on them. Adopting sustainable practices like waste reduction, water consumption, and healthy lifestyles is known to reduce the negative impact on the triple bottom line (Khalil et al., 2022). These three dimensions of sustainable tourism are illustrated in Fig. 1. In other words, sustainability in tourism would ensure optimal utilisation of natural resources; conservation of the social & cultural heritage in various host countries; and contribution to poverty alleviation by providing employment and earning opportunities to its citizens.

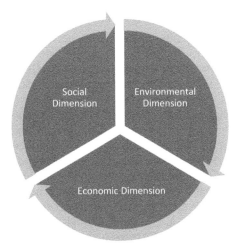

Fig. 1. Sustainable Tourism Dimensions. *Source*: Author's compilation.

i.   *Environmental dimension:* Environment may include the natural environment (air, land, minerals, water, etc.); farmed environment (agricultural systems); wildlife (tourist attraction, natural woodlands, birds and animals); and built environment (human settlements like villages, towns, and cities). There is a strong coordinated relationship between tourism and the environment as they are strategically linked (Swarbrooke, 2010).

ii. *Economic dimension:* Tourism is a major industry that contributes to many countries' GDP and foreign currency earnings. There are both economic benefits and costs associated with tourism. Though the economic benefits are comparatively easier to calculate, the economic costs are difficult to trace, specifically in the long run. Sustainable tourism aims to maximise tourist spending, while keeping a stringent check on income leakages in the local economy (Swarbrooke, 2010).

iii. *Social dimension:* the sociocultural impacts of tourism occur gradually over a long period of time. These impacts are mostly intangible; however, they are irreversible and cause permanent damage to host communities. The social dimension involves implementing equity amongst all stakeholders, ensuring equal opportunities between employees and tourists, and finally, observing a high degree of ethics with tourists, the government, and the host country population (Swarbrooke, 2010).

Recent researchers (Prakash et al., 2023) have also discovered that the adoption of sustainable practices like minimising air-borne pollution; preservation of energy; conservation of water; and effective management of waste disposals are very likely to positively and significantly impact customer experience and eventually their revisit intentions. Moreover, employees also have been reported to be happier and more connected to their organisations, this leading to a positive work culture (Prakash et al., 2023).

SUSTAINABLE DEVELOPMENT GOALS

In the year 2015, all the member countries of the United Nations resolved to ensure peace and prosperity for their citizens and for Mother Earth by embracing the framework of 17 sustainable development goals (SDGs). These SDGs require all member nations to collaborate and partner to ensure sustainable growth, globally (United Nations, 2023). These SDSs are: 'No poverty; Zero hunger; Good health and well-being; Quality education; Gender equality; Clean water and sanitization; Affordable and clean energy; Decent work and economic growth; Industry, innovation, and infrastructure; Reduced inequalities; Sustainable cities and communities; Responsible consumption and production; Climate action; Life below water; Life on land; Peace, justice and strong institutions; and finally Partnerships for the goals' (United Nations, 2015). The distinctive aspects of these SDGs are that they are universal, indivisible and transformative (Fauzi et al., 2023) in nature. The tourism sector, though contributes directly or indirectly to all the goals, has specifically been included as a target in the 8th, 12th and 14th SDGs. Thus, the tourism sector's benefits are critical in achieving the SDGs. These three crucial SDGs along with the associated tourism themes (Mason et al., 2022) are depicted in Table 1.

THE 2030 AGENDA FOR SUSTAINABLE DEVELOPMENT

The 17 SDGs, effective from the 1 January 2016 act as a torchlight to member countries on the path of sustainable development (United Nations, 2015). It also requires all member countries to join hands and pledge common action to achieve sustainable development. Under the 8th SDG, it is advised to ensure that member countries implement sustainable forms of tourism that help in job creation and promoting local cultures. The 12th SDG, on the other hand, intends to monitor the impact of sustainable development on the tourism industry by developing and implementing relevant tools. Finally, the 14th SDG

Table 1.   Tourism Themes and the SDGs.

SDG No.	Sustainable Development Goals	Associated Tourism Themes
SDG 8	'Decent work and economic growth'	• Leisure tourism • Employee's rights and wage systems • Social tourism • Native-owned and operated tourism business
SDG 12	'Responsible consumption and production'	• Conscious consumerism • Quality certification • Economic growth • Partnerships
SDG 14	'Life below water'	• Areas protected for marine life • Tourism pertaining to marine life • Blue Economy (Water)

Source: Author's compilation.

focuses on the justifiable usage of marine and aquatic resources, as coastal and maritime tourism is one of the largest segments of the tourism sector (United Nations, 2015). Sustainability is crucial to SDGs and reinforces that all goals focused on the environment are essential to effective implementation (Khemka & Kumar, 2020). Moreover, the active participation and involvement of all concerned stakeholders are imperative in achieving sustainable tourism development (Jamkhaneh et al., 2022).

IMPLEMENTATION PROGRESS

As per the annual report published by the UN Secretary-General in 2023, exactly at a midpoint of 2030 agenda implementation, it is observed that though there has been some progress in a few areas, a majority of them still are far from their logical accomplishments; this regressed or negative progress highlights a cause of deep worry (United Nations General Assembly Economic and Social Council, 2023). With respect to SDG 8, it is noted that the share of tourism in global GDP has halved in 2020 due to the COVID-19 pandemic. However, there has been a slow growth of 6% on its path of recovery (United Nations General Assembly Economic and Social Council, 2023). Similarly, for SDG 12, it seems that the recovery is off track with disruptions in global supply chains and changes in consumer behaviour. SDG 14 also seemingly regressed with oceans being endangered by acidification and plastic pollution. Thus, it may be seen that the overall status is quite worrisome and demands the member countries to join hands and work in close coordination towards the path of sustainable recovery.

FINDINGS AND CONCLUSION

The three crucial aspects on which the member countries need to work to ensure timely and affable implementation of the 2030 framework of SDGs with respect to promoting sustainable tourism are as follows:

i.   Equipping the government and empowering strategic institutions to embrace sustainable practices to ensure comprehensive transformation;
ii. Arranging policy matters and prioritising critical investment decisions in line with the relevant SDGs;
iii. Ensuring increased financing and a conducive environment for developing countries to implement the necessary strategies.

Various schools of thought propagating the need for sustainable tourism may either discourage the current levels of travel undertaken by propagating the use of teleconferencing services and alternative modes of transportation to protect local environments and cultures; or by encouraging tourists to be sensitive to the destination culture and environment (Belz & Peattie, 2009).

REFERENCES

Belz, F.-M., & Peattie, K. (2009). *Sustainability marketing: A global perspective*. John Wiley and Sons.

Caradonna, J. L. (Ed.). (2018). *Routledge handbook of the history of sustainability* (1st ed.). Routledge.

Fauzi, M. A., Abdul Rahman, A. R., & Lee, K. C. (2023). A systematic bibliometric review of the United Nation's SDGS: Which are the most related to higher education institutions? *International Journal of Sustainability in Higher Education, 24*(3), 637–659.

Jamkhaneh, H. B., Shahin, R., & Shahin, A. (2022). Assessing sustainable tourism development through service supply chain process maturity and service quality model. *International Journal of Productivity and Performance Management, 72*(7), 2046–2068.

Khalil, N., Abdullah, S. N., Haron, S. N., & Hamid, M. Y. (2022). A review of green practices and initiatives from stakeholder's perspectives towards sustainable hotel operations and performance impact. *Journal of Facilities Management, 7*(41), 307–316.

Khemka, N. M., & Kumar, S. (2020). *Social development and the sustainable development goals in South Asia*. Routledge Taylor and Francis Group.

Mason, P., Augustyn, M., & King, A. S. (2022). Tourism destination quality and the UN Sustainable Development Goals: Tourism Agenda 2030. *Tourism Review, 78*(2), 443–460.

Prakash, S., Sharma, V.P., Singh, R., Vijayvargy, L. and Nilaish. (2023). Adopting green and sustainable practices in the hotel industry operations- an analysis of critical performance indicators for improved environmental quality. *Management of Environmental Quality, 34*(4), 1057–1076.

Swarbrooke, J. (2010). *Sustainable tourism management*. Rawat Publications.

United Nations. (2015). *Transforming our world: The 2030 agenda for sustainable development*. United Nations.

United Nations. (2023, May 6). The sustainable development goals. https://sdgs.un.org/goals

United Nations General Assembly Economic and Social Council. (2023). *Progress towards the sustainable development goals: Towards a rescue plan for people and planet*. United Nations.

UNWTO. (2023, May 6). *Sustainable development*. https://www.unwto.org/sustainable-development

CHAPTER 3

SUSTAINABILITY THROUGH HUMAN RESOURCE MANAGEMENT: A CONCEPTUAL FRAMEWORK

Nikita Agrawal, Kashish Beriwal and Nisha Daga

Guru Gobind Singh Indraprastha University, Vivekananda Institute of Professional Studies, Delhi, India

ABSTRACT

Introduction: *Sustainable human resource management (SHRM) as a practice is nowadays seen as an essential factor contributing to an individual's and organisation's growth. At the organisational level, the people concerned face many pressures to inculcate SHRM practices from various authorities and stakeholders.*

Purpose: *This chapter explains SHRM as a concept through an extensive literature review along with the evolutionary stages and multi-lateral perspectives of SHRM. The factors affecting this concept are Economic, Social, and Environmental; its driving forces like Employees, Government and Market Pressure; Employee Outcomes, namely Employee retention, satisfaction, motivation and Employee Presence; Organisational outcomes – Business level, Workers' satisfaction, improved environmental outcomes better correlations, etc.; and value created by SHRM in terms of both employee and organisation are thereby explained.*

Sustainable Development Goals: The Impact of Sustainability Measures on Wellbeing
Contemporary Studies in Economic and Financial Analysis, Volume 113B, 27–42
Copyright © 2024 by Nikita Agrawal, Kashish Beriwal and Nisha Daga
Published under exclusive licence by Emerald Publishing Limited
ISSN: 1569-3759/doi:10.1108/S1569-37592024000113B003

Methodology: *A specific procedure has been employed since the chapter has been based on literature review. The process of systematic literature review has been followed, which lays down the process followed by the authors – right from the Scope Formulation to the Illustration of Conceptual Framework.*

Findings: *A conceptual model is represented as a basis of the literature review, which the organisation can use and apply to develop SHRM practices, and finally, the precise effects of the research findings are suggested alongside ideas for future research.*

Keywords: Sustainable human resource management; SHRM; employee outcome; organisational outcome; value creation; driving forces of SHRM; value creation of SHRM; social factors affecting SHRM; economic factors affecting SHRM

INTRODUCTION

The evolution of every concept and every practice is constant. Thus, the concept of human resource management (HRM) has evolved. Development has been there at every stage, from HRM to SHRM. It is turning out to be progressively specific that an HRM framework comprises a significant part that can help an associate become more successful and achieve an upper hand (Becker & Huselid, 1998).

For many years, sustainability has been a point of discussion in management. Nowadays, SHRM is a vital idea in the corporate world, particularly with a concentration on empowering people and organisations to meet their present necessities without creating any harm to the atmosphere for people in the coming years (Garza-Reyes et al., 2019; Nadeem et al., 2017). Sustainability has often been defined as an idea for making new arrangements, monetary frameworks and associations more reasonable in the long term with minimal damage to the community and the rest of the world's prosperity (Ehnert et al., 2014). Sustainability transfers the attention towards the ability of HRM to maintain the foundation of human resources and for the feasibility of the organisation. New angles of SHRM are now being taken into consideration by researchers. Researchers have highlighted how SHRM can exhibit a thorough examination of a plan on the formal kinship and a commitment towards a supportable turn of events (Ehnert, 2009; Zaugg et al., 2001).

This chapter extends the previous reviews of the literature on SHRM by suggesting a conceptual framework with driving forces as mediating factors. The chapter is divided into various headings. Various headings include a systematic review of the literature, the study's objective, a discussion of SHRM as a concept and a presentation of various perspectives given over time by various researchers. Then, the chapter explains the conceptual framework and the discussion of the conceptual framework is presented in the chapter, which also includes subsections explaining the factors affecting SHRM. Furthermore, the sections discuss the forces that drive SHRM, the outcomes given forward by this model, the value created through SHRM practice and finally, the conclusion derived from the research and future scope of the research. The study aims to investigate the notion of SHRM as a systematic literature review (SLR) with the factors affecting it. The driving forces are also explained by the outcomes of employees and organisations due to SHRM and the value created. At last, the particular ramifications of the discoveries are proposed, alongside ideas for potential headings of additional exploration.

SYSTEMATIC LITERATURE REVIEW APPROACH

For the fulfilment of the scope laid down for the current study, an approach of SLR by Garza-Reyes (2015) was observed. Fig. 1 displays the facets that the SLR went through.

Fig. 1 depicts the SLR process, starting with formulating the scope of the research that revolves around sustainable human resource management (SHRM). Moving forward, papers from 1984 to 2022 were extensively read for the location of studies. Electronic databases like John Wiley, Elsevier, JSTOR, Science Direct, Taylor and Francis, Springer and IGI were explored. Initial keywords taken into consideration were barriers, human resources, employees, sustainability, human resource management, triple bottom line, environmental human resource management and organisational value. Through various combinations, keywords related to organisational and employee outcomes and SHRM were used. The next phase in the SLR, as shown in Fig. 1, was the selection of studies and the

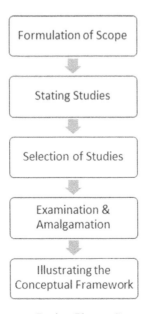

Fig. 1.   Systematic Literature Review Phases. *Source*: Authors' Compilation.

papers published with aspects of environmental, economic and social sustainability, organisational and employee outcome, and implementation of the aspects of SHRM in Human Resource Management (HRM) were taken into consideration. After this, the identification of the concepts of SHRM, its indicators, implementation of these indicators, barriers, drivers, employee and organisational outcomes, and values was done. At last, a conceptual framework was designed to show the indicators and outcomes of SHRM. One thousand seventy-five research papers were yielded.

After the removal of duplications, the number of papers selected was 568. Abstracts of all these papers were precisely read, and 372 papers were further eliminated. One hundred ninety-six papers were thoroughly re-evaluated so that the applicability of the research would be assured, out of which 125 papers were at last chosen.

OBJECTIVE OF STUDY

This chapter explains SHRM as a concept through a literature review. This chapter also explains the factors affecting the concept of SHRM, its driving forces, employee outcome, organisational outcome and value created by SHRM. The evolution and different perspectives of SHRM are discussed in the chapter, which helps understand how the idea of SHRM has changed over the years. The chapter provides a better understanding of how people have different perspectives on SHRM as well as the different kinds of models developed in previous years. COVID has had a significant impact on organisations, and human resources faced the greatest challenge, so the concept of sustainability in human resources has emerged as the holy grail for organisations to preserve their position and go further than that and achieve more. The study's goal is to systematically review the literature on the concept of SHRM and the factors that influence it. The outcomes of employees and organisations result from SHRM and the value created. This chapter also aims to create a conceptual framework that connects the concept of SHRM with the generation of value. Finally, the specific implications of the discoveries are proposed, along with ideas for potential areas of further investigation.

SUSTAINABLE HUMAN RESOURCE MANAGEMENT

SHRM has been, for many years, a very new concept. Due to this, only a few pieces of research were done on SHRM (Sosik et al., 2002; Wehling et al., 2009). The fundamental concept under the primary discussion of SHRM is that organisations look for various types of results to fulfil the expectations and needs of people affiliated with the organisation (Järlström et al., 2018). These outcomes can be social, human, employee-based ecological or environmental. It is possible that for the organisation, one or more outcomes may be more critical for it than the other outcomes. Numerous associations are enthusiastic about detailing their monetary, social and environmental manageability execution (Schaltegger & Wagner, 2006; Sena & Shani, 2008). The approach is based on an open-systems model that applies Brundtland's definition of sustainable development.

The central idea of this method is to be responsible not only for a single stakeholder group, such as owners, but also for a more significant number of them, in this example, employees. That understanding necessitates approaching employees in a sociable manner, encouraging employee well-being and minimising the burden of work (Ehnert, 2009).

As mentioned previously, SHRM has long been in its emerging stage. However, many evolutions have also been made in this regard. From definitions to categories to different dimensions of SHRM, many authors have explored every bit of it. The four tables below show the evolutions, perspectives and relations of SHRM with both employees and the organisation.

Table 1 presents an evolution in SHRM from HRM and gives various angles of SHRM. While SHRM was a very new concept, Wesley R. de Souza Freitas et al. (2011) presented historical views on HRM and concluded how empirical research should be done for the assessment and practices of SHRM. Then, for many years, the idea of SHRM started to get refined, and various other authors presented new angles. Esther Villajos et al. (2019) gave a model representing the mediating factor of ideals in the relationship of HRM practices to ensure that HRM practices are effective. It is essential to understand the role that ideals play. This model represents the mediating factor of ideals in the relationship between HRM practices and employee satisfaction. By understanding how ideals impact each component of HRM, practices can be better optimised to create a positive impact on employee satisfaction. 2020 came with many downfalls; the organisation and its stakeholders faced challenges. Catering to this, new aspects of SHRM were presented by Anil Kumar et al. (2020) in the conceptual framework titled 'Sustainability Adoption through Sustainable Human Resource Management: A Systematic Literature Review and Conceptual Framework'. This chapter presented the indicators with the barriers faced while applying SHRM components like economic, environmental and social. The benefits of the same are also presented. Ina Aust (Ehnert) et al. (2020) presented another new and fresh angle of SHRM, that is, Common Good HRM, which relates to a systematic working

Table 1. Evolutions and Angles of SHRM.

S.No.	Author	Year	Dimension
1.	Wesley Ricardo de Souza Freitas et al.	2011	Evolution of SHRM from HRM
2.	Esther Villajos et al.	2019	The mediating role of SHRM is termed to be unique and peculiar.
3.	Anil Kumar et al.	2020	Environmental, social, and economic sustainability, benefits and barriers.
4.	Ina Aust (Ehnert) et al.	2020	Green HRM, triple bottom line

Source: Authors' calculations.

environment and supports leaders to direct their attention to ecological and societal impacts.

Table 2 proposes some relevant perspectives that various authors have presented through published papers all these years. Zaugg et al. (2001)'s model of The Three Pillars of SHRM is validated empirically and academically. This model talks about how employees act in a participatory way regarding decision-making and in a responsible way concerning an organisation. He also extends the importance of balance in workers' professional and personal lives with the autonomy to take forward their well-being. Enhert (2009c) has presented normative interpretations efficient for human capital – the unseen and unquantifiable values that an employee beholds. These values include a worker's skill set, experience and other qualitative aspects. This chapter embarks on the dependence of an organisation upon its environment. De Prins et al. (2014) presented the 'Respect, Openness, and Continuity (ROC) model' that caters to the importance of employees who are the internal stakeholders of an organisation, respecting them, openness in terms of environmental awareness, individualism in an organisation and a continuous focus on both economic and social sustainability as a long-term approach. Maruappanadar and Kramar (2014) recognised four results – hierarchical, social, personal and biological. An organisation's hierarchy results from interaction among all the social, environmental, personal and biological paradigms. He presents SHRM as an example of arranging/arising HR procedures/rehearses planned to aid in pursuing monetary, social

Table 2. Perspectives of SHRM.

S.No.	Author's Name	Year	Model Presented	Dimension
1.	Zaugg et al.	2001	The Three Pillars of SHRM	Worker's employability, balance in work-life, professional progress requiring personal autonomy.
2.	Ehnert	2009	Paradox framework for SHRM	Efficient interpretations, normative sustainability interpretations and human capital.
3.	Mariappanadar and Kramar	2014	Sustainable HRM	'defacement' of HRM that is 'efficiency-oriented' on externalities and stakeholders
4.	de Prins et al.	2014	Respect, Openness and Continuity (ROC) model	Employee Recognition, Environmental Knowledge and its impact on HRM. Take a sustained view of the situation (economic and societal sustainability as well as individual employability)
5.	Tabatabaei et al.	2017	Sustainable HRM Model on BSC	Strategies of sustainable human resource management, HRM that is sustainable in the context of strategic management.

Source: Authors' calculations.

and biological benchmarks while rebuilding the human resource base through time. Tabatabaei et al. (2017) presented the strategies of SHRM and a strategic environment for HRM.

The strategic environment for HRM is to create high-level and proactive management of human resources. HRM is developing, managing and allocating personnel resources to obtain organisational goals.

Fig. 2 gives out a conceptual framework for SHRM. The framework includes the factors of SHRM, its driving forces and the outcomes of SHRM, which include employee outcomes, organisational outcomes and the value created by implementing sustainable human resource (HR) practices. The framework also emphasises that sustainability necessitates a comprehensive approach to managing human resources that goes beyond tackling compliance issues. When developing and implementing sustainable HR policies and procedures, it is critical to consider all the facets of an organisation's human resources strategy. This will ensure that everyone involved in HRM understands and values the importance of sustainability in their work.

SHRM is the practice of managing people in an organisation in a way that positively impacts employee well-being, organisational effectiveness and value creation. The driving forces behind SHRM are organisations' need to remain competitive through innovation, employees' desire for job security and organisations' societal responsibility. SHRM outcomes include increased organisational efficiency, improved employee performance and higher customer satisfaction/loyalty. Implementing SHRM practices can result in significant benefits such as

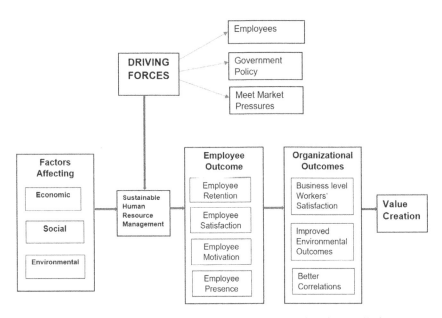

Fig. 2. Conceptual Model/Framework. *Source*: Authors' Compilation.

lower recruitment and retention costs, lower legal expenses related to workplace accidents or misconduct, increased productivity due to better strategic planning and coordination among teams and a more remarkable ability to respond quickly and effectively when business changes necessitate adjustments in staffing levels or operational procedures.

DISCUSSION

Factors Affecting

Those approaches and activities that serve as the foundation of a sustainable HRM aim at recruiting, developing, selecting, deploying and releasing employees economically and socially responsible. The Brundtland Commission proclaims that the three objectives that can be achieved through sustainability are economic, social and environmental, without harming nature (Ehnert, 2009). Many researchers have described economic, social and environmental sustainability as the main factor and three pillars of SHRM. The above pillars and sustainability characteristics are crucial to understanding the purpose of SHRM and the processes that could be incorporated into this HRM approach (Kramar, 2022). Companies are releasing the need for sustainability and its positive effect on the organisation. As a result, an increasing number of organisations are finding ways to implement sustainability in all their operations that affect the economic, social and environmental needs of society.

Economic

Economic sustainability is often linked with reducing costs, economising resources for the coming generations and more helpful administration of the resources (Garza-Reyes et al., 2019; Munasinghe, 1993; Nadeem et al., 2019). SHRM uses sustainability as a factor that benefits all the stakeholders of an organisation, like its employees, managers, customers, etc. SHRM also uses sustainability to achieve long-term economic sustainability that benefits society and the financial condition of the people. Following Nadeem et al. (2018), developing sustainability means making progress in socio-economic and environmental terms without depleting natural resources and making morally just, socially acceptable and commercially successful decisions.

Social

Society plays a huge part in everything that is happening around us, be it personal or professional; Society is there to cater to the needs of society, help them and vice versa. Social sustainability ensures the well-being and development of existing and future generations. A better quality of life can be attained by reducing social inequalities, which is what organisations strive for. A community's capacity to survive and thrive is enhanced when informal and formal systems, processes and community alliances work together to create healthy, liveable communities for today's and tomorrow's generations. A sustainable social community is about equity, connectedness, diversity, democracy and maintaining a good life quality for all its members.

Environmental

Sustainable environmental practices seek to create healthy surroundings, reduce negative impacts and solve issues related to the environment. Organisations, both corporate and non-corporate, are focusing on implementing green HRM in their practices to improve the environmental performance of their company (Jabbour & de-Sousa Jabbour, 2016; Udokporo et al., 2020). Numerous kinds of research emphasise the need for green HRM practices (Ahmad, 2015; Masri & Jaaron, 2017; Mittal & Sangwan, 2014; Opatha & Arulrajah, 2014; Prasad, 2013; Sathyapriya et al., 2013).

The research evidence underscores the importance of green human resource practices, including green recruiting, hiring, performance, reward systems and cooperative relations for achieving positive environmental impacts. Guerci et al. (2016) observed significant positive effects of participation in green activities, performance and compensation in green work regarding environmental performance.

DRIVING FORCES

Sustainability is the need of the hour, and companies are realising this because of the many driving forces that directly or indirectly affect the work of these organisations. There is no denying that the digital revolution has transformed many facets of our lives. However, its influence on HRM has disappointed. Businesses must adopt a more SHRM approach to remain competitive in today's dynamic market. Table 3 shows some of the labels that are the driving forces of SHRM. Employees and their performance act as a driving force for SHRM (Laudal, 2011; Podgorodnichenko et al., 2020). According to Laudal (2011), Jones et al. (2014) and Anlesinya and Susomrith (2020), Government policies, regulatory pressure, customer pressure, etc., are some major driving forces of SHRM. Adopting SHRM undoubtedly has many benefits as it helps improve their public image, gain the public's trust and become a responsible company in the eyes of their customers.

Table 3. Driving Forces of SHRM.

Label	References
Employees	Laudal (2011), Podgorodnichenko et al. (2020)
Government Policy	Laudal (2011), Jones et al. (2014), Anlesinya and Susomrith (2020)
Customer Pressure	Anlesinya and Susomrith (2020)

OUTCOMES

Employee Outcome

Employees, also known as human resources, are the backbone of any organisation. The quality of human resources is directly proportionate to the organisation's outcomes. In addition to ecological health and economic prosperity, social equity contributes directly to enhancing employee value. The conceptual approaches and actions seek to achieve SHRM outcomes like employee retention, employee satisfaction, employee presence and employee motivation, which contribute to socioeconomically and ethically responsible recruitment, selection, training and management of employees. The mentioned outcomes of SHRM will increase the organisation's performance and improve its image in the market. Various authors argue that SHRM positively changes workforce performance, profitability, employee retention, success and performance. Sustainability shows that for an organisation to remain viable, social and ecological objectives should be considered in addition to its financial results. It highlights the importance of integrating these objectives into HRM.

Sustainable HR practices include giving employees the freedom to take up their challenges and encouraging them to give suggestions about improving their environment. They also help to create awareness among employees about their rights and safety. Social sustainability provides employees with a better work-life balance, a high quality of life and learnings that help them in their lives; such improvements in the workers' lives show a positive effect on their commitment to the organisation, which turns into bringing even better results for the company as well as high employee retention which improves their employer branding.

It has now become vividly confident that SHRM practices and employees are interrelated. Table 4 shows the relationship between SHRM and employees presented by many authors from 2012 to 2020. Bettine Lis (2012) presented a module dimensioning how corporate social responsibility plays a relevant part in the organisation for attracting the efficient stakeholders of the company,

Table 4. Employees and Sustainable Human Resource Management.

S.No.	Author	Year	Dimension
1.	Adriana Ana Maria Davidescu et al.	2020	Job satisfaction and performance among employees, the effect of various sorts of adaptability.
2.	Chiara Pellegrini et al.	2018	Drafting of HRM techniques to magnify employees' allegiance to support organisational change for sustainability.
3.	Guerci et al.	2015	Perception of employees in regards to corporate sustainability, decreasing the positive connections between inspiration-improving practices and selfish environment
4.	Bettina Lis	2012	How CSR can be a successful tool to captivate the right employees, and how with SHRM the employers can become the right choice.

that is, employees. CSR with SHRM allows employees to be the 'employer of choice'. Guerci et al. (2015) presented a paper showing empirical research on employees' viewpoints on corporate sustainability.

It also suggests ways to convert the direct relationship between improving practices and employees' egos into an indirect one. Chiara Pellegrini et al. (2018) designed a module of HRM strategies to expand employees' loyalty to support any change in the organisation due to sustainability. The most recent paper by Adriana Ana et al. in 2020 explains how job satisfaction and performance are influenced by the adaptability of various flexibility techniques especially in the COVID-19 era. It also explains how the current HRM practices need to be redesigned in light of future work events. There are many other papers published about employee relations with SHRM practices that talk about employee satisfaction and loyalty (Strenitzerova et al., 2019), the idea of CSR, and SHRM to understand employee branding (Budhiraja et al., 2020) and more. Some employee dimensions and SHRM dimensions are also presented later in this chapter.

ORGANISATIONAL OUTCOMES

Kang et al. (2007) propose that an organisation's success depends on its capability to offer its customers something unique and meaningful, which increases its value in their minds. This customer value can only be attained if the organisation uses its human resources fully. To do this, the firm realises that they have to provide opportunities to the employees which help them overcome their difficulties and encourage them to participate in entrepreneurial activities. SHRM includes cultivating an organisational culture that accepts diversity, allowing employees to experiment and incentivising them to become innovative. SHRM helps connect the lines between the employee's creativity and the organisation's innovativeness.

In addition to developing employee skills through training, competitions, etc., SHRM usage can also motivate employees through punishment and reward systems, which also help in increasing employee involvement. As a result of SHRM practices, organisational productivity is greatly improved, bringing business-level worker satisfaction, improved environmental outcomes and better correlations in the business. Though SHRM practices may be hard to instantly incorporate in an organisation as change is always slow and steady, applying these changes to their HRM system may be slow. However, it helps the company cope with these changing times and helps the organisation in multiple ways. Hence, the organisational outcomes of implementing SHRM in the company outweigh the problems that might occur.

SHRM and an organisation are closely related. For many years, research has been done concerning organisational relationships with SHRM. Nyameh Jerome presented a paper in 2013 that showed SHRM's impact on the organisation's success and vice versa. It has aptly explained how an organisation's practices also play a crucial part in sustainable development. Vihari et al. (2018) found a correlation between SHRM practices and the flexibility of an organisation. Year by year, the conceptualisations have differed. Babel'ová et al. (2019) presented a paper that showed the resolution of issues through SHRM and how to maintain the continuous development of an organisation.

The year 2020 brought a complete change in the ongoing times and presented an entirely new working system for the organisation. Manuti et al. (2020) presented a paper, 'Everything Will Be Fine': A Study on the Relationship between Employees' Perception of SHRM Practices and positive organisational behaviour during COVID-19 explains how the era seriously impacted an organisation and its employees. This review plans to examine workers' view of reasonable HRM at the edge of the COVID-19 crisis, investigating if and how many impressions of inclusion and authoritative help with individual adapting procedures related to hierarchical change could impact positive hierarchical practices. Karman (2020) gave a conceptual framework to link the SHRM with organisational value. The chapter concludes that SHRM is prominent in achieving an organisation's value and benefits. Table 5 depicts certain works of authors related to the interrelation of organisations and SHRM.

INTER-RELATEDNESS

Both organisations and employees are inter-related. If there is any change in one of the two factors, the effect can be seen in the second factor. In the same way, an organisation and its employees are related. Any change in the former impacts or affects the latter and vice versa. SHRM practices, fortunately, have a positive impact. Training, benefit and reward are the three components of SHRM practices, critical for workplace satisfaction and organisational sustenance (Cho & Choi, 2021). Human evolution as an intricately descriptive characteristic of individual psychology about a social and organisational context is dependent on and

Table 5.   Organisation and SHRM.

S.No.	Author	Year	Dimension
1.	Nyameh Jerome	2013	How SHRM impacts an organisation's success and the organisation's role in sustainable development.
2.	Nitin Simha Vihari et al.	2018	Correlation between organisational alterability and SHRM exercises
3.	Zdenka Gyurák Babel'ová et al.	2019	Maintaining the development and potential of an organisation, resolving selected issues and identifying objectives.
4.	Amelia Manuti et al.	2020	How SHRM and hierarchical help together can adapt to methodologies including association, particularly in the Covid period.
5.	Agnieszka Karman	2020	Connection of the possibility of SHRM with hierarchical worth and decide the strength of an HRM framework

Made by the author based on Literature Review.

reflected in the triangulation amongst SHRM, work satisfaction and the organisation's performance (Tortia et al., 2022). If organisations start following SHRM practices even in the minutest of things, it will help the organisation to be more efficient and will eventually help the firm earn a good profit margin. When an organisation gets a good profit margin, the employees get a good raise. In the same way, if the employees start implementing SHRM practices, they become more efficient, and eventually, the performance of an organisation as a whole improves.

VALUE CREATED

The concept of value creation refers to the merit that is attained through the process. The need for SHRM practices is urgent; enhancing human resources gives a company an edge in this competitive world. SHRM processes are precious for organisations due to their learning abilities, rarity, robustness and tacit technique. SHRM creates value both directly and indirectly. It increases the quality of life by creating social value via initiatives such as fair wages, healthcare, other insurances, etc. It also helps strengthen community relations by implementing and promoting charity, fundraising and the involvement of society in such practices. SHRM is something that must be tailored to the needs of the organisation to get the optimum results. The incorporation of SHRM also fulfils the needs of the stakeholders. With increasing awareness about the need for sustainability it helps the organisation distinguish itself and its competitors, and it also makes them more appealing as employers. Following sustainable HR practices provides an advantage to the organisations and creates positive branding for the company. By implementing these practices, the company can establish a reputation as a responsible employer committed to providing a safe and healthy workplace. Furthermore, long-term HR policies reduce liability in the event of workplace injuries or accidents. Besides that, by incorporating sustainability initiatives into the hiring process, the company will be more likely to attract talented individuals who value sustainability initiatives.

CONCLUSION

The research shows the notion of SHRM and its importance in positively impacting the organisation. Through the systematic review approach, this research shows the factors affecting SHRM, the driving forces that help the SHRM approach to remain the need of the hour for the organisations and its positive impact on the employees and the organisation. SHRM practices help achieve employee retention, satisfaction, motivation and presence on an internal level, and they bring business-level worker satisfaction, improved environmental outcomes and better correlations in the business. Adopting SHRM creates excellent value for the company as it gives them an edge in the cutthroat business world as the consumers are more aware than ever and tend to lean towards companies with a good brand image and a favourable environmental impact. However, the research is based on secondary value, and the future scope for the research is that the results could be tested empirically, which would also help in determining the things that may hold more importance to the framework than others and to what extent they impact the organisation.

REFERENCES

Ahmad, S. (2015). Green human resource management: Policies and practices. *Cogent Business & Management, 2*(1), 1030817.

Anlesinya, A., & Susomrith, P. (2020). Sustainable human resource management: A systematic review of a developing field. *Journal of Global Responsibility, 11*(3), 295–324.

Becker, B. E., & Huselid, M. A. (1998). High performance work systems and firm performance: A synthesis of research and managerial implications. *Research in Personnel and Human Resources Management, 16*, 53–101.

Budhiraja, S., & Yadav, S. (2020). Employer branding and employee-emotional bonding – The CSR way to sustainable HRM. In S. Vanka, S. Singh & M. B. Rao (Eds.), *Sustainable human resource management* (pp. 133–149). Springer.

Cho, Y., & Choi, Y. (2021). When and how does sustainable HRM improve customer orientation of frontline employees? Satisfaction, empowerment, and communication. *Sustainability, 13*(7), 3693.

Davidescu, A. A., Apostu, S. A., Paul, A., & Casuneanu, I. (2020). Work flexibility, job satisfaction, and job performance among Romanian employees – Implications for sustainable human resource management. *Sustainability, 12*(15), 6086.

De Prins, P., Van Beirendonck, L., De Vos, A., & Segers, J. (2014). Sustainable HRM: Bridging theory and practice through the 'Respect Openness Continuity (ROC)' model. *Management Revue, 25*(4), 263–284.

De Souza Freitas, W. R., Jabbour, C. J. C., & Santos, F. C. A. (2011). Continuing the evolution: Towards sustainable HRM and sustainable organizations. *Business Strategy Series, 12*(5), 226–234.

Ehnert, I. (2009). *Sustainable human resource management*. Physica-Verlag.

Ehnert, I., Harry, W., & Zink, K. J. (2014). Sustainability and HRM. In I. Ehnert, W. Harry, & K. Zink (Eds.), *Sustainability and human resource management* (pp. 3–32). Springer.

Garza-Reyes, J. A. (2015). Lean and green-a systematic review of the state of the art literature. *Journal of Cleaner Production, 102*(1), 18–29.

Garza-Reyes, J. A., Salomé Valls, A., Nadeem, S. P., Anosike, A., & Kumar, V. (2019). A circularity measurement toolkit for manufacturing SMEs. *International Journal of Production Research, 57*(23), 7319–7343.

Guerci, M., Longoni, A., & Luzzini, D. (2016). Translating stakeholder pressures into environmental performance – The mediating role of green HRM practices. *The International Journal of Human Resource Management, 27*(2), 262–289.

Guerci, M., Radaelli, G., Siletti, E., Cirella, S., & Rami Shani, A. B. (2015). The impact of human resource management practices and corporate sustainability on organizational ethical climates: An employee perspective. *Journal of Business Ethics, 126*(2), 325–342.

Gyurák Babeľová, Z., Stareček, A., Koltnerová, K., & Cagáňová, D. (2020). Perceived organizational performance in recruiting and retaining employees with respect to different generational groups of employees and sustainable human resource management. *Sustainability, 12*(2), 574.

Jabbour, C. J. C., & de Sousa Jabbour, A. B. L. (2016). Green human resource management and green supply chain management: Linking two emerging agendas. *Journal of Cleaner Production, 112*, 1824–1833.

Järlström, M., Saru, E., & Vanhala, S. (2018). Sustainable human resource management with salience of stakeholders: A top management perspective. *Journal of Business Ethics, 152*(3), 703–724.

Jones, P., Hillier, D., & Comfort, D. (2014). Sustainability in the global hotel industry. *International Journal of Contemporary Hospitality Management, 26*(1), 5–17.

Kang, S. C., Morris, S. S., & Snell, S. A. (2007). Relational archetypes, organizational learning, and value creation: Extending the human resource architecture. *Academy of Management Review, 32*(1), 236–256.

Karman, A. (2020). Understanding sustainable human resource management–organizational value linkages: The strength of the SHRM system. *Human Systems Management, 39*(1), 51–68.

Kramar, R. (2022). Sustainable human resource management: Six defining characteristics. *Asia Pacific Journal of Human Resources, 60*(1), 146–170.

Kumar, A., Bhaskar, P., Nadeem, S. P., Tyagi, M., & Garza-Reyes, J. A. (2020). Sustainability adoption through sustainable human resource management: A systematic literature reviews and conceptual framework. *International Journal of Mathematical, Engineering and Management Sciences, 5*(6), 1014–1031.

Laudal, T. (2011). Drivers and barriers of CSR and the size and internationalization of firms. *Social Responsibility Journal, 7*(2), 234–256.

Lis, B. (2012). The relevance of corporate social responsibility for a sustainable human resource management: An analysis of organizational attractiveness as a determinant in employees' selection of a (potential) employer. *Management Revue, 23*(3), 279–295.

Manuti, A., Giancaspro, M. L., Molino, M., Ingusci, E., Russo, V., Signore, F., Zito, M., & Cortese, C. G. (2020). "Everything will be fine": A study on the relationship between employees' perception of sustainable HRM practices and positive organizational behavior during COVID19. *Sustainability, 12*(23), 10216.

Mariappanadar, S., & Kramar, R. (2014). Sustainable HRM: The synthesis effect of high performance work systems on organisational performance and employee harm. *Asia-Pacific Journal of Business Administration, 6*(3), 206–224.

Masri, H. A., & Jaaron, A. A. (2017). Assessing green human resources management practices in Palestinian manufacturing context: An empirical study. *Journal of Cleaner Production, 143*, 474–489.

Mittal, V. K., & Sangwan, K. S. (2014). Prioritizing drivers for green manufacturing: Environmental, social and economic perspectives. *Procedia Cirp, 15*, 135–140.

Munasinghe, M. (1993). Environmental economics and biodiversity management in developing countries. *Ambio, 22*(2/3), 126–135.

Nadeem, S. P., Garza-Reyes, J. A., Anosike, A. I., & Kumar, V. (2017). Spectrum of circular economy and its prospects in logistics. In *Proceedings of the 2017 international symposium on industrial engineering and operations management (IEOM)*, Bristol, UK (pp. 440–451).

Nadeem, S. P., Garza-Reyes, J. A., & Glanville, D. (2018). The challenges of the circular economy. In E. Conway & D. Byrne (Eds.), *Contemporary issues in accounting* (pp. 37–60). Palgrave Macmillan.

Nadeem, S. P., Garza-Reyes, J. A., Kumar, V., & Anosike, A. I. (2019). Coalescing the lean and circular economy. In *Proceedings of the 9th international conference on industrial engineering and operations management (IEOM)* (pp. 1–12). IEOM Society.

Opatha, H. H. P., & Arulrajah, A. A. (2014). Green human resource management: Simplified general reflections. *International Business Research, 7*(8), 101–112.

Pellegrini, C., Rizzi, F., & Frey, M. (2018). The role of sustainable human resource practices in influencing employee behavior for corporate sustainability. *Business Strategy and the Environment, 27*(8), 1221–1232.

Podgorodnichenko, N., Akmal, A., Edgar, F., & Everett, A. M. (2020). Sustainable HRM: Toward addressing diverse employee roles. *Employee Relations: The International Journal, 44*(3), 576–608.

Prasad, R. S. (2013). Green HRM-partner in sustainable competitive growth. *Journal of Management Sciences and Technology, 1*(1), 15–18.

Sathyapriya, J., Kanimozhi, R., & Adhilakshmi, V. (2013). Green HRM-delivering high performance HR systems. *International Journal of Marketing and Human Resource Management, 4*(2), 19–25.

Schaltegger, S., & Wagner, M. (2006). Integrative management of sustainability performance, measurement and reporting. *International Journal of Accounting, Auditing and Performance Evaluation, 3*(1), 1–19.

Sena, J., & Shani, A. R. (2008). Utilizing technology to support sustainability. In P. Docherty, & A. B. Mira Kira (Eds.), *Creating Sustainable Work Systems* (pp. 110–126). Routledge.

Sosik, J. J., Avolio, B. J., & Jung, D. I. (2002). Beneath the mask: Examining the relationship of self-presentation attributes and impression management to charismatic leadership. *The Leadership Quarterly, 13*(3), 217–242.

Strenitzerová, M., & Achimský, K. (2019). Employee satisfaction and loyalty as a part of sustainable human resource management in postal sector. *Sustainability, 11*(17), 4591.

Tabatabaei, S. A. N., Omran, E. S., Hashemi, S., & Sedaghat, M. (2017). Presenting sustainable HRM model based on balanced scorecard in knowledge-based ICT companies (the case of Iran). *Economics & Sociology, 10*(2), 107–124.

Tortia, E. C., Sacchetti, S., & López-Arceiz, F. J. (2022). A human growth perspective on sustainable HRM practices, worker well-being and organizational performance. *Sustainability, 14*(17), 11064.

Udokporo, C. K., Anosike, A., Lim, M., Nadeem, S. P., Garza-Reyes, J. A., & Ogbuka, C. P. (2020). Impact of lean, agile and green (LAG) on business competitiveness: An empirical study of fast moving consumer goods businesses. *Resources, Conservation and Recycling, 156*, 104714.

Vihari, N. S., Rao, M. K., & Jada, U. (2018). Empirical linkage between sustainable HRM and organisational flexibility: A SEM-based approach. *International Journal of Business Innovation and Research, 17*(1), 65–86.

Villajos, E., Tordera, N., & Peiró, J. M. (2019). Human resource practices, eudaimonic well-being, and creative performance: The mediating role of idiosyncratic deals for sustainable human resource management. *Sustainability, 11*(24), 6933.

Wehling, C., Guanipa Hernandez, A., Osland, J., Osland, A., Deller, J., Tanure, B., & Sairaj, A. (2009). An exploratory study of the role of HRM and the transfer of German MNC sustainability values to Brazil. *European Journal of International Management, 3*(2), 176–198.

Zaugg, R. J., Blum, A., & Thom, N. (2001). *Sustainability in human resource management*. Evaluation Report. Survey in European companies and institutions, Switzerland.

CHAPTER 4

DETERRENTS TO DIGITAL SUSTAINABILITY IN MSMEs

Kriti Dhingra[a] and Kanika Dhingra Sardana[b]

[a]Vivekananda Institute of Professional Studies, New Delhi, India
[b]IINTM, New Delhi, India

ABSTRACT

Introduction: *Sustainability and Industry 4.0 have recently influenced the global economy. With the Industrial Revolution 4.0, there has been a significant focus on digital sustainability in enterprises. Micro, small and medium enterprises (MSMEs) are the most vulnerable sections regarding new transformations.*

Purpose: *Even during the COVID-19 pandemic, when all businesses had no option other than to adopt digitisation, MSMEs faced tremendous issues to make this shift. Despite the immense focus on digital sustainability, some deterrents exist to its adoption in MSMEs. Contemporary research focuses on determining the critical deterrents to digital sustainability in MSMEs.*

Methodology: *This chapter employs the interpretive structural modelling technique, and Matrice impacts Croises Multiplication Appliqué a classement (MICMAC) analysis to identify and further classify the deterrents to digital sustainability in MSMEs.*

Sustainable Development Goals: The Impact of Sustainability Measures on Wellbeing
Contemporary Studies in Economic and Financial Analysis, Volume 113B, 43–56
Copyright © 2024 by Kriti Dhingra and Kanika Dhingra Sardana
Published under exclusive licence by Emerald Publishing Limited
ISSN: 1569-3759/doi:10.1108/S1569-37592024000113B004

Findings: *Legal barriers and firms' economic conditions are identified as the major deterrents. Eliminating these deterrents would help minimise the minor ones too. To deliver global sustainability goals, digital sustainability must be duly adopted everywhere.*

Keywords: Digital sustainability; Industry 4.0; SMEs; interpretive structural modelling; MICMAC analysis; digitalisation

1. INTRODUCTION

With the outburst of the COVID-19 pandemic, the world economy has been hardly hit. The mobility restrictions had deeply affected all the economic activities. Almost all the service sectors have been affected by the pandemic. However, the pandemic has unusually stirred the need to use digital technologies (Dannenberg et al., 2020). People are using virtual conferences to meet, e-marketplaces to purchase goods and services, students learning remotely, etc. Digital technologies are helping people to maintain a new momentum to adjust to the new normal.

In recent years, several studies have focused on using digital technologies in businesses because of the Industrial Revolution 4.0. With the advent of this revolution a decade ago, the way businesses work has completely revolutionised (Stock & Seliger, 2016). The Industrial Revolution 4.0 technologies aim to maximise output and efficiency using minimal resources. Ever since the first industrial revolution, everyone globally has faced challenges in manufacturing more goods from restricted and diminishing natural resources to fulfil the growing consumption demand, negatively affecting the environment (Beier et al., 2020; Müller & Voigt, 2018). Thus, the impact of Industry Revolution 4.0 on sustainability is gaining much importance nowadays.

Sahut et al. (2019) enlightened the immense interest in the enablers to facilitate digitisation of businesses and government policies and its impact on economic growth. OERs, crowdsourcing, data mining and modern technology are critical enablers (Steininger, 2019). However, the COVID-19 pandemic is added to the enabler list for this adoption. These enablers are changing both the consumer's and organisations' way of functioning, hence leading to the augmented transformation of medium- and small-scale enterprises (MSMEs) and large organisations (Gavrila & Ancillo, 2021; del Olmo-García et al., 2020).

Digital sustainability is a novel approach that harnesses a notable influential force for social change, referred to as digitalisation, to bring whatever is required sustainably. With the help of digitalisation, we can easily track the consequences of consuming our needs. Today, where we are destroying our planet with overconsumption of natural resources, digitalisation can provide us with a treasured tool. Bradley (2007) defined digital sustainability as:

'Encompassing the wide range of issues and concerns that contribute to the longevity of digital information' throughout the 'overall life cycle, technical, and sociotechnical issues associated with the creation and management of the digital item'.

Since MSMEs are considered as the backbone of the economy in several developing and developed countries, it is essential to understand the adoption of digitalisation in these enterprises. With complete digitalisation, the MSMEs could connect globally and reduce the polarising effect of the economic disruption caused by the pandemic. However, a few apprehensions exist, especially from the MSMEs, in adopting digital sustainability. The current research focuses on identifying the significant deterrents to adopting digital sustainability in MSMEs. Eliminating the major deterrents would also impact the minor ones, leading to the successful adoption of digitalisation. Interpretive structural modelling (ISM) technique and MICMAC analysis have corroborated the significant deterrents to adopting digital sustainability in MSMEs.

2. LITERATURE REVIEW

The economy has seen a comprehensive digital revolution in the industry during the past 10 years. The Industrial Revolution 4.0 is a compelling phenomenon, not just a mere media event (Ardito et al., 2018; Buer et al., 2018). Since this revolution, digital transformation has been grasping the attention of different industries globally (Ghobakhloo et al., 2021; Nascimento et al., 2018). This shift to digital transformation to the concept of digital sustainability.

MSMEs are the major backbones of any developing country's economy. As a result, in the modern digital world, it is crucial to research the adoption of digital sustainability in this industry (Mukhoryanova et al., 2021), specifically after the pandemic, where technology was the only source to connect businesses with people. There have been many studies on digital sustainability in different territories globally and how digitalisation multiplied during the pandemic.

Muhamad et al. (2021) steered an e-survey among different industrial sectors (services, retail, manufacturing and tourism) in Malaysia. He showed a substantial increase in digitalisation in various enterprises during the pandemic compared to before the pandemic.

Mohapatra et al. (2022) conducted a study in the manufacturing sector. He mentioned in his study that during the pandemic, the importance of digital technology was well understood, and customers also gained confidence in using digital technology during this time.

Jorge-Vázquez et al. (2021) researched the Agri-Food Cooperative Sector in Europe. The study suggested that company digitalisation was undoubtedly of interest and that this interest boosts an organisation's profitability in terms of effectiveness and competition.

Massaro (2021) conducted his study in medical practices. He mentioned that digital transformation can help solve many problems in this line. Apart from this, digitalisation may offer new development patterns like blockchains, which reduces issues in data management.

Many studies investigated the impact of mobility restrictions and the adoption of digital sustainability in small businesses (Hidalgo et al., 2021; Parilla, 2021; Tudy, 2021).

Reyes (2022), in his study, recognised the viewpoint of top-level management of the nation's leading corporations to assess the pandemic's economic impact and government actions for them.

Though there have been several studies enlisting the benefits of digital sustainability for MSMEs, very few have reported whether this adoption is being optimally implemented. There have been several deterrents that have existed for the proper adoption of digital sustainability in MSMEs. Eliminating the major ones would help minimise the minor ones, leading to a successful adoption. The significant deterrents identified from the literature have been mentioned in Table 1.

3. RESEARCH METHODOLOGY

The significant deterrents were identified using the literature and reconfirmed with experts in the respective area to finalise the major deterrents in adopting digital sustainability in MSMEs.

3.1. Interpretive Structural Modelling

The major deterrents to adopting digital sustainability in MSMEs were identified using the literature. Furthermore, the renowned ISM technique to identify the most significant barriers. Identifications of the significant barriers help find a relationship between them and the other barriers.

The ISM technique was developed by Warfield in 1974. The ISM approach is a collaborative learning procedure that helps improve the order and path of the complicated relations among variables in a system (Sage, 1977). This technique can be used to determine if and how the variables in a complicated situation relate (Dalvi-Esfahani et al., 2017; Gan et al., 2018; Rajaprasad & Chalapathi, 2015). Here, unlike and related variables that affect a system under a specific consideration are structured in an extensive systemic model. The resultant model will portray the structure of a complicated issue in a thoroughly designed form using graphics and words (Azevedo et al., 2019; Kannan, 2018; Mangla et al., 2018). ISM has been used in various fields. Abuzeinab et al. (2017) investigated various

Table 1. Deterrents to Adoption of Digital Sustainability in MSMEs.

S. No.	Deterrent	References
1.	Lack of top management support	Agag (2019), Alsaad et al. (2018), Al-Tit and Nakhleh
2.	Limitation of employees' IT knowledge	(2014), Arshad et al. (2018), Awa et al. (2015a, 2015b), Chuang et al. (2007), Corbitt et al. (2003),
3.	Legal barriers/ Government Regulations	Daniel et al. (2002), Dwivedi et al. (2009), Eid (2011), Ekanem and Abiade (2018), Gefen (2000),
4.	Lack of IT infrastructure	Ghobakhloo et al. (2011), Gibbs et al. (2003),
5.	Lack of internet security	Hallikainen and Laukkanen (2018), Hussein et al.
6.	Content barriers	(2019), Raudeliūnienė et al. (2018), Scupola (2009),
7.	Lack of customer readiness	Van Huy et al. (2012), Wymer and Regan (2005),
8.	Economic conditions of the firm	Al-Tit et al. (2014).

Source: Authors' compilation.

barriers to sustainable models using ISM in the UK. The relationships between several impediments to the adoption of smart grid technology were examined by Luthra et al. (2014). The interaction of barriers in implementing OHSAS 18001 was examined by Rajaprasad and Chalapathi (2015) in India.

The steps for developing a model using the ISM technique are as follows:

1. Identify the barriers to digital sustainability in MSMEs.
2. Set up contextual relationships amongst the various barriers identified from the literature. Create the structural self-interaction matrix (SSIM) of variables that show a pairwise relation amongst the barriers.
3. Build the reachability matrix (RM) using the structural self-interaction matrix. Furthermore, remove the transitive relations.
4. Split the RM into separate levels.
5. Create a digraph based on the relationships in RM.
6. Convert the digraph to an ISM model by correctly substituting each node with its associated statement.
7. Analyse the developed ISM model and verify that there are no conceptual contradictions. Modify the model if needed.

Each step is explained in detail below.

Step 1: Identify the Barriers in Adoption of Digital Sustainability in MSMEs
Extensive literature was reviewed to identify the significant deterrents to adopting digital sustainability in MSMEs. Furthermore, semi-structured focus group interviews were undertaken with specialists in the area to validate the barriers. The significant barriers identified were lack of backing from upper management, Limited Information Technology expertise among the staff, Legal barriers/ Government Regulations, Lack of security measures on the internet, Inadequate IT infrastructure, Content barriers, Lack of customer readiness and Economic conditions of the firm. The identified barriers and their references are listed in Table 1. Furthermore, this table is used to find relations among the barriers.

Step 2: Setting Conceptual Relations and Creating SSIM
The barriers identified in Step 1 are organised as a matrix. The pairwise relationship is developed amongst the barriers, starting from the first barrier one at a time. Contextual relations are established among the barriers. The relation between two barriers (i1 and i2) is represented using the following symbols:

- V is used if barrier i1 helps attain barrier i2.
- A is used if barrier i2 helps attain barrier i1.
- X is used if both barriers i1 and i2 help attain each other.
- O is used if barriers i1 and i2 are not associated.

The SSIM developed based on relationships is depicted in Table 2. The established relationships among different deterrents to digital sustainability in MSMEs are shown in this table. Furthermore, Table 2 is used for constructing RM.

Table 2. Structural Self-Interaction Matrix (SSIM).

Barrier No.	1	2	3	4	5	6	7	8
1	V	X	A	V	A	O	O	A
2		V	O	A	O	O	O	A
3			V	O	V	O	V	O
4				V	X	O	O	A
5					V	O	V	A
6						V	V	A
7							V	O
8								V

Source: Authors' calculations.

Step 3: Constructing RM
In Table 3, RM is constructed by substituting '0s' and '1s' in the SSIM. The substitutions made are as follows:

- If the value in cell (i1,i2) in SSIM is 'V', then (i1,i2) will become '1' and (i2,i1) will become '0' in the initial RM.
- If the value in cell (i1,i2) in SSIM is 'A', then (i1,i2) will become '0', and (i2,i1) will become '1' in the initial RM.
- If the value in cell (i1,i2) in SSIM is 'X', then both (i1,i2) and (i2,i1) will become '1' in the initial RM.
- If the value in cell (i1,i2) in SSIM is 'O', then (i1,i2) and (i2,i1) will become '0' in the initial RM.

Furthermore, this initial reachability matrix is checked for transitive relations. The final reachability matrix is attained after the concept of transitivity is applied. The final reachability matrix is shown in Table 4, with transitive relations marked with 1*. The driving and dependence power is also shown in this table. The number of barriers a particular barrier may assist in attaining, including

Table 3. Reachability Matrix.

Barrier No.	1	2	3	4	5	6	7	8
1	1	1	0	1	0	0	0	0
2	1	1	0	0	0	0	0	0
3	1	0	1	1	1	0	1	0
4	0	1	0	1	1	0	0	0
5	1	0	0	1	1	0	1	0
6	0	0	0	0	0	1	1	0
7	0	0	0	0	0	0	1	0
8	1	1	0	1	1	1	0	1

Source: Authors' calculations.

Table 4. Final Reachability Matrix.

Barrier No.	1	2	3	4	5	6	7	8
1	1	1	0	1	1*	0	0	0
2	1	1	0	1*	1*	0	1*	0
3	1	1*	1	1	1	0	1	0
4	0	1	0	1	1	0	0	0
5	1	1*	0	1	1	0	1	0
6	0	0	0	0	0	1	1	0
7	0	0	0	0	0	0	1	0
8	1	1	0	1	1	1	1*	1

Source: Authors' calculations.

itself, is known as its driving power. It can be calculated by adding the number of 1s in a row. A particular barrier may get assisted in attaining, including itself, is known as its dependency power. It can be calculated by adding the total number of 1s in a column.

Step 4: Split the RM into Separate Levels
Level partitioning is done to identify different levels in a model. The reachability set, antecedent set and intersection set are used to identify the level partition of a variable in order to define the hierarchy. The variables in the reachability set will include itself and others it may affect. The antecedent set will consist of variables that may impact it, including itself. The intersection set will consist of all the standard variables of the reachability and antecedent set. Reachability and antecedent sets can be obtained from the RM, and intersection sets can be generated from them. The level of each variable can be determined by comparing the reachability and intersection set. Variables with identical reachability and intersection set are put in level 1. These variables are then removed from the further iterations, and the exact steps are repeated to obtain further levels. Tables 5–8 depict the level partitioning. Barriers 4 and 7 are shown in Table 5 at the

Table 5. RM Partitioning (Iteration 1).

Barrier No.	Reachability Set	Antecedent Set	Intersection	Level
1	1,2,3,5,8	1,2,4,5	1,2,5	
2	1,2,3,4,5,8	1,2,4,5,7	1,2,4,5	
3	3	1,2,3,4,5,7	3	
4	1,2,3,4,5,8	2,4,5	2,4,5	I
5	1,2,3,4,5,8	1,2,4,5,7	1,2,4,5	
6	6,8	6,7	6	
7	2,5,6,7	7	7	I
8	8	1,2,4,5,6,7,8	8	

Source: Authors' calculations.

Table 6.   RM Partitioning (Iteration 2).

Barrier No.	Reachability Set	Antecedent Set	Intersection	Level
1	1,2,3,5,8	1,2,5	1,2,5	II
2	1,2,3,5,8	1,2,5	1,2,5	II
3	3	1,2,3,5	3	
5	1,2,3,5,8	1,2,5	1,2,5	
6	6,8	6	6	II
8	8	1,2,5,6,8	8	

Source: Authors' calculations.

Table 7.   RM Partitioning (Iteration 3).

Barrier No.	Reachability Set	Antecedent Set	Intersection	Level
3	3	3,5	3	
5	3,5,8	5	5	III
8	8	5,8	8	

Source: Authors' calculations.

Table 8.   RM Partitioning (Iteration 4).

Barrier No.	Reachability Set	Antecedent Set	Intersection	Level
3	3	3	3	IV
8	8	8	8	IV

Source: Authors' calculations.

initial level. Table 6 lists the second-level barriers 1, 2 and 6. Barrier 5 is shown at the third level in Table 7.

Table 8 shows barriers 3 and 8 at the utmost level.

Step 5: Construction of Digraph
After level partitioning, a digraph shows the directional relations amongst different barriers (variables). Level 4 creates the root node, demonstrating that barriers 3 and 8 are the most important obstacles and have an impact on all other barriers. The digraph is depicted in Fig. 1. This diagram shows numerous barriers organised into levels ranging from level 1 to level 4.

Step 6: Digraph Conversion to the ISM Model
The ISM model is further developed using the digraph by replacing the nodes' variables with the statements. Fig. 2 depicts the ISM model showing the barriers to adopting digital sustainability in MSMEs. It can be seen from the figure that the organisation's economic conditions and Legal barriers/government regulations are the significant barriers.

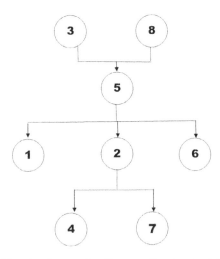

Fig. 1 Digraph Showing Interaction Between Barriers to Adoption of Digital Sustainability in MSMEs. *Source*: Authors' calculations.

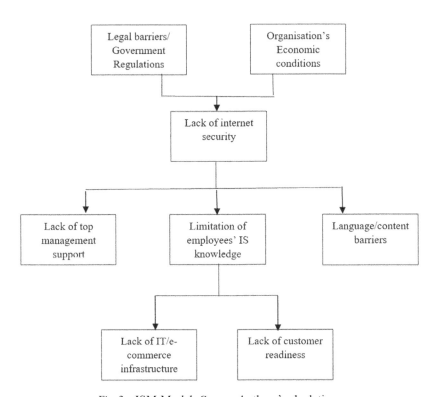

Fig. 2 ISM Model. *Source*: Authors' calculations.

Step 7: Reviewing of the ISM Model
The focus group members evaluated the model created and concurred with the findings. The model was then completed. Further structural analysis of the created model for barrier classification was done using MICMAC analysis.

3.2. MICMAC Analysis

Matrice d'Impacts Croises Multiplication Appliqué a classement (MICMAC) approach can be used to investigate the distribution of effects across reaction paths, loops for the construction of hierarchies for participants in an element set and more (Wang et al., 2008). Various elements' driving and dependency power are typically examined during MICMAC analysis. Each factor can be placed in one of the categories:

Autonomous factors: These variables' driving and dependence powers are weak. Cluster I represents autonomous factors. Language/content barrier falls under this category.

Dependent factors: These variables have a strong dependence but weak driving power. Cluster II represents dependent factors. Legal barriers/government regulations and the organisation's economic condition fall under this category.

Linkage factors: These variables' driving and dependence powers are strong. Cluster III represents linkage factors. Lack of top management support, limited employees' IT knowledge and lack of internet security fall under this category.

Independent factors variables possess weak dependence power but strong driving power. Cluster IV represents this category. Lack of IT infrastructure and lack of customer readiness fall under this category.

The MICMAC analysis for the factors is depicted in Fig. 3.

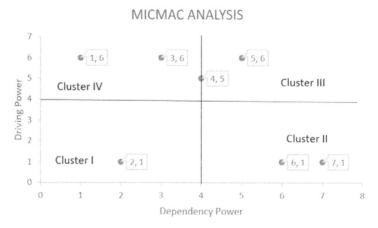

Fig. 3   Matrice d'Impacts Croises Multipication Appliqué a Classement (MICMAC) Analysis. *Source*: Authors' calculations.

4. CONCLUSION

Digital sustainability and Industry 4.0 have recently grown to play a significant role in the world economy. Nowadays, many studies are being conducted to understand the sustainability aspects with a specific focus on digital technologies.

In the current research work, significant deterrents to adopting digital sustainability have been identified using the literature. Furthermore, the ISM technique is used to identify the significant deterrents and their relation with the other ones.

Identification of these deterrents would help the firms to eliminate them and further reduce the minor ones. With the world revolving around technology, especially after the pandemic, where everything is technology-driven, it is very important that there should be complete digital sustainability in both large-scale firms and MSMEs. MSMEs should focus on minimising the barriers to adopting digital sustainability and promoting digitalisation.

5. LIMITATIONS AND FUTURE SCOPE

The limitation of the current study is that significant deterrents reported are in the Indian context. The study can further explore with problems faced by MSMEs across the world. In future, the authors would like to explore the driving factors for digital sustainability in MSMEs as well.

REFERENCES

Abuzeinab, A., Arif, M., & Qadri, M. A. (2017). Barriers to MNEs green business models in the UK construction sector: An ISM analysis. *Journal of Cleaner Production, 160*, 27–37.

Agag, G. (2019). E-commerce ethics and its impact on buyer repurchase intentions and loyalty: An empirical study of small and medium Egyptian businesses. *Journal of Business Ethics, 154*(5), 389–410. https://doi.org/10.1007/s10551-017-3452-3

Alsaad, A., Mohamad, R., & Ismail, N. A. (2018). The contingent role of dependency in predicting the intention to adopt B2B E-commerce. *Information Technology for Development, 25*(4), 686–714. https://doi.org/10.1080/02681102.2018.1476830

Al-Tit, A. A., & Nakhleh, H. (2014). The role of e-marketing in the development of internet user attitudes toward tourist sites in Saudi Arabia. *Journal of Administrative and Economic Sciences, 7*(2), 25–44. https://doi.org/10.12816/0009659

Ardito, L., Petruzzelli, A. M., Panniello, U., & Garavelli, A. C. (2018). Towards Industry 4.0: Mapping digital technologies for supply chain management-marketing integration. *Business Process Management Journal, 25*(2), 323–346.

Arshad, Y., Chin, W. P., Yahaya, S. N., Nizam, N. Z., Masrom, N. R., & Ibrahim, S. N. S. (2018). Small and medium enterprises' adoption for e-commerce in Malaysia tourism state. *International Journal of Academic Research in Business and Social Sciences, 8*(10), 1457–1557. https://doi.org/10.6007/IJARBSS/v8-i10/5311

Awa, H. O., Ojiabo, O. U., & Emecheta, B. C. (2015a). Integrating TAM, TPB and TOE frameworks and expanding their characteristic constructs for e-commerce adoption by SMEs. *Journal of Science & Technology Policy Management, 6*(1), 76–94. https://doi.org/10.1108/JSTPM-04-2014-0012

Awa, H., Awara, N., & Lebari, E. (2015b). Critical factors inhibiting electronic commerce (EC) adoption in Nigeria: A study of operators of SMEs. *Journal of Science and Technology Policy Management, 6*(2), 143–164. https://doi.org/10.1108/JSTPM-07-2014-0033

Azevedo, S. G., Sequeira, T., Santos, M., & Mendes, L. (2019). Biomass-related sustainability: A review of the literature and interpretive structural modeling. *Energy*, *171*, 1107–1125.

Beier, G., Ullrich, A., Niehoff, S., Reißig, M., & Habich, M. (2020). Industry 4.0: How it is defined from a sociotechnical perspective and how much sustainability it includes – A literature review. *Journal of Cleaner Production*, *259*, 120856.

Bradley, K. (2007). Defining digital sustainability. *Library Trends*, *56*(1), 148–163.

Buer, S. V., Strandhagen, J. O., & Chan, F. T. (2018). The link between Industry 4.0 and lean manufacturing: Mapping current research and establishing a research agenda. *International Journal of Production Research*, *56*(8), 2924–2940.

Chuang, T. T., Nakatani, K., Chen, J. C., & Huang, I. L. (2007). Examining the impact of organisational and owner's characteristics on the extent of e-commerce adoption in SMEs. *International Journal of Business and Systems Research*, *1*(1), 61–80. https://doi.org/10.1504/IJBSR.2007.014770

Corbitt, B. J., Thanasankit, T., & Yi, H. (2003). Trust and e-commerce: A study of consumer perceptions. *Electronic Commerce Research and Applications*, *2*(3), 203–215. https://doi.org/10.1016/S1567-4223(03)00024-3

Dalvi-Esfahani, M., Ramayah, T., & Nilashi, M. (2017). Modelling upper echelons' behavioural drivers of Green IT/IS adoption using an integrated interpretive structural modelling – Analytic network process approach. *Telematics and Informatics*, *34*(2), 583–603.

Daniel, E., Wilson, H., & Myers, A. (2002). Adoption of e-commerce by SMEs in the UK: Towards a stage model. *International Small Business Journal*, *20*(3), 253–270. https://doi.org/10.1177/0266242602203002

Dannenberg, P., Fuchs, M., Riedler, T., & Wiedemann, C. (2020). Digital transition by COVID-19 pandemic? The German food online retail. *Tijdschrift Voor Economische en Sociale Geografie*, *111*(3), 543–560.

del Olmo-García, F., Crecente, F., & Sarabia, M. (2020). Macroeconomic and institutional drivers of early failure among self-employed entrepreneurs: An analysis of the euro zone. *Economic Research-Ekonomska istraživanja*, *33*(1), 1830–1848.

Dwivedi, Y., Lal, B., & Williams, M. (2009). Managing consumer adoption of broadband: Examining drivers and barriers. *Industrial Management & Data Systems*, *109*(3), 357–369. https://doi.org/10.1108/02635570910939380

Eid, M. I. (2011). Determinants of e-commerce customer satisfaction, trust, and loyalty in Saudi Arabia. *Journal of Electronic Commerce Research*, *12*(1), 78–93.

Ekanem, I., & Abiade, G. E. (2018). Factors influencing the use of e-commerce by small enterprises in Nigeria. *International Journal of ICT Research in Africa and the Middle East (IJICTRAME)*, *7*(1), 37–53.

Gan, X., Chang, R., Zuo, J., Wen, T., & Zillante, G. (2018). Barriers to the transition towards off-site construction in China: An Interpretive structural modeling approach. *Journal of Cleaner Production*, *197*, 8–18.

Gavrila, S. G., & Ancillo, A. D. L. (2021). Entrepreneurship, innovation, digitization and digital transformation toward a sustainable growth within the pandemic environment. *International Journal of Entrepreneurial Behavior & Research*, *28*(1), 45–66.

Gefen, D. (2000). E-commerce: The role of familiarity and trust. *Omega*, *28*(6), 725–737. https://doi.org/10.1016/S0305-0483(00)00021-9

Ghobakhloo, M., Arias-Aranda, D., & Benitez-Amado, J. (2011). Adoption of e-commerce applications in SMEs. *Industrial Management & Data Systems*, *111*(8), 1238–1269. https://doi.org/10.1108/02635571111170785

Ghobakhloo, M., Fathi, M., Iranmanesh, M., Maroufkhani, P., & Morales, M. E. (2021). Industry 4.0 ten years on: A bibliometric and systematic review of concepts, sustainability value drivers, and success determinants. *Journal of Cleaner Production*, *302*, 127052.

Gibbs, J., Kraemer, K. L., & Dedrick, J. (2003). Environment and policy factors shaping global e-commerce diffusion: A cross-country comparison. *The Information Society*, *19*(1), 5–18. https://doi.org/10.1080/01972240309472

Hallikainen, H., & Laukkanen, T. (2018). National culture and consumer trust in e-commerce. *International Journal of Information Management*, *38*(1), 97–106. https://doi.org/10.1016/j.ijinfomgt.2017.07.002

Hidalgo, D. T., Marquez, F. P. B., Sarmenta, P. B., Alvarez, J. K. A., Ong, D. U., & Balaria, F. E. (2021). Impact of Covid-19 on micro and small entrepreneur (MSE) graduates of the Kapatid mentor me program of the department of trade and industry. *International Journal of Advanced Engineering, Management and Science, 7,* 19–26.

Hussein, L. A., Baharudin, A. S., Jayaraman, K., & Kiumarsi, S. (2019). B2B e-commerce technology factors with mediating effect perceived usefulness in Jordanian manufacturing SMES. *Journal of Engineering Science and Technology, 14*(1), 411–429.

Jorge-Vázquez, J., Chivite-Cebolla, M., & Salinas-Ramos, F. (2021). The digitalization of the European agri-food cooperative sector. Determining factors to embrace information and communication technologies. *Agriculture, 11*(6), 514.

Kannan, D. (2018). Role of multiple stakeholders and the critical success factor theory for the sustainable supplier selection process. *International Journal of Production Economics, 195,* 391–418.

Luthra, S., Garg, D., & Haleem, A. (2014). Sustainable purchasing in Indian automobile industry: An ISM approach. *Manufacturing Excellence: Imperatives for Emerging Economies,* 95–108.

Mangla, S. K., Luthra, S., Rich, N., Kumar, D., Rana, N. P., & Dwivedi, Y. K. (2018). Enablers to implement sustainable initiatives in agri-food supply chains. *International Journal of Production Economics, 203,* 379–393.

Massaro, M. (2021). Digital transformation in the healthcare sector through blockchain technology. Insights from academic research and business developments. *Technovation, 20,* 102386.

Mohapatra, B., Tripathy, S., Singhal, D., & Saha, R. (2022). Significance of digital technology in manufacturing sectors: Examination of key factors during COVID-19. *Research in Transportation Economics, 93,* 101134.

Muhamad, S., Kusairi, S., Man, M., Majid, N. F. H., & Kassim, W. Z. W. (2021). Digital adoption by enterprises in Malaysian industrial sectors during COVID-19 pandemic: A data article. *Data in Brief, 37,* 107197.

Mukhoryanova, O., Kuleshova, L., Rusakova, N., & Mirgorodskaya, O. (2021). Sustainability of micro-enterprises in the digital economy. In *E3S Web of Conferences* (Vol. 250, p. 06008). EDP Sciences.

Müller, J. M., & Voigt, K. I. (2018). Sustainable industrial value creation in SMEs: A comparison between industry 4.0 and made in China 2025. *International Journal of Precision Engineering and Manufacturing-Green Technology, 5*(5), 659–670.

Nascimento, D. L. M., Alencastro, V., Quelhas, O. L. G., Caiado, R. G. G., Garza-Reyes, J. A., Rocha-Lona, L., & Tortorella, G. (2018). Exploring Industry 4.0 technologies to enable circular economy practices in a manufacturing context: A business model proposal. *Journal of Manufacturing Technology Management, 30*(3), 607–627.

Parilla, E. S. (2021, August). Effects of COVID-19 pandemic on micro, small, and medium-sized enterprises in the Province of Ilocos Norte Philippines. *RSF Conference Series: Business, Management and Social Sciences, 1*(2), 46–57.

Rajaprasad, S. V. S., & Chalapathi, P. V. (2015). Factors influencing implementation of OHSAS 18001 in Indian construction organizations: Interpretive structural modeling approach. *Safety and health at work, 6*(3), 200–205.

Raudeliūnienė, J., Davidavičienė, V., Tvaronaviciene, M., & Radeckytė, V. (2018). A study of success factors of women's leadership in e-commerce. *Terra Economicus, 16*(3), 131–149.

Reyes, L. G. (2022). Philippine private sector response, strategies, and state-business relations toward economic recovery and growth post-COVID-19. *Business and Politics, 24*(1), 18–35.

Sage, A. P. (1977) *Interpretive Structural Modelling: Methodology for Large Scale Systems* (pp. 91–164). McGraw-Hill.

Sahut, J.-M., Iandoli, L., & Teulon, F. (2019). The age of digital entrepreneurship. *Small Business Economics, 56,* 159–169.

Scupola, A. (2009). SMEs' e-commerce adoption: Perspectives from Denmark and Australia. *Journal of Enterprise Information Management, 22*(1/2), 152–166. https://doi.org/10.1108/17410390910932803

Steininger, D. M. (2019). Linking information systems and entrepreneurship: A review and agenda for IT-associated and digital entrepreneurship research. *Information Systems Journal, 29*(2), 363–407.

Stock, T., & Seliger, G. (2016). Opportunities of sustainable manufacturing in industry 4.0. *Procedia CIRP*, *40*, 536–541.

Tudy, R. A. (2021). From the corporate world to freelancing: The phenomenon of working from home in the Philippines. *Community, Work & Family*, *24*(1), 77–92.

Van Huy, L., Rowe, F., Truex, D., & Huynh, M. Q. (2012). An empirical study of determinants of e-commerce adoption in SMEs in Vietnam: An economy in transition. *Journal of Global Information Management (JGIM)*, *20*(3), 23–54.

Wang, G., Wang, Y., & Zhao, T. (2008). Analysis of interactions among the barriers to energy saving in China. *Energy Policy*, *36*(6), 1879–1889.

Wymer, S. A., & Regan, E. A. (2005). Factors influencing e-commerce adoption and use by small and medium businesses. *Electronic Markets*, *15*(4), 438–453. https://doi.org/10.1080/10196780500303151

CHAPTER 5

IMPACT OF GLOBAL CURRENCIES ON THE SUSTAINABILITY OF THE INDIAN STOCK MARKET

Isha Narula, Ankita Dawar and Khushi Sehgal

Vivekananda Institute of Professional Studies, Delhi, India

ABSTRACT

Introduction: *The Stock Exchange is an economic indicator of sustainability in the global market over an extended period. The Indian economy has observed a downfall in foreign currency in quarter 2 of 2022, as per the reports of the International Monitory Fund. The central banks of many countries have been facing crises because of a piercing decline in their reserves, which is additionally affecting their sustainable performance. The Indian economy is one of the most potentially sound economies emerging as a global leader, and this study is an attempt to understand the economy's vulnerability to foreign factors.*

Purpose: *The research explores the impact of the US Dollar, EURO and Japanese Yen on Bombay Stock Exchange and the National Stock Exchange Index.*

Methodology: *Four variables have been considered for the conduct of the study: Sensex, Nifty, inflation and foreign exchange. Sensex and Nifty have been taken as dependent variables, while foreign exchange and inflation have been taken as independent variables.*

The regression analysis has been performed using Microsoft Excel: *The variables used for the study are monthly values from January 2011 to December 2020. The specific period is selected to avoid the impact of COVID-19 on the stock market, avoiding biases in the results.*

Sustainable Development Goals: The Impact of Sustainability Measures on Wellbeing
Contemporary Studies in Economic and Financial Analysis, Volume 113B, 57–74
Copyright © 2024 by Isha Narula, Ankita Dawar and Khushi Sehgal
Published under exclusive licence by Emerald Publishing Limited
ISSN: 1569-3759/doi:10.1108/S1569-37592024000113B005

Findings: *All the variables are affecting the performance of each other up to a certain level.*

Practical Implication: *The research chapter will help the investor understand the relationship between many variables and their impact on the stock market, which will assist them in gaining higher profits.*

Keywords Foreign exchange rate; BSE; NSE; sustainable economy; international currency; multiple regression; globalisation

INTRODUCTION

Worldwide globalisation and liberalisation were the revolutionising turning points in the antiquity of the Indian economy, which contributed to the smooth, efficient and sustainable functioning of the stock markets. It opened new gateways for extensive opportunities for Indian exporters and importers as well. The obliteration of foreign exchange controls by the Indian government opened doorways for portfolio diversification and assisted investors in sustainable investment programmes. The flexible foreign exchange schemes adopted by the economy were another significant step towards raising investor awareness, but they also enlarged the risk associated with foreign investments. Many steps have been taken by the government to keep the money active in the market by having regulatory procedures by the Stock Exchange Board of India and introducing derivative markets in India. These steps dynamically subsidised the market's depth and width. Global currencies significantly influence the performance of economies as they are the vital elements that shake the earnings and profitability of enterprises that drive intercontinental trade. Below are some of how global currencies can stimulate stock markets:

Exchange rates: Exchange rates among currencies can disturb the earnings of companies that drive transnationally. For example, if a US-based company generates revenue in euros, a strengthening euro against the US dollar will increase the company's revenue when converted back into US dollars. This can lift the business's stock price as stockholders develop an optimistic outlook for their earnings.

Inflation: Inflation rates can move clients' purchasing power, which can significantly influence the sales and earnings of corporations. If a country experiences high inflation, the value of its currency may decline, making imported goods more expensive. This can upset businesses' earnings that count on imported goods or have noteworthy set-ups in nations with extraordinary inflation tariffs.

Interest rates: Interest rates can touch the price of borrowing for corporations and ultimately sway their profitability. Advanced interest rates can upsurge the price of borrowing and, hence, diminish profits and subordinate stock prices. On the contrary, inferior interest rates can make it inexpensive for firms to borrow and can escalate profits and enhance stock prices.

In a nutshell, the impression of global currencies on stock markets is indicative and multifaceted. It is a prerequisite for investors to deliberate an extensive variety of influences, comprising exchange rates, inflation rates and interest rates while constructing their portfolio. The literature delivers many proofs about the relationship between the sustainability of the stock market and global currencies. The present study has used multiple tests to understand the impact of global currencies on policymaking, portfolio diversification and investor awareness.

LITERATURE REVIEW

Kaur (2017) undertook the influence of inflation and foreign exchange rates on the performance of companies in an Indian setting. It was found that an increase in inflation leads to an increase in the stock market. High inflation allows investors to receive higher returns than the other avenues with interest rates. However, the same cannot be said for the exchange rate. There is no relationship between returns and exchange rates.

Ray and Vani (2012) found out that the interest ratio has a positive connotation with the stock market. Their analysis confirms that inflation has a significant bearing on the investors' psyche. However, the study could not deny a plausible relationship between exchange rate and market returns.

Sireesha (2013) observes that the inflation rate movement influences stock market returns. The observation of such rates delivers an investor a hedge against increasing inflation rates. It also found out that the exchange rate affects the returns. A plausible reason is the inflow of foreign portfolio investors.

Polisetty et al. (2016) concluded that the relationship between stock returns and foreign exchange is shallow.

Singh (2014) found that exchange rates have an opposing effect on the sustainability of economies. Ongoing solidification of the dollar, the value of the rupee depreciates. The Indian economy weakened because of a diminution in the worth of Indian currency.

Data Methodology

Four variables have been considered for the study, that is, Sensex, Nifty, inflation and foreign exchange. Sensex and Nifty have been taken as dependent variables, while foreign exchange and inflation have been taken as independent variables.

Regression analysis has been performed using Microsoft Excel. The variables used for the study are monthly values from January 2011 to December 2020. The specific time period is selected to avoid the impact of COVID on the stock market. As per studies, the impact of COVID-19 was maximum after 2020. Specific data are selected to avoid bias in the result.

Objectives of the Study

- To investigate the relationship between foreign exchange rates with the BSE Sensex and the NSE nifty.
- To investigate the relationship between inflation and the BSE Sensex and the NSE nifty.

HYPOTHESIS

1. *H0*. There is no significant association between the NSE nifty and the Indian Rupee – US Dollar.

   H1. There is a significant association between the NSE nifty and the Indian Rupee – US Dollar.

2. *H0*. There is no significant association between the NSE nifty and the Indian Rupee – EURO.

   H1. There is an association between the NSE nifty and the Indian Rupee – EURO.

3. *H0*. There is no significant association between the NSE nifty and the Indian Rupee – Japanese Yen.

   H1. There is an association between the NSE nifty and the Indian Rupee – Japanese Yen.

4. *H0*. There is no significant association between the BSE Sensex and the Indian Rupee – US Dollar.

   H1. There is an association between the BSE Sensex and the Indian Rupee – US Dollar.

5. *H0*. There is no significant association between the BSE Sensex and the Indian Rupee – EURO.

   H1. There is an association between the BSE Sensex and the Indian Rupee – EURO.

6. *H0*. There is no significant association between the BSE Sensex and the Indian Rupee – Japanese Yen.

   H1. There is an association between the BSE Sensex and the Indian Rupee – Japanese Yen.

REGRESSION

Regression is an arithmetical procedure employed to model the connection between a dependent variable and one or more independent variables. It aims to comprehend the strength of the connection among variables and make extrapolations or guesstimate values of the dependent variable grounded on the values of the independent variables.

Tables 1 and 2 represent the results of regression analysis. The R^2 for NSE nifty and INR-USD is 0.6589, which signifies that there is a moderate correlation between NSE nifty and INR-USD. This means a change in INR-USD will reasonably affect NSE's nifty returns. Therefore, *H0* is rejected, and *H1* is rejected.

Fig. 1 represents the relationship between the INR and USD. The figure represents a direct relationship between the two variables. An increase in one variable

Table 1. NSE Nifty and INR-USD – Regression Analysis Results.

Regression Statistics					
Multiple R				0.828188921	
R^2				0.685896889	
Adjusted R^2				0.683234998	
Standard Error				1319.163689	
Observations				120	

	df	SS	MS	F	Significance F
Regression	1	448400387	448400387	257.672815	1.87314E-31
Residual	118	205342754.8	1740192.837		
Total	119	653743141.8			

Table 2. NSE Nifty and INR-USD – Regression Analysis Results.

	Coefficients	Standard Error	*t* Stat	P-value	Lower 95%	Upper 95%	Lower 95.0%	Upper 95.0%
Intercept X	-6716.461476	947.4712385	-7.088828877	1.06861E-10	-8592.712476	-4840.210475	-8592.712476	-4840.210475
Variable 1	239.3109656	14.90830599	16.05219035	1.87314E-31	209.7884609	268.8334702	209.7884609	268.8334702

Source: Compiled by authors.

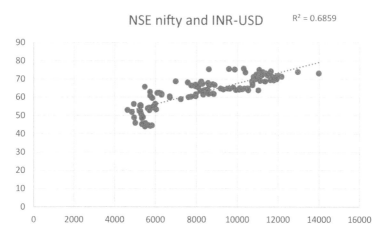

Fig. 1   Relationship Between the INR and USD. *Source*: Compiled by authors.

illustrates an increase in other variable too. The values are more clustered around the regression line.

Tables 3–5 represent the relationship between NSE and INR-EURO through regression analysis. The value for R^2 is 0.3313, which signifies that there is a weak relationship between NSE nifty returns and the INR-EURO exchange rate. This means INR-EUR rate will have weak effect on NSE nifty returns. Therefore, *H0* is accepted, and *H1* is rejected.

Fig. 2 represents the relationship between INR and EURO graphically. To produce the figure, daily Nifty prices and INR-EURO rate are considered. It shows a direct relationship between the two variables.

Tables 6–8 demonstrate the results of NSE and INR-JPY regression analysis. The value of R^2 is 0.0404 which denotes that there is a very weak correlation between NSE nifty and INR-JPY. This means that INR-JPY exchange rate will not affect NSE's nifty returns. Therefore, *H0* is accepted, and *H1* is rejected.

Fig. 3 represents the relationship between NSE and INR-JPY graphically. The daily prices of Nifty and INR_JPY are considered and a direct relationship between the two variables is depicted around the regression line.

Tables 9–11 demonstrate the results of NSE and INR-CPI regression analysis. The value of R^2 is 0.8787, which denotes that there is a very strong correlation between NSE nifty and CPI. This means that CPI will affect NSE nifty returns. Therefore, *H0* is rejected, and *H1* is accepted.

Fig. 4 represents the relationship between NSE and INR-CPI graphically. The graph represents the relationship between inflation rate Nifty returns. There is a direct relationship between the two variables.

Tables 12–15 demonstrate the results of regression analysis between BSE and INR-USD. The value of R^2 is 0.6899 which denotes that there is moderate correlation between BSE Sensex and INR-USD. This means that the INR-USD

Table 3. NSE Nifty and INR-EURO – Regression Analysis.

Regression Statistics	
Multiple R	0.575560606
R^2	0.331270011
Adjusted R^2	0.325602808
Standard Error	1924.810455
Observations	120

Table 4. NSE Nifty and INR-EURO – Regression Analysis.

	df	SS	MS	F	Significance F
Regression	1	216565497.8	216565497.8	58.45387817	6.13421E-12
Residual	118	437177644	3704895.288		
Total	119	653743141.8			

Table 5. NSE Nifty and INR-EURO – Regression Analysis.

	Coefficients	Standard Error	*t* Stat	*P*-value	Lower 95%	Upper 95%	Lower 95.0%	Upper 95.0%
Intercept X	-7263.782121	2052.259803	-3.539406711	0.000574725	-11327.81526	-3199.748984	-11327.81526	-3199.748984
Variable 1	206.6708707	27.03165301	7.645513598	6.13421E-12	153.1408384	260.200903	153.1408384	260.200903

Source: Compiled by authors.

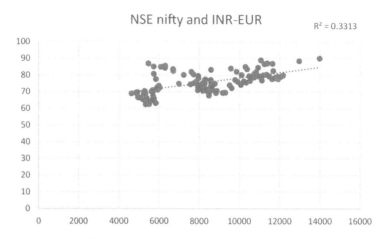

Fig. 2   Relationship Between INR and EURO. *Source*: Compiled by authors.

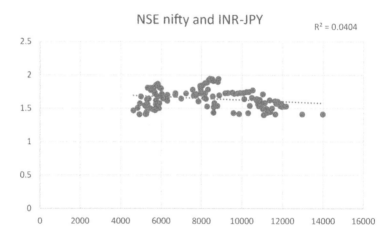

Fig. 3   Relationship Between NSE and INR-JPY. *Source*: Compiled by authors.

exchange rate will moderately affect BSE's nifty returns. Therefore, *H0* is rejected, and *H1* is accepted.

Fig. 5 represents the relationship between BSE and INR-USD graphically. BSE returns and INR-USD show a direct relationship. Returns are clustered around regression line.

Tables 16–18 represent the regression analysis results between BSE and INR-EURO. The value of R^2 is 0.3566, which denotes that there is a weak correlation between BSE Sensex and INR-EUR. This means that the INR-EUR exchange rate will not affect BSE Sensex returns. Therefore, *H0* is accepted, and *H1* is rejected.

Table 6. NSE Nifty and INR-JPY – Regression Analysis.

Regression Statistics	
Multiple R	0.201032297
R^2	0.040413984
Adjusted R^2	0.032281899
Standard Error	2305.709157
Observations	120

Table 7. NSE Nifty and INR-JPY – Regression Analysis.

	df	SS	MS	F	Significance F
Regression	1	26420365.08	26420365.08	4.969695339	0.027688158
Residual	118	627322776.7	5316294.718		
Total	119	653743141.8			

Table 8. NSE Nifty and INR-JPY – Regression Analysis.

	Coefficients	Standard Error	t Stat	P-value	Lower 95%	Upper 95%	Lower 95.0%	Upper 95.0%
Intercept X	13760.46089	2427.53501	5.66849122	1.03892E-07	8953.280675	18567.6411	8953.280675	18567.6411
Variable 1	-3281.38926	1471.949361	-2.22928135	0.027688158	-6196.249733	-366.5287874	-6196.249733	-366.5287874

Source: Compiled by authors.

Table 9. NSE Nifty and CPI – Regression Analysis.

Regression Statistics	
Multiple R	0.937150542
R^2	0.878251139
Adjusted R^2	0.877219369
Standard Error	821.2871413
Observations	120

Table 10. NSE Nifty and CPI – Regression Analysis.

	df	SS	MS	F	Significance F
Regression	1	5741150658.7	5741150658.7	851.2082436	8.61388E-56
Residual	118	79592483.08	674512.5685		
Total	119	65374314.18			

Table 11. NSE Nifty and CPI – Regression Analysis.

	Coefficients	Standard Error	t Stat	P-value	Lower 95%	Upper 95%	Lower 95.0%	Upper 95.0%
Intercept X	-4827.751402	458.5009631	-10.52942478	1.10695E-18	-5735.708136	-3919.794668	-5735.708136	-3919.794668
Variable 1	130.4727424	4.47200883	29.17547332	8.61388E-56	121.6169632	139.3285217	121.6169632	139.3285217

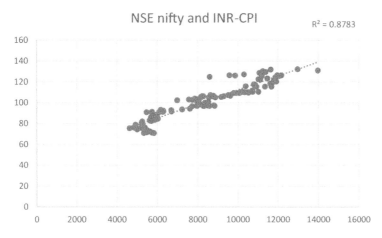

Fig. 4   Relationship Between NSE and INR-CPI. *Source*: Compiled by authors.

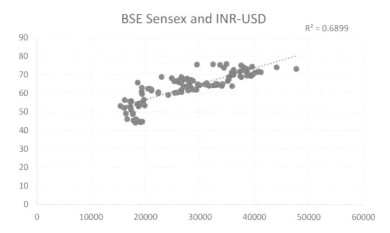

Fig. 5   Relationship Between BSE and INR-USD. *Source*: Compiled by authors.

Fig. 6 represents the relationship between **BSE** and **INR-EUR** graphically. BSE returns and **INR-EURO** shows a direct relationship and hence the relationship is positive. An increase in one variable has a direct impact on the other.

Tables 19–21 represent the regression analysis results between **BSE** and **INR-JPY**. The value of R^2 is 0.0508, which denotes a very weak correlation between BSE Sensex and **INR-JPY**. This means that the INR-JPY exchange rate will not affect BSE Sensex returns. Therefore, *H0* is accepted, and *H1* is rejected.

Table 12. BSE Sensex and INR-USD – Regression Analysis.

ANOVA	df	SS	MS	F	Significance F
Regression	1	5101556516	5101556516	262.5112617	8.77873E-32
Residual	118	2293172738	1943667.27		
Total	119	7394729255			

Table 13. BSE Sensex and INR-USD – Regression Analysis.

Regression Statistics	
Multiple R	0.830596721
R^2	0.689890913
Adjusted R^2	0.68726287
Standard Error	4408.363333
Observations	120

Table 14. BSE Sensex and INR-USD – Regression Analysis.

ANOVA	df	SS	MS	F	Significance F
Regression	1	5101556516	5101556516	262.5112617	8.77873E-32
Residual	118	2293172738	1943667.27		
Total	119	7394729255			

Table 15. BSE Sensex and INR-USD – Regression Analysis.

	Coefficients	Standard Error	t Stat	P-value	Lower 95%	Upper 95%	Lower 95.0%	Upper 95.0%
Intercept X	−23121.5083	3166.246541	−7.302497775	3.59948E-11	−29391.53848	−16851.147816	−29391.53848	−16851.47816
Variable 1	807.1996423	49.82037488	16.20219929	8.77873E-32	708.5417365	905.8575481	708.5417365	905.8575481

Source: Compiled by authors.

Table 16. BSE Sensex and INR-EUR – Regression Analysis.

Regression Statistics	
Multiple R	0.597173595
R^2	0.356616303
Adjusted R^2	0.351163899
Standard Error	6349.728573
Observations	120

Table 17. BSE Sensex and INR-EUR – Regression Analysis.

ANOVA	df	SS	MS	F	Significance F
Regression	1	2637081007	2637081007	65.40533108	6.05908E-13
Residual	118	4757648248	40319052.95		
Total	119	7394729255			

Table 18. BSE Sensex and INR-EUR – Regression Analysis.

	Coefficients	Standard Error	t Stat	P-value	Lower 95%	Upper 95%	Lower 95.0%	Upper 95.0%
Intercept X	−26789.11426	6770.169331	−3.956934155	0.000130078	−40195.89271	−13382.33581	−40195.89271	−13382.33581
Variable 1	721.1844774	89.17431794	8.087356248	6.05908E-13	544.5950502	897.7739046	544.5950502	897.7739046

Source: Compiled by authors.

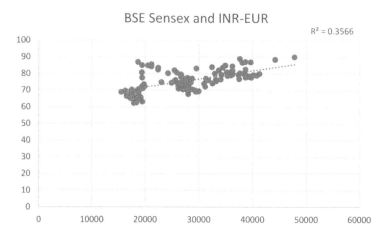

Fig. 6   Relationship Between BSE and INR-EUR. *Source*: Compiled by authors.

Fig. 7 represents the relationship between BSE and INR-JPY graphically. BSE returns and INR-JPY show a direct relationship and hence the relationship is positive. An increase in one variable has a direct impact on the other.

Tables 22–24 present regression analysis results between BSE and CPI. The value of R^2 is 0.8867, which denotes a strong correlation between BSE Sensex and CPI. This means that CPI will affect BSE Sensex returns. Therefore, *H0* is rejected, and *H1* is accepted.

Fig. 8 represents the relationship between BSE and INR-CPI graphically. BSE returns and INR-CPI show a direct relationship and hence the relationship is positive. An increase in the inflation rate leads to an increase in stock market prices.

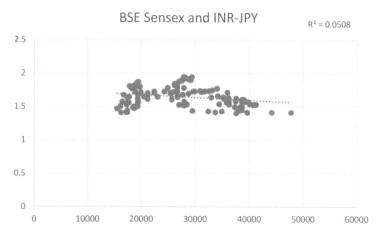

Fig. 7.   Relationship Between BSE and INR-JPY. *Source*: Compiled by authors.

Table 19. BSE Sensex and INR-JPY – Regression Analysis.

Regression Statistics

Multiple R	0.225302551
R^2	0.05076124
Adjusted R^2	0.042716843
Standard Error	7712.725359
Observations	120

Table 20. BSE Sensex and INR-JPY – Regression Analysis.

	df	SS	MS	F	Significance F
Regression	1	375365624.3	375365624.3	6.310136644	0.013356091
Residual	118	7019363630	59486132.46		
Total	119	7394729255			

Table 21. BSE Sensex and INR-JPY – Regression Analysis.

	Coefficients	Standard Error	t Stat	P-value	Lower 95%	Upper 95%	Lower 95.0%	Upper 95.0%
Intercept X	48083.81706	8120.23961	5.921477612	3.21509E-08	32003.5319	64164.10221	32003.5319	64164.10221
Variable 1	−12368.459	4923.752473	−2.511998536	0.013356091	−22118.82939	−2618.088619	−22118.82939	−2618.088619

Source: Compiled by authors.

Table 22. BSE Sensex and CPI – Regression Analysis.

Regression Statistics

Multiple R	0.94167098
R^2	0.886744235
Adjusted R^2	0.885784441
Standard Error	2664.098596
Observations	120

Table 23. BSE Sensex and CPI – Regression Analysis.

	df	SS	MS	F	Significance F
Regression	1	6557233538	6557233538	923.8895698	120303E-57
Residual	118	837495716.8	7097421.329		
Total	119	7394729255			

Table 24. BSE Sensex and CPI – Regression Analysis.

	Coefficients	Standard Error	t Stat	P-value	Lower 95%	Upper 95%	Lower 95.0%	Upper 95.0%
Intercept X	−16835.91167	1487.289491	−11.31986192	1.46191E-20	−19781.14978	−13890.67357	−19781.14978	−13890.67357
Variable 1	440.927496	14.50631654	30.39555181	1.20303E-57	412.2010399	469.653952	412.2010399	469.653952

Source: Compiled by authors.

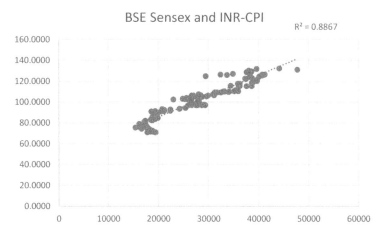

Fig. 8 Relationship Between BSE and INR-CPI. *Source*: Compiled by authors.

CONCLUSION

It can be concluded that

- CPI (consumer price index) has a robust influence on the returns of Nifty and Sensex.
- INR-USD exchange rate has a moderate influence on the returns of Nifty and Sensex.
- INR-EUR exchange rate weakly influences the returns of nifty and Sensex.
- INE-JPY returns have negligible influence on the returns of nifty and Sensex.

Tables 25 and 26 summarise the relationship between all the variables (extracted from the regression analysis) employed in the study.

Table 25. Correlation Among Variables.

	INR-USD	INR-EUR	INR-JPY	CPI
BSE Sensex	0.6899	0.3566	0.0508	0.8867
NSE Nifty	0.6859	0.3313	0.0404	0.8783

Table 26. Relationship Among Variables.

	INR-USD	INR-EUR	INR-JPY	CPI
BSE Sensex	Moderate	Weak	No	Strong
NSE Nifty	Moderate	Weak	No	Strong

Source: Compiled by authors.

On the basis of the above-mentioned results, it can be stated that Indian currency is mildly affected by global currency fluctuations and hence investors who are willing to trade in the currency market can take advantage of foreign currency fluctuations to predict the market and bag reasonable profits.

REFERENCES

International Monetary Fund. (2022). *World economic outlook: Countering the cost-of-living crisis.* International Monetary Fund.

Kaur, M. (2017). An impact of inflation and exchange rate on stock returns: Evidence from India. *Scholarly Research Journal for Interdisciplinary Studies, 4*(37), 8232–8239.

Polisetty, A., Kumar, D., & Kurian, M. S. (2016). Influence of exchange rate on BSE Sensex & NSE Nifty. *IOSR Journal of Business and Management, 18,* 10–15.

Ray, P., & Vani, V. (2012). What moves Indian stock markets: A study on the linkage with real economy in post-reform era. Paper presented in *The Sixth Annual Conference on Money and Finance in The Indian Economy* (pp. 25–27).

Singh, P. (2014). Indian stock market and macroeconomic factors in current scenario. *International Journal of Research in Business Management, 2*(11), 43–54.

Sireesha, P. (2013). Effect of select macro economic variables on stock returns in India. *ERN: Other Econometric Modeling: International Financial Markets – Emerging Markets, 2*(6), 13.

CHAPTER 6

SELF-BRAND CONNECTION AND BRAND LOYALTY AS AN OUTCOME OF SUSTAINABLE CAUSE-RELATED MARKETING: A CONCEPTUAL FRAMEWORK

Anu Bhardwaj, Nidhi Gupta and Seema Wadhawan

Jagannath International Management School, New Delhi, India

ABSTRACT

Introduction: *In today's world of increasing competition, diminishing product differentiation, higher customer expectations, easy product replacements and lowering brand loyalty, organisations are evolving new marketing strategies for economic, societal and sustainability. Cause-related marketing (hereafter referred to as CRM), a strategic sustainable philanthropic practice, is the upcoming form of CSR. CRM plays an instrumental role in achieving self-brand connection and brand loyalty.*

Purpose: *To explore, integrate and interconnect concepts of CRM and self-brand connection to get more insights into the imperative role of CRM strategy in developing self-brand connections that can lead to brand loyalty in the most sustainable way. For this, CRM and self-brand connection, as proposed by societal marketing and branding literature, were explored. This chapter is a propositional inventory where the researcher has explored the antecedents of CRM strategy and its role in developing brand loyalty through self-brand connection.*

Sustainable Development Goals: The Impact of Sustainability Measures on Wellbeing
Contemporary Studies in Economic and Financial Analysis, Volume 113B, 75–90
Copyright © 2024 by Anu Bhardwaj, Nidhi Gupta and Seema Wadhawan
Published under exclusive licence by Emerald Publishing Limited
ISSN: 1569-3759/doi:10.1108/S1569-37592024000113B006

Methodology: *This chapter is centred upon the existing literature on sustainability, CRM and branding to understand better the relationships between dimensions and consequences of CRM and its interlinkage with brand loyalty.*

Findings: *The literature recommends that selected dimensions: Cause-brand fit, product type, altruistic motivation and brand credibility determine the effectiveness of CRM strategy. It also establishes the profound impact of attitude towards brand, brand perception and brand distinctiveness on self-brand connection. A theoretical framework based on the existing literature represents an amalgamated groundwork for developing effective, sustainable CRM strategies in conjunction with the self-brand connection. The proposed framework is distinct as no study conjoins the abovementioned concepts and aims to comprehend whether this integration is brand loyalty.*

Keywords: CSR; cause-related marketing; sustainability; self-brand connection; brand loyalty; brand distinctiveness; attitude towards brands

1. INTRODUCTION

According to Porter and Kramer (2011), 'creating shared value' has become the core of business strategies. Business and community development were considered separate, and all the contributions towards this development were considered philanthropic (Paul & Mukhopadhyay, 2010). However, CSR is a new buzzword as many companies are initiating charitable programmes to show their consciousness towards society. Cause-related marketing (CRM) is one of the dimensions of CSR, where a company partners with a cause for a relationship that can benefit both the company and the customer. In CRM, the organisation promises to contribute a pre-decided portion of the profit from the generated sales to the non-profit organisation. This association between organisation and cause is termed as CRM. Integrating an organisation's marketing function with social cause is an established strategy (Edmondson & Lafferty, 2007; Nan & Heo, 2007), known as CRM, that is, cause-related marketing (Drumwright, 1996). CRM allows companies to work towards sustainability by contributing towards social and environmental well-being. Contributions made by the companies have grown many folds over that decade. As (per the IEG) Sponsorship Report (2020), the sponsorship contribution to social causes in North America has grown to $2.23 billion in 2019 from $120 million in 1990 and reached $10 Billion in 2020 amid COVID-19.

CRM is an upcoming strategy implemented to develop a distinctive brand with a personality that fulfils the self-definitional needs of consumers (Berger et al., 2006; Du et al., 2007; Fournier, 1998) and leads to self-brand connection. As per Escalas and Bettman (2003), 'self-brand connection is defined as the degree to which consumers incorporate a brand into their self-concept'. It has also been extensively acknowledged that brands can personify, inform and communicate desired consumer identity. Hence, researchers want to investigate the concept of self-brand connection and its implications on companies and consumers. Studies have empirically tested the connection between CSR and customer-company identification (Lichtenstein et al., 2004; Marin & Ruiz, 2007; Sen & Bhattacharya, 2001; Sen et al., 2006). However, evidence has not been found where the integration between CRM and self-brand connection has been explored.

Researchers have investigated the consumer's brand association in the past; however, exploring the integration of CRM and self-brand connection and loyalty is vital. It is crucial as organisations implement sustainable business practices, and CRM is a vital strategy. This association is a vital predictor of consumer behaviour, such as repeating a purchase and spreading word of mouth (Donavan et al., 2006; Kuenzel & Halliday, 2008).

This chapter explores the possible theoretical relationship between CRM and self-brand connection, which has been divided into four objectives. The first is to understand the concept of CRM and the dimensions affecting its success. Second, to investigate the extent to which CRM strategy influences the three selected CRM consequences, that is attitude towards the brand, brand perception and brand distinctiveness. Third, to analyse the influence of these selected CRM consequences on self-brand connection and fourth, to propose a conceptual framework grounded on the existing literature representing an integrated framework for developing effective CRM strategies in conjunction with self-brand connection with brand loyalty as the outcome. This chapter is structured in four sections. First, the concept of CRM and self-brand connection is defined and discussed. Second, it provides the theoretical background of all the constructs and their interlinkages and makes research propositions. Third, the researcher proposes the conceptual framework for the study based on an extensive literature review. Finally, it is concluded by discussing the research's academic and managerial implications and proposing future research directions.

2. LITERATURE REVIEW
2.1. Cause-Related Marketing

Organisations worldwide are working towards a sustainable way of doing business where economic and social objectives can be achieved. Marketers are coming up with strategies that can create a connection between customers and brands. Thus, creating a brand with a social outlook is an effectual differentiation and positioning strategy. The strategy with which an organisation can behave both socially and profitably is through sponsoring the activities. CRM can be implemented in different ways (Gupta & Pirsch, 2006; Liu & Ko, 2011); however (Varadarajan & Menon, 1988, p. 60), pioneer researchers in the field of CRM defined it as 'the process of formulating and implementing marketing activities that are characterised by an offer from the firm to contribute a specified amount to a designated cause when customers engage in revenue-providing exchanges that satisfy organisational and individual objectives'.

As per Drumwright (1996), integrating a social dimension with a marketing strategy is becoming discernible. Consumers are showing interest towards CSR activities (Benezra, 1996), and organisations have discovered that consumers' perception towards CSR impacts their attitudes and purchase intent (Brown & Dacin, 1997).

2.2. CRM – An Effective Marketing Strategy

CRM strategy changes the organisation's orientation towards sustainable practices (Laužikas & Dailydaitė, 2013). CRM can be a strategy to build a long-term differentiation strategy and can enhance the value of the brand. Varadarajan and Menon (1988) mentioned that companies are interested in CRM for those causes that customers prefer (Collins, 1993). They emphasised that CRM provides a competitive advantage, positive word of mouth and enhanced goodwill. Literature has emphasised the impact of CRM in enhancing brand awareness (Varadarajan & Menon, 1988), improving brand attitude and improving brand image (Cornwell & Maignan, 1998; Polonsky & Speed, 2001). As per Nielsen's corporate social responsibility survey (2014), 66% of respondents say that they will choose to purchase products from organisations that have executed strategies where we contribute back to society. So, being an effective marketing strategy, CRM will not only give more business to the companies but also better connection with customers, brand credibility, better image, brand loyalty and competitive edge.

2.3. Self-Brand Connections

This is an evolving concept, and as per Escalas and Bettman (2003), it is the degree to which consumers incorporate a brand into their self-concepts. In addition (Escalas & Bettman, 2003; Moore & Homer, 2008) consumers use brands to express themselves and develop their self-concept (Escalas & Bettman, 2003; McCracken, 1989; Moore & Homer, 2008), which can lead to the creation of an extensive connection between self-identity of consumers and brand (Escalas & Bettman, 2003). As per Belk (1988) and Sirgy (1982), there is a well-acknowledged scope of 'self' influencing the behaviour of the consumer. They also added that the development of self-brand connections possibly aids in creating brand equity.

The earlier research suggests that when the association between the consumer and the brand is high, the consumer is expected to develop a self-brand connection. Consumers often choose a brand consistent with their self-images (Chaplin & John, 2005). So, it can be interpreted that consumers like to develop relationships with those brands that help them cultivate a sense of who they are (Fournier, 1998). This sense of self-identity can be of various types like past, current and future self-identity, which means who one was, who one is and who one wants to be (Ahuvia, 2005; Batra et al., 2012; Belk, 1988). Consumers like to express their feelings and experiences for the brand they like. It was also observed that consumers with stronger self-brand connections display stronger relations with the brand. Consequently, they strengthen their association with the brand by repeating their purchase. Therefore, the researcher believes that the self-brand connection is positively connected with loyalty towards the brand.

3. CONCEPTUAL BACKGROUND AND PROPOSITION DEVELOPMENT

Through a systematic review of existing literature, the researcher identified and analysed four dimensions and three consequences of CRM strategy. For this chapter, both theoretical and empirical papers published in reputed journals were considered to find the dimension impacting the success of CRM, the consequences of CRM and the relationship between CRM and self-brand connection. This chapter is one of a kind where the theoretical relationship between CRM and self-brand connection has been established. Thus, researchers constitute the proposition based on theoretical backup.

3.1. Dimensions of Cause-Related Marketing

3.1.1. Cause-Brand Fit

Varadarajan and Menon (1988) and Ellen et al. (2000) defined fit as an alleged link between the company's position and image and the cause's image and constituency. Basil and Herr (2006) mentioned that when fit or congruence between brand and cause is strong, the behaviour is more favourable than a fit that does not go well. Bigné-Alcañiz et al.'s (2011), for the success of CRM campaigns, cause-brand fit is one of the most essential factors (Nan & Heo, 2007; Trimble & Rifon, 2006).

In their studies, Becker-Oslen et al. (2006) mentioned that CRM strategy can negatively impact purchase intention if a consumer perceives a weak fit. According to Lafferty et al. (2004), a lack of fit between the alliance partners influence consumer's evaluation, that is, if the fit is high, it leads to a favourable attitude towards CRM. From this, we can conclude that the degree of favourableness or unfavourableness towards a brand/company depends on the company-cause fit.

P1. Cause-brand fit has a positive impact on CRM strategy.

3.1.2. Type of Product

Strahilevitz and Myers (1998) mentioned two types of products: hedonic and utilitarian. Hedonic Products are purchased for experiential consumption and are judged for the pleasure they can give. For example, ice cream and movie tickets, whereas utilitarian products provide utility and are purchased for performance. Hedonic products may result from extravagance compared to functional products (Luchs et al., 2010; Strahilevitz, 1999; Subrahmanyan, 2004). As per Chang (2008) and Strahilevitz and Myers (1998), the success of CRM is high when it is implemented for hedonic products as it helps to counterbalance the guilt related to enjoyable consumption (Chang, 2008; Kim et al., 2005).

Charity is more effective when it is related to hedonic products, whereas they also found that consumers prefer price discounts for utilitarian products (Strahilevitz & Myers, 1998).

P2. Type of product has a positive impact on CRM strategy.

3.1.3. Altruistic Motivation

As per Forehand and Grier (2003), there can be two motives for which CRM strategy is implemented by the companies: one where the societal concern is high (altruistic motives), the other is when concern is more for the promoting the brand (egoist motive). Ellen et al. (2006) found that consumer shows dominance of one motive at a time, which profoundly impacts their evaluation of a brand. They also mentioned that organisations can have intrinsic or extrinsic motives for CRM determinations. Intrinsically motivated companies believe that CRM initiatives are self-satisfying (Du et al., 2007). Whereas extrinsically motivated companies expect benefits from their environment.

Rifon et al. (2004) attribution theory was used by Ellen et al. (2000) to understand and explain how consumers will assess companies' CRM campaigns (Becker-Olsen et al., 2006). As per them, consumers assess and react to CRM initiatives by drawing inferences regarding the company's real intentions behind engaging in social campaigns and organisations that implement CRM strategically, that is, for a longer duration and with higher commitment from the management. Such companies are intrinsically motivated. Forehand and Grier (2003) mentioned that if the consumer feels that the brand's motivation involved in a CRM practice is egoist, their evaluation of that brand is negative. As per Ellen et al. (2000), consumers' response towards CRM is favourable if they are intrinsically motivated. Hence, consumers' motivational attribution influences their reactions positively towards CRM strategy (Barone et al., 2007; Gao, 2009).

P3. Altruistic motivation has a positive impact on CRM strategy.

3.1.4. Brand Credibility

Credibility is the authenticity of the entity's intentions, trustworthiness and expertise (Tülin & Swait, 2004). Elyria Kemp and Bui (2011) – whenever a brand is considered credible, it is repeatedly purchased, and consumers become committed to it. Brands become so meaningful that consumers develop a desired self-image or self-concept.

If the company implementing CRM is perceived as trustworthy, then the success is high. As per Yoon et al. (2006), corporate credibility is the characteristic of a company's reputation built on expertise, trustworthiness and likeability. According to Bigné-Alcañiz et al. (2009), credibility can be increased by informing the public about CRM initiatives through independent sources and relating this act with the altruistic motivation of the company.

Godfrey (2005) mentioned that organisation invests in CSR initiatives to create positive ethical assets and the company's idiosyncratic intangible benefits such as reputation and credibility.

P4. Brand credibility has a positive impact on CRM strategy.

3.2. Consequences of CRM

3.2.1. Attitude Towards Brand

Schiffman and Kanuk (2007) defined 'attitude as a predisposition to behave in a consistently favourable or unfavourable manner towards an object (e.g. a product category, a brand, a service, an advertisement)'. Purchase decisions are highly influenced by attitude, so it interests all consumer researchers. Ross et al. (1992) mentioned that CRM generates a favourable attitude towards the company implementing CRM initiatives. Babu and Mohiuddin (2008) also mentioned that CRM considerably influences consumers' attitudes only when they are well aware of such initiatives. Literature suggests that CRM can be one of the vital strategies to change the attitude towards the brand/company, which has been confirmed by Till and Nowak (2000).

P5. CRM strategy has a positive impact on attitude towards the brand.

3.2.2. Brand Perception

Consumers are becoming socially concerned and are responsible for their purchases (Smith, 2008). So, the perception of the consumer is positive towards CRM. According to Zeithaml (1988) and Aaker (1991), perception affects the evaluation of a company's product/offering. This evaluation is done on parameters like product quality, experience and fulfilment of needs (Yoo et al., 2000). As per Boone and Kurtz (2011), 92% of consumers support a company that acts socially responsibly. Stroup and Neubert (1987) also mentioned in their work that consumer perception of the firm that is implementing CRM may improve, and this way, companies can also support worthy causes. According to Dodds et al. (1991), perceived quality influences consumers choice of purchase. If the quality of the product is perceived better, it will influence consumer choice vis-à-vis competitors.

P6. CRM strategy has a positive impact on brand perception.

3.2.3. Brand Distinctiveness

Marin and Ruiz (2007) stated that differentiating a brand by traditional means, such as change in features, price and quality, is difficult. When a customer perceives uniqueness, it may nurture feelings of pride. Zhou and Nakamoto (2007) stated that brand distinctiveness is the level by which a brand is perceived to be different from others. Subsequently, such emotions cause higher self-connection with the brand. A brand is perceived to be unique if it offers the customer something new or any additional benefit (social or economic). Besides, for a consumer, uniqueness is often related to more excellent value and high quality (Netemeyer et al., 2004). Literature suggests that CRM helps in creating a distinctive image of the company.

P7. CRM strategy has a positive impact on brand distinctiveness.

3.3. Consequences of CRM Affecting Self-Brand Connection

As per the conceptual model, brand perception, brand attitude and brand distinctiveness are the consequences of CRM that lead to self-brand connection. Literature suggests that brand perception, brand attitude and brand distinctiveness lead to higher self-brand connection, which results in brand loyalty. Bigné-Alcañiz et al. (2009) mentioned that perceived company image and CRM programme influence consumers' perception of brand attractiveness. In such situations, customers start relating themselves with the organisation, leading to higher purchase intentions and involvement with the cause that finally leads to repeat purchases.

3.3.1. Attitude Towards Brand and Self-Brand Connection

Consumers are expected to connect with a brand when their attitude towards that brand is favourable. Humans are internally driven to achieve distinctiveness and characteristically identify with positive things and concepts (Tajfel, 1974). Therefore, whenever there is a positive perception and attitude towards the brand, consumers will likely align with that brand. As per Low and Lamb (2000), the attitude of consumers towards a brand can be captured as a characteristic of the connotation consumers confer on the brand. As per Keller (1993), attitude can serve a value-expressive function that helps consumers to express their self-concepts.

P8. Attitude towards the brand has a positive impact on self-brand connection.

3.3.2. Brand Perception and Self-Brand Connection

As per Escalas and Bettman (2003), if the perceptions of a brand are unique, it will result in an enhanced self-brand connection. Different cues related to the brand are given to consumers by the companies to form an image (perception) that stimulates comparing self-image with a brand image (Sirgy, 1982). Escalas and Bettman (2003), consumers choose from the alternate brands and consider the one where there is high congruence between the perception of brand and self-image, and can help self-brand connection. In their study, Bigné-Alcañiz et al. (2012) mentioned that perceived company image and CRM programme influence consumers' perception of brand attractiveness. In such situations, customers start relating themselves to the organisation, leading to higher purchase intentions and involvement with the cause, finally leading to repeat purchases.

P9. Brand perception has a positive impact on self-brand connection.

3.3.3. Brand Distinctiveness and Self-Brand Connection

According to Aaker (1991) and Keller (1993), brands can be of great value to the company and form an essential base for differentiating. Consumers differentiate a brand by assessing them on various features, often generated through advertising claims, word of mouth and past experiences (Netemeyer et al., 2004). This perception of uniqueness impacts consumers' choices (Kalra & Goodstein, 1998). Bhattacharya and Sen (2003) mentioned that if consumers perceive a brand as distinctiveness, it will likely become attractive. If consumers perceive the brand to be more attractive, their identification with it is high (Bergami & Bagozzi, 2000).

P10. Brand distinctiveness has a positive impact on self-brand connection.

3.4. Brand Connection and Brand Loyalty

In a competitive environment, repeat purchases and brand loyalty are challenging goals. Organisations create brand loyalty as they provide lots of benefits like repeat purchases, positive word of mouth and recommendations (Dick & Basu, 1994). As per Sirdeshmukh et al. (2002), brand loyalty is the intention of customers to act in a way that indicates a motivation to endure affiliation with the brand. Miller (2002) mentioned that organisations committed to CRM will have Brand loyalty. Bhattacharya and Sen (2003) state that self-brand connection impacts customer loyalty. Bloom et al. (2006) mentioned the benefits of CRM, like better effectiveness in marketing strategies, enabling companies to keep high prices and achieve higher market share and better stakeholder management. Zdravkovic et al. (2010) stated that CRM can give the organisation a dual advantage, that is, higher sales and loyalty. However, all CRM arrangements do not result in a positive outcome. Customer loyalty consists of sharing the higher part of the pocket, positive publicity and repeat purchases.

When a customer identifies with a brand, his loyalty increases (Cooper et al., 2010). As per Escalas and Bettman (2003), sometimes consumer becomes dedicated to brands that represent their desired self-concepts (Escalas, 2004). Bhattacharya and Sen (2003), when a customer identifies with a brand, the connection with it can be reinforced as it fulfils their self-definition needs.

P11. Self-brand connection has a positive impact on Brand Loyalty.

3.5. Conceptual Framework

Based on the extensive literature review of self-brand connection and CRM, an integrative conceptual framework of relationships has been developed to thoroughly understand the dimensions and consequences of CRM and their interlinkage with self-brand connection (Fig. 1). This framework consists of four dimensions and three outcomes of CRM that are less explored and profoundly impact the success of CRM and self-brand connection. Finally, the literature suggests that self-brand connection influences brand loyalty.

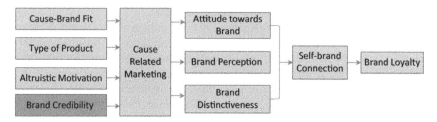

Fig. 1   Collaborative Model of Cause-Related Marketing and Self-Brand
Connection. *Source*: Authors' compilation.

4. THEORETICAL CONTRIBUTIONS

This study contributes to the existing literature in the field of CRM. Due to the
growing importance of CRM, there is a huge potential to explore this concept
further. According to Amoako et al. (2022), a sustainable business outlook is
required in all business decisions, including marketing strategies, as effective and
sustainable marketing plans like CRM are instrumental in achieving sustainability. Consumers have become socially conscious, so they support CRM strategy
as they show prosocial behaviour. Hoeffler and Keller (2002), though CRM, is
becoming a successful marketing strategy, and not all initiatives have a positive
outcome. To our understanding, this study is the first of its kind that undertakes a
systematic and extensive review of the literature that helped to explore and docu-
ment the dimensions that have a profound impact on the success of CRM and
also studied consequences of CRM that have a considerable impact on self-brand
connection.

It also examined the systemised dynamics of CRM and self-brand connection.
One of the most important contributions of this research is to develop an integrated framework of the different variables. These variables have been deliberated
earlier but in distinct papers, so by bringing these different variables together, this
framework provides a holistic view of CRM and its possible significance. It is first
to discuss that CRM can lead to self-brand connection, an upcoming consumer
behaviour and branding research. Self-brand connection is significant for a mar-
keter as it contributes to the loyalty and equity of a brand.

To conclude, a company implementing CRM will positively impact the consumer's attitude towards the brand and brand distinctiveness, leading to a self-
brand connection. However, to be brand loyal, customers must feel connected
to the brand, motivating them to get into a long-term relationship. Moreover,
there is a paucity of research in the area of CRM and self-brand connection, and
research scholars can use this framework for further investigations.

5. MANAGERIAL CONTRIBUTIONS

This chapter makes an insightful contribution to a detailed understanding of
the relationship between CRM and sustainability. Here, CRM and self-brand

connections have been explored. This relationship is crucial as it is vital for the company's sponsorship of sustainable issues. This chapter has various significant managerial implications. At first, the proposed framework helps managers to understand the factors that contribute to the success of CRM strategy. Considering the suggestions, managers can plan their CRM activities and investments accordingly. This study also suggests that organisations should aim to build strong connections between consumers and brands as this will foster positive attitudes and forgiveness for the company's brands (Escalas & Bettman, 2003). This chapter makes an insightful contribution by focusing on the need to understand brand association and its impact on self-brand connection and help organisations gain sustainable competitive advantage. This chapter will be valuable for future researchers to corroborate the determinants by conducting quantitative research.

6. LIMITATION AND FUTURE SCOPE

As with any other paper, this chapter also has some limitations that further open the avenues for research. Here, a model based on an extensive literature review is developed to understand the selected dimensions impacting the success of CRM and the possible consequences it can have. Other unexplored dimensions can be further explored and included in the framework. Researchers conjoined CRM and self-brand connection for the first time and proposed that the consequences of CRM can lead to self-brand connection. However, in further studies, other CRM consequences can also be examined, and their relationship with self-brand connection can be discovered.

Further investigations into the construct will help the academic and corporate world to get better insights into how self-brand connection in the context of CRM would help gain benefits like loyalty. Research scholars can also conduct further studies by taking self-brand connection as a mediating variable. Another limitation of this study is that this study is not culture-specific. Many researchers (Malhotra et al., 1996; McSweeney, 2002) have mentioned that every culture differs and influences people's beliefs and thought processes differently. Since each nation is different, it is vital to understand the people, society and organisations (Malhotra et al., 1996; McSweeney, 2002; Sekaran, 1983). Thus, to make the framework cross-cultural, research must be conducted by replicating the study in different cultures. Finally, in future, the researcher proposes to validate the model that will capture the proposed conceptualisation of CRM and its impact on loyalty. Furthermore, the proposed hypotheses in the present study can be tested empirically to estimate the reliability and validity and to understand the relationship between CRM and self-brand connection.

7. CONCLUSION

For this research, an extensive literature review of CRM, an effective CSR strategy to achieve sustainability, was undertaken. CSR initiatives like CRM are popular among organisations as they provide popularity, financial security, improved market presence and more funds. These funds are utilised for the societal causes to which the organisation is committed. CRM also plays a pivotal role in sustainable development, as contributing towards social causes is the main objective of this strategy. From the thorough review of dimensions affecting CRM success, four less-explored dimensions were selected for the study. The study also explored various consequences of CRM and investigated three consequences that lead to self-brand connection.

Furthermore, to understand the interrelationships between selected variables, 11 prepositions were developed. The study suggests that CRM strategy can have better results if implemented for hedonic products rather than utilitarian products. The effectiveness of a CRM programme will increase if the fit between brand and cause is high (Hamlin & Wilson, 2004). Perception of altruistic motivation is one of the most fundamental factors that can lead to the success or failure of a CRM programme. If a consumer does not perceive CRM initiative as altruistic, then CRM can even lead to a negative impact. Brand credibility is also an essential antecedent to the success of a CRM initiative. The literature shows that CRM leads to a better brand perception and, hence, a positive attitude. CRM is an effective strategy for creating brand distinctiveness. The study also recommends self-brand connection as an outcome of CRM and advocates that companies committed to CRM campaigns generate brand loyalty (Miller, 2002). This study further opens the avenues for research scholars, as theoretical and empirical research is scarce.

REFERENCES

Aaker, D. A. (1991). *Managing brand equity: Capitalizing on the value of a brand name* (pp. 71–77). Free Press.

Ahuvia, A. C. (2005). Beyond the extended self: Loved objects and consumers' identity narratives. *Journal of Consumer Research, 32*(1), 171–184.

Amoako, G. K., Dzogbenuku, R. K., Doe, J., & Adjaison, G. K. (2022). Green marketing and the SDGs: Emerging market perspective. *Marketing Intelligence & Planning, 40*(3), 310–327.

Babu, M. M., & Mohiuddin, M. (2008). *Cause-related marketing and its impact on the purchasing behaviour of the customers of Bangladesh: An empirical study*. [AIUB Bus Econ Working Paper, Series No. 2008-05]. http://orp.aiub.edu/WorkingPaper/WorkingPaper.aspx?year=2008

Barone, J. M., Norman, T. A., & Miyazaki, D. A. (2007). Consumer response to retailer use of cause-related marketing: Is more fit better? *Journal of Retailing, 83*(4), 437–445.

Basil, D. Z., & Herr, P. M. (2006). Attitudinal balance and cause-related marketing: An empirical application of balance theory. *Journal of Consumer Psychology, 16*(4), 391–403.

Batra, R., Ahuvia, A., & Bagozzi, R. P. (2012). Brand love. *Journal of Marketing, 76*(2), 1–16.

Becker-Olsen, K. L., Cudmore, B. A., & Hill, R. P. (2006). The impact of perceived corporate social responsibility on consumer behaviour. *Journal of Business Research, 59*(1), 46–53.

Benezra, K. (1996). Cause and effect marketing. *Brandweek, 37*(17), 38–40.

Bergami, M., & Bagozzi, R. (2000). Self-categorization, affective commitment and group self-esteem as distinct aspects of social identity in the organization. *The British Journal of Social Psychology, 39*, 555–577.

Berger, I., Cunningham, P., & Drumwright, M. (2006). Identity, identification, and relationship through social alliances. *Journal of the Academy of Marketing Science, 34*, 128–137. https://doi.org/10.1177/0092070305284973

Bhattacharya, C. B., & Sen, S. (2003). Consumer–company identification: A framework for understanding consumers' relationships with companies. *Journal of Marketing, 67*, 76–88.

Bigné-Alcañiz, E., Currás-Pérez, R., & Sanchez-Garcia, I. (2009). Brand credibility in cause-related marketing: The moderating role of consumer values. *Journal of Product & Brand Management, 18*(6), 437–447.

Bigné-Alcañiz, E., Currás-Pérez, R., Ruiz-Mafé, C., & Sanz-Blas, S. (2011). Cause-related marketing influence on consumer response: The moderating effect of cause brand fit. *Journal of Marketing Communications, 18*(4), 265–283.

Bigné-Alcañiz, E., Currás-Pérez, R., Ruiz-Mafé, C., & Sanz-Blas, S. (2012). Cause-related marketing influence on consumer responses: The moderating effect of cause–brand fit. *Journal of Marketing Communications, 18*(4), 265–283.

Belk, R. W. (1988). Possessions and the extended self. *Journal of Consumer Research, 15*(2), 139–168.

Bloom, P. N., Hoeffler, S., Keller, K. L., & Meza, C. E. B. (2006). How social-cause marketing affects consumer perceptions. *MIT Sloan Management Review, 47*(2).

Boone, L. E., & Kurtz, D. L. (2011). *Contemporary marketing* (pp. 57–65). South-Western College Publishing.

Brown, T. J., & Dacin, P. A. (1997). The company and the product: Corporate associations and consumer product responses. *Journal of Marketing, 61*(1), 68–84.

Chang, C. T. (2008). To donate or not to donate? Product characteristics and framing effects of cause-related marketing on consumer purchase behaviour. *Psychology and Marketing, 25*(12), 1089–1110.

Chaplin, L. N., & John, D. J. (2005). The development of self-brand connections in children and adolescents. *Journal of Consumer Research, 32*(1), 119–129.

Collins, M. (1993). Global corporate philanthropy – Marketing beyond the call of duty. *European Journal of Marketing, 27*(2), 46–58.

Cooper, H., Schembri, S., & Miller, D. (2010). Brand self-identity narratives in the James Bond movies. *Psychology & Marketing, 27*(6), 557–567.

Cornwell, T. B., & Maignan, I. (1998). An international review of sponsorship research. *Journal of Advertising, 27*(1), 1–21.

Dick, A. S., & Basu, K. (1994). Customer loyalty: Toward an integrated conceptual framework. *Journal of the Academy of Marketing Science, 22*(2), 99–113.

Dodds, W. B., Monroe, K. B., & Grewal, D. (1991). Effects of price, brand and store information on buyers' product evaluations. *Journal of Marketing Research, 28*(3), 307–319.

Donavan, T. D., Janda, S., & Suh, J. (2006). Environmental influences in corporate brand identification and consequences. *Journal of Brand Management, 14*, 125–136.

Drumwright, M. (1996). Company advertising with a social dimension: The role of noneconomic criteria. *Journal of Marketing, 60*(4), 71–87.

Du, S., Bhattacharya, C., & Sen, S. (2007). Reaping relational rewards from corporate social responsibility: The role of competitive positioning. *International Journal of Research in Marketing. 24*(3), 224–241. https://doi.org/10.1016/j.ijresmar.2007.01.001

Edmondson, D. R., & Lafferty, B. A. (2007). Cause related marketing: A model of consumer's attitude toward the cause-brand alliance. *Distinguished Teaching Competition-Sponsored by Sherwin-Williams, 67*, 20.

Ellen, P. S., Mohr, L. A., & Webb, D. J. (2000). Charitable programs and the retailer: Do they mix? *Journal of Retailing, 76*(3), 393–406.

Ellen, P. S., Webb, D. J., & Mohr, L. A. (2006). Building corporate associations: Consumer attributions for corporate socially responsible programs. *Journal of the academy of Marketing Science, 34*(2), 147–157.

Escalas, J. E. (2004). Narrative processing: Building consumer connections to brands. *Journal of Consumer Psychology, 14*(1 and 2), 168–180.

Escalas, J. E., & Bettman, J. (2003). You are what they eat: The influence of reference groups on consumers' connections to brands. *Journal of Consumer Psychology, 13*(3), 339–348.

Forehand, M., & Grier, S. (2003). When is honesty the best policy? The effect of stated company intent on consumer skepticism. *Journal of Consumer Psychology, 13*(3), 349–356. https://doi.org/10.1207/S15327663JCP1303_15

Fournier, S. (1998). Consumers and their brands: Developing relationship theory in consumer research. *The Journal of Consumer Research, 24*(4), 343–373.

Godfrey, P. C. (2005). The relationship between corporate philanthropy and shareholder wealth: A risk management perspective. *Academy of Management Review, 30*, 777–798.

Gao, Y. (2009). Corporate social responsibility and consumers' response: The missing linkage. *Baltic Journal of Management, 4*(3), 269–287.

Gupta, S., & Pirsch, J. (2006). Taxonomy of cause-related marketing research: Current findings and future research directions. *Journal of Non-profit and Public Sector Marketing, 15*(1), 25–43.

Hamlin, R. P., & Wilson, T. (2004). The impact of cause branding on consumer reactions to products: Does product/cause fit really matter? *Journal of Marketing Management, 20*(7/8), 663–681.

Hoeffler, S., & Keller, K. L. (2002). Building brand equity through corporate societal marketing. *Journal of Public Policy & Marketing, 21*(1), 78–79.

IEG. (2020). *Executive summary.* Retrieved July 26, 2021, from https://www.sponsorship.com/Latest-Thinking/Sponsorship-Infographics/Executive-Summary-page.aspx

Kalra, A., & Goodstein, R. C. (1998). The impact of advertising positioning strategies on consumer price sensitivity. *Journal of Marketing Research, 35*(2), 210–224.

Keller, K. L. (1993). Conceptualizing, measuring and managing customer-based brand equity. *Journal of Marketing, 57*(1), 1–22.

Kemp, E., & Bui, M. (2011). Healthy brands: Establishing brand credibility, commitment and connection among consumers. *Journal of Consumer Marketing, 28*(6), 429–437.

Kim, H., Kim, J., & Han, W. (2005). The effects of cause-related marketing on company and brand attitudes. *Seoul Journal of Business, 11*(2), 83–117.

Kuenzel, S., & Halliday, S. V. (2008). Investigating antecedents and consequences of brand identification. *Journal of Product and Brand Management, 17*, 293–304.

Lafferty, B. A., Goldsmith, R. E., & Hult, G. T. M. (2004). The impact of the alliance on the partners: A look at cause brand alliances. *Psychology & Marketing, 21*(7), 509.

Laužikas, M., & Dailydaitė, S. (2013). Benefits of social capital for sustainable innovation capabilities. *Journal of Security and Sustainability Issues, 2*, 85–97.

Lichtenstein, D., Drumwright, M., & Braig, B. (2004). The effect of corporate social responsibility on customer donations to corporate-supported non-profits. *Journal of Marketing, 68*(October), 16–32.

Liu, G., & Ko, W.-W. (2011). Analysis of cause-related marketing implementation strategies through social alliance: Partnership conditions and strategic objectives. *Journal of Business Ethics, 100*(2), 253–281.

Low, G. S., & Lamb, C. W. (2000). The measurement and dimensionality of brand associations. *Journal of Product & Brand Management, 9*(6), 350–368.

Luchs, M. G., Naylor, R. W., Irwin, J. R., & Raghunathan, R. (2010). The sustainability liability: Potential negative effects of ethicality on product preference. *Journal of Marketing, 74*(5), 18–31.

Malhotra, K. N., Agarwal, J., & Peterson, M. (1996). Methodological issues in cross-cultural marketing research: A state-of-the-art review. *International Marketing Review, 13*(5), 7–43.

Marin, L., & Ruiz, S. (2007). I need you, too! Corporate identity attractiveness for consumers and the role of social responsibility. *Journal of Business Ethics, 71*, 245–260.

McCracken, G. (1989). Who is the celebrity endorser? Cultural foundations of the endorsement process. *Journal of Consumer Research, 16*(3), 310–321.

McSweeney, B. (2002). Hofstede's model of national cultural differences and their consequences: A triumph of faith – A failure of analysis. *Human Relations, 55*(1), 89–118.

Miller, B. A. (2002). Social initiatives can boost loyalty. *Marketing News, 36*(21), 14–15.

Moore, D. J., & Homer, P. M. (2008). Self-brand connections: The role of attitude strength and autobiographical memory primes. *Journal of Business Research, 61*(7), 707–714.

Nan, X., & Heo, K. (2007). Consumer responses to corporate social responsibility (CSR) initiatives – Examining the role of brand-cause fit in cause-related marketing. *Journal of Advertising, 36*(2), 63–74.

Netemeyer, R., Krishnan, B., Pullig, C., Wang, G., Yagci, M., Dean, D., Ricks, J. M., & Wirth, F. (2004). Developing and validating measures of facets of customer-based brand equity. *Journal of Business Research, 57*(2), 209–244.

Nielsen's Corporate Social Responsibility Survey. (2014). Retrieved April 10, 2020, from http://www.nielsen.com/us/en/insights/reports/2014/doing-well-by-doing-good.html

Paul, P., & Mukhopadhyay, K. (2010). Growth via intellectual property rights versus gendered inequity in emerging economies: An ethical dilemma for international business. *Journal of Business Ethics, 91*(3), 359–378.

Polonsky, M., & Speed, R. (2001). Linking sponsorship and cause-related marketing. Complementarities and conflicts. *European Journal of Marketing, 35*(11/12), 1361–1385.

Porter, M. E., & Kramer, M. R. (2011). Creating shared value. *Harvard Business Review, 89*(1/2), 62–77.

Rifon, N. J., Choi, S. M., Trimble, C. S., & Li, H. (2004). Congruence effects in sponsorship: The mediating role of sponsor credibility and consumer attributions of sponsor motive. *Journal of Advertising, 33*(1), 29–42.

Ross, J. K. III, Patterson, L. T., & Stutts, M. A. (1992). Consumer perception of organization that use cause related marketing. *Journal of the Academy of Marketing Science, 20*(1), 93–97.

Schiffman, L. G., & Kanuk, L. L. (2007). *Consumer behavior* (9th ed.). Prentice Hall, Inc. ISBN-978-81-203-3086-3.

Sekaran, U. (1983). Methodological and theoretical issues and advancements in cross-cultural research. *Journal of International Business Studies, 14*(2), 61–73.

Sen, S., & Bhattacharya, C. (2001). Does doing good always lead to doing better? Consumer reactions to corporate social responsibility. *Journal of Marketing Research, 38*(2), 225–243. https://doi.org/10.1509/jmkr.38.2.225.18838

Sen, S., Bhattacharya, C., & Korschun, D. (2006). The role of corporate social responsibility in strengthening multiple stakeholder relationships: A field experiment. *Journal of the Academy of Marketing Science, 34*(2), 158–166. https://doi.org/10.1177/0092070305284978

Sirdeshmukh, D., Singh, J., & Sabol, B. (2002). Consumer trust, value, and loyalty in relational exchanges. *Journal of Marketing, 66*, 15–37.

Sirgy, M. J. (1982). Self-concept in consumer behaviour: A critical review. *Journal of Consumer Research, 9*(3), 287–300.

Smith, N. C. (2008). Consumers as drivers of corporate social responsibility. In A. Crane, D. Matten, A. McWilliams, J. Moon, & D. S. Siegel (Eds.), *The Oxford handbook of corporate social responsibility*. Oxford Academic. https://doi.org/10.1093/oxfordhb/9780199211593.003.0012

Strahilevitz, M. (1999). The effects of product type and donation magnitude on willingness to pay more for a charity-linked brand. *Journal of Consumer Psychology, 8*(3), 215–241.

Strahilevitz, M., & Myers, J. (1998). Donations to charity as purchase incentives: How well they work may depend on what you are trying to sell. *Journal of Consumer Research, 24*(4), 434–446.

Stroup, M., & Neubert, R. L. (1987). The evolution of social responsibility. *Business Horizons, 30*(March–April), 22–24.

Subrahmanyan, S. (2004). Effects of price premium and product type on the choice of cause-related brands: A Singapore perspective. *Journal of Product & Brand Management, 13*(2), 116–124.

Tajfel, H. (1974). Social identity and intergroup behaviour. *Social Science Information, 13*(2), 65–93.

Till, B. D., & Nowak, L. I. (2000). Toward effective use of cause-related marketing alliances. *Journal of Product and Brand Management, 9*(7), 472–484.

Trimble, C. S., & Rifon, N. J. (2006). Consumer perceptions of compatibility in cause-related marketing messages. *International Journal of Non-profit and Voluntary Sector Marketing, 11*(1), 29–47.

Tülin, E., & Swait, J. (2004). Brand credibility and its role in brand choice and consideration. *Journal of Consumer Research, 31*(1), 191–199.

Varadarajan, P. R., & Menon, A. (1988). Cause-related marketing: A coalignment of marketing strategy and corporate philanthropy. *Journal of Marketing, 52*(July), 58–74.

Yoo, B., Donthu, N., & Lee, S. (2000). An examination of selected marketing mix elements and brand equity. *Journal of the Academy of Marketing Science, 28*(2), 195–121.

Yoon, Y., Gürhan-Canli, Z., & Schwarz, N. (2006). The effect of corporate social responsibility (CSR) activities on companies with bad reputations. *Journal of Consumer Psychology, 16*(4), 377–390.

Zdravkovic, S., Magnusson, P., & Stanley, S. M. (2010). Dimensions of fit between a brand and a social cause and their influence on attitude. *International Journal of Research in Marketing*, *27*, 151–160.

Zeithaml, V. (1988). Consumer perceptions of price quality and value: A means-end model and synthesis of evidence. *Journal of Marketing*, *55*(3), 2–22.

Zhou, K. Z., & Nakamoto, K. (2007). The effect of enhanced and unique features on new product preference: The moderating role of product familiarity. *Journal of the Academy of Marketing Science*, *35*(1), 53–62.

CHAPTER 7

A SYSTEMATIC STUDY OF CAUSAL INTERACTION BETWEEN NATURAL GAS, INDIA'S GDP AND SUSTAINABLE GROWTH

Anita Tanwar

Chitkara Business School, Chitkara University, Rajpura, Punjab, India

ABSTRACT

Introduction: *India has the 15th-largest domestic natural gas consumption (NGC), critical to sustainable economic growth. Promoting natural gas will have a crucial impact on production in all industries.*

Purpose: *This research gives an overview of NGC and gross domestic product (GDP) in India from 1990 to 2021 and investigates the association and nature of causality between NGC and GDP in India.*

Methodology: *For the years 1990 through 2021, we used annual statistics from the NGC and the GDP of India. Both research variables data have been taken from the World Bank Indicator.*

Findings: *There is no causality and correlation between natural gas and GDP in India.*

Practical Implications: *Based on the research, the Government of India can create different policies for substituting natural gas for other energy sources*

Sustainable Development Goals: The Impact of Sustainability Measures on Wellbeing
Contemporary Studies in Economic and Financial Analysis, Volume 113B, 91–105
Copyright © 2024 by Anita Tanwar
Published under exclusive licence by Emerald Publishing Limited
ISSN: 1569-3759/doi:10.1108/S1569-37592024000113B007

to have a healthier impact on a sustainable environment in the short and long term. In the future, researchers can work on environmental degradation and GDP.

Keywords: GDP; causality; growth rate; sustainable growth; natural gas consumption; causality; energy

JEL Codes: N70; O40; F62; F64

1. INTRODUCTION

Sustainable Environment is the fossil fuel for the economy that involves different characteristics as discussed below:

1. It emits significantly less carbon dioxide when burned than coal, cutting emissions by half.
2. It has efficient power-generation capabilities.
3. It satisfies the expanding demand from the industrial sector.
4. Its reserves are dispersed across numerous regions.

As a result, natural gas is lauded as the best fuel option because it aligns with sustainability and financial concerns (UNCTAD, 2012). This resource also has the potential to spur sustainable industrial development in underdeveloped countries, opening the door for sustainable economic growth, higher incomes and lower poverty levels. However, maintaining a consistent and sustainable gas supply to these emerging nations is still a significant concern. Many developing countries have untapped gas reserves, both large and small. Furthermore, several locations continue to burn off gas created during crude oil production, resulting in significant environmental implications. India's natural gas industry began to take off after discovering gas reserves in Gujrat and Assam (Kar & Gupta, 2017). In the 1970s, natural gas was discovered in the Bombay High Fields in India. Most of the natural gas is generated in the eastern offshore, Gujarat overseas, and Bombay High. Gas production in the Krishna and Godavari basins began in the middle of the 2000s. The government of India has control over gas prices (Sen, 2015).

A growing body of research examines the relationships between energy usage and other critical economic indicators with substantial policy ramifications. While many studies focus on aggregate energy data, natural gas has gained popularity (Apergis & Payne, 2010; Fadiran et al., 2019; Ghandat, 2015; Solarin & Ozturk, 2016; Vivoda, 2012; Xie at al., 2014). The natural gas industry in India began to take off after finding gas reserves in Gujrat and Assam. It was discovered in the Bombay High Fields in India in the 1970s. Most of the natural gas is generated in the eastern offshore, Gujarat overseas and Bombay High. Gas production in the Krishna and Godavari basins began in the middle of the 2000s (Ghandat, 2015). The Government in India has control over gas prices.

In contrast, according to research by Chen et al. (2019), using natural gas is particularly significant for the nation's energy productivity and sustainable economic growth. According to predictions, natural gas will dominate the global energy landscape before 2040, making up 4.9 trillion cubic metres, or 26.9%, of total energy consumption (Galadima & Aminu, 2020; Rahman et al., 2020; Ye, 2020).

Second, the International Energy Agency (IEA, 2020) views natural gas as a transitional fuel to accomplish a more sustainable energy transition. Furthermore, renewables are heavily promoted as having a significant potential share, with India needing comprehensive programs to replace coal and oil, respectively. Despite later events undermining this energy trend, nuclear power still provides much electricity. For their energy needs, rapidly developing nations like China and India rely on renewable energy sources such as natural gas (Kong et al., 2019; latin et al., 2011; Leather et al., 2013; Qzturk et al., 2010; Shahbaz et al., 2015; Saint Akadiri et al., 2019; Wang et al., 2020; Weijermars et al., 2017). Natural gas use is still increasing throughout the world as a result of its cleaner energy as compared to different fossil fuels (Leather et al., 2013). One of the top three most used fuels in the world is natural gas. According to the 2018 statistical report, gas comprised 23.4% of the world's energy consumption in 2017. Third, natural gas has emerged as a feasible and appealing energy option for other fossil fuels (Zhao et al., 2019). Natural gas is more flexible and secure than other fuels, is less expensive and is easier to store, which is the leading cause of this (Destek, 2016; Solarin & Shahbaz, 2015; Tyagi et al., 2023). Gas-fired plants require less time and capital than green energy facilities, making investment decisions easier for many enterprises (Bartoli et al., 2009; Shahbaz et al., 2013). Finally, because it emits less CO_2, utilising natural gas to create power is less harmful to the environment than using other non-renewable resources. Fourth, India is presently the third-biggest producer of carbon, with a yearly production of 1.5 metric tons (Ahmad et al., 2016; Dangwal et al., 2023; Kaur et al., 2023). Du Can et al. (2019) and TNN (2018), among others, claim that natural gas is a cleaner fuel that will help reduce greenhouse gas emissions. However, due to enormous indigenous reserves, coal has historically dominated India's energy supply, and due to the combination's reliance on coal and natural gas, it only accounted for 6% of all renewable energy consumption in 2016 (Energy Outlook for India, 2018). For the reasons listed above, this work focuses on the form of knowledge in three separate ways. First and foremost, this is India's first comprehensive investigation into the connections between natural gas and GDP. The association between India's GDP and its use of natural gas will be examined second. Third, from 1990 through 2021, the researcher utilised the most current and readily available data.

This research chapter is planned as follows, except for the introduction: Section 2 discusses the existing research, notable gaps and our study strategy. Section 3 presents the current scenario for natural gas consumption (NGC). Section 4 shows the rationale and scope of the research. Section 5 shows the objectives of the study. Section 6 summarises empirical data, the unit root test, causation, and the Auto-Regressive Distributive Lag (ARDL) model. Section 7 summarises the findings, while Section 8 discusses closing observations and implications.

2. LITERATURE REVIEW

Consumption of energy and GDP are strongly linked. Moreover, this relationship has only recently come to the attention of specialists. Only some studies, nevertheless, have examined India's domestic natural gas usage and its connection to GDP. The relationship that exists between NGC and GDP has been related in four ways:

(a) NGC → GDP (Unidirectional causality from NGC to GDP)
(b) NGC ← GDP (Unidirectional causality from GDP to NGC)
(c) NGC ↔ GDP (Bidirectional causality occurs between NGC and GDP)
(d) NGC ——— GDP (No causality occurs between NGC and GDP)

NGC denotes natural gas domestic consumption, while GDP is gross domestic product. Tables 1–4 describe the numerous kinds of literature on possible causal relationships or hypotheses between NGC and GDP in different nations. To identify the type of causal relationship and association between NGC and GDP, various authors used various research tools such as Engle-Granger Causality, ARDL

Table 1.   Empirical Researches That Proves Growth Hypothesis.

Name of the Author and Year of Research	Nation with Time Period of Research	Methodology	Variables
Lee and Chang (2005)	Taiwan (1954–2003)	Cointegration test and Granger Causality	Natural gas and GDP
Sari et al. (2008)	USA (2001–2005)	Augmented Dickey–Fuller test and bound test	Coal, natural gas, industrial production, energy, fossil fuel and wood
Yang and Zhao (2014)	India (1955–1998)	Granger causality test and cointegration test	Energy, electricity, natural gas, coal and GDP
Asghar (2008)	ASEAN (1971–2003)	ECM, DF, TY	Energy, gas consumption, coal, petroleum, electricity and GDP
Li et al. (2019)	China (2000–2014)	Panel data	Natural gas and GDP
Işik (2010)	Turkey (1977–2008)	Autoregressive distribute lag and Johansen test.	Natural gas and GDP
Ighodaro (2010)	Nigeria (1970–2005)	Cointegration test and Granger Causality	Health expenses, natural gas and GDP
Shahbaz et al. (2013)	Pakistan (1972–2010)	Autoregressive distribute lag and Johansen test	Natural gas, per capita income, exports and gross domestic product
Abid and Mraihi (2015)	Tunisia (1980–2007)	Johansen cointegration and Granger Causality	Natural gas and gross domestic product

Source: Author's compilation.

Table 2. Empirical Researches That Describes Conservation Hypothesis.

Name of the Author and Year of Research	Nation with Time Period of Research	Methodology	Variables
Lotfalipour et al. (2010)	Iran (1967–2007)	Vector auto regression, Augmented Dickey–Fuller test, PERRON, SIM, PHILLIP and MWALT	Energy, GDP and natural gas
Khan and Ahmad (2008)	Pakistan (1972–2007)	Johansen test	Natural gas price and GDP
Sari et al. (2008)	U.S. (2001–2005 monthly)	ARDL and causality test	Natural gas, employment and industrial production
Adeniran et al. (2019)	Nigeria (1980–2006)	Sims test	Natural gas and GDP
Das et al. (2013)	Bangladesh (1980–2010)	Johansen cointegration and Causality	Natural gas and gross domestic product

Source: Author's compilation.

Table 3. Empirical Researches That Describes Feedback Hypothesis.

Name of the Author and Year of Research	Nation with Time Period of Research	Methodology	Variables
Zamani (2007)	Iran (1967–2003)	Granger Causality	Energy, natural gas consumption, petroleum, industrial energy, Industrial and agricultural value added and GDP
Solarin and Ozturk (2016)	OPEC Countries (1980–2012)	Granger Causality	Natural gas and GDP
Payne (2011)	U.S. (1949–2006)	T-Y test	NGC and GDP
Apergis and Payne (2010)	67 countries (1992–2006)	Cointegration and causality test	Capital formation, natural gas, labour and gross domestic product
Hu and Lin (2008)	Taiwan (1982–2006)	Cointegration test	Gas consumption and GDP
Saboori and Sulaiman (2013)	Malaysia (1980–2013)	Autoregressive model, Johansen test and causality test	GDP, natural gas and CO_2 emission
Shahiduzzaman and Alam (2014)	Australia (1970–2009)	ARDL and Johansen test	Natural gas, capital, energy, employment and gross domestic product
Farhani et al. (2014)	Tunisia (1980–2010)	ARDL, Toda-Yamamoto Test, cointegration test	Natural gas, capital, labour and gross domestic product
Solarin and Shahbaz (2015)	Malaysia (1971–2012)	ARDL and Causality test	Natural gas, capital, trade and GDP
Ozturk and AI-Mulali (2015)	Gulf Countries (1980–2012)	Pedroni test and Causality test	Natural gas, capital, FDI, trade and GDP

Source: Author's compilation.

Table 4.   Empirical Researches That Provides Mixed Results Between Natural
Gas Consumption and GDP in More than One Country.

Name of the Author and Year of Research	Nation with Time Period of Research	Methodology	Relationship Between Variables
Furuoka (2016)	China and Japan (1980–2012)	ARDL test, Granger test and Toda-Yamamoto	NGC ↔ GDP for Japan NGC ↔ GDP for Japan
Hossein et al. (2012)	Organisation of the Petroleum Exporting Countries (1980–2009)	Causality test	Diverse results found in short time, In long run no existence of causality
Fatai et al. (2004)	Australia, India, Indonesia, the Philippines and Thailand (1960–1999)	Juselius, ARDL Test, Granger Causality test	NGC ——— GDP
Kum et al. (2012)	Group of seven countries (1970–2008)	Bootstrap-corrected and Toda-Yamammoto Causality test	NGC ——— GDP = Canada and Japan NGC → GDP = Italy NGC ← GDP = UK NGC↔ GDP = France, Germany and USA

Source: Author's compilation.

bound test, error correction model, ordinary least square, vector autoregressive model, cointegration theory, **ARDL, PERRON, SIM, PHILLIP, MWALT** and Toda-Yamamoto causality test.

Table 1 lists empirical studies that examine growth theories in particular nations chronologically. Table 2 shows the conservation hypothesis in a specific nation. Table 3 lists research on the feedback hypothesis in a particular nation. Table 4 provides a chronological order of empirical research demonstrating the linkage between natural gas and GDP in various nations.

With varied degrees of success, researchers have tried to look into the association and causality between NGC and GDP. The Engle and Granger cointegration and Granger tests are used to analyse energy, electricity, natural gas, coal and GDP. This work led to the discovery of the growth theory. The association between NGC and GDP in Thailand, Australia, the Philippines and New Zealand was a significant focus of Fatai's research in 2004. Natural gas consumption and GDP have not been proven to correlate strongly in Asian countries.

Important note:

(a) NGC → GDP (Unidirectional causality from NGC to GDP)
(b) NGC ← GDP (Unidirectional causality from GDP to NGC)
(c) NGC ↔ GDP (Bidirectional causality occurs between NGC and GDP)
(d) NGC ——— GDP (No causality occurs between NGC and GDP)

The researcher's literature analysis reveals that no study analysing the connection between natural gas and India's GDP is available.

3. PRESENT SCENARIO OF CONSUMPTION OF NATURAL GAS IN INDIA

Consumption of natural gas is critical to India's economic growth since India has the 15th highest domestic use of natural gas. As of 2017, in terms of proven gas reserves, India ranks 22nd in the globe, with 43 trillion cubic feet, or over 1% of the global total of 6,923 trillion cubic feet. India has confirmed reserves that are 22.1 times the country's annual consumption. As a result, it has approximately 22 years of natural gas remaining. In this study, we look at how India could improve its trade balance and lessen its dependency on gas imports in a 1.5 °C low-gas future. Depending on the pricing and import assumptions used, India would save between $9 and $24 billion in gas imports in 2030 if it adopted a 1.5 °C sustainable pathway. According to various import assumptions, it would lead to average annual import expenditures of USD5–12 billion between 2021 and 2030. Because it is a fossil fuel, gas is inefficient as a 'bridge' fuel for reducing emissions. Fossil gas is still expanding and attracting investments all around the world (India Natural Gas, 2017). The promotion of natural gas will have a substantial impact on production in all industries, whether directly or indirectly. With an annual output of 1.5 metric tonnes, as of right now, India produces the third-most carbon per year (Ahmad et al., 2016). Natural gas is essential to pollution reduction because it is a cleaner fuel (TNN, 2018). Because of its enormous indigenous reserves, coal has dominated India's energy supply. Due to the dominance of crude oil and coal in the mix, natural gas consumption was only 6% of energy consumption (Energy Outlook India, 2018). Consumption of natural gas in India improved from 27.6 BCM in 2002 to 54.6 BCM in 2012 (CAGR of 7%) due to increased demand from consumer clusters and an increase in supply (Money Control, 2013). Domestic use of natural gas increased between 1990 and 2007, then decreased between 2008 and 2009 before increasing again until 2020 (World Bank Indicators, 2022). Fig. 1 shows the causality between domestic natural gas and yearly GDP. The figure demonstrates the positive association between NGC and GDP by showing that they are moving in the same direction. It implied that NGC and GDP have one kind of unidirectional relationship or another. The researcher will be able to comprehend the genuine association between variables with the help of the analysis provided in the section that follows the article.

4. STUDY'S RATIONALE AND SCOPE

Natural gas only accounts for roughly 6% of total energy consumption. According to Kumar et al. (2020), the Government of India plans to raise natural gas to 15% by 2030. In its Intended Nationally Determined Contributions displayed at the PACC, India vowed to enhance its contribution of renewable energy volume (GOI, 2015). Therefore, the utilisation of natural gas energy can rise. The natural gas industry in India began to take off after the discovery of gas reserves in Gujrat and Assam (Kar & Gupta, 2017). Natural gas was discovered in the Bombay High fields in India in the 1970s. Most of the natural gas is generated in the eastern offshore, Gujarat overseas and Bombay High. Gas production in the

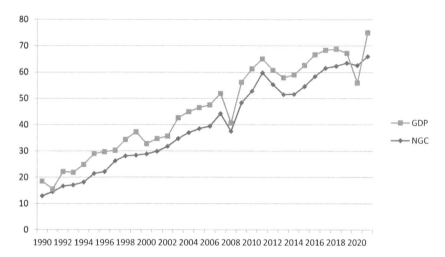

Fig. 1   Relationship Between Natural Gas Domestic Consumption and GDP
Annual %. (International Energy Agency). *Source*: Author's compilation.

Krishna and Godavari basins began in the middle of the 2000s. The government
in India has control over gas prices (Sen, 2015).

The two industries in India that use the most gas are undoubtedly the ones that
produce energy and fertilisers. Following these came 'other industries', including
the steel, refinery and manufacturing sectors (Ewing & Thomson, 2007; Kar &
Gupta, 2017). Compressed natural gas, a product of the gas industry that is still
growing, is used for cooking and transportation. An increase in domestic natural
gas consumption suggests that manufacturing operations are expanding and people's living conditions are improving, which may imply economic advancement.
Nevertheless, increased NGC may or may not be a significant factor in India's GDP.

The prior literature study did not demonstrate a connection between these two
criteria in India's evidence. Therefore, examining the nature of the causal link
between India's natural gas and GDP is the goal of this study. When deciding
how to develop and implement various domestic utility policies for natural gas,
policymakers may need to comprehend the connection and degree of causality
between India's natural gas and GDP.

5. OBJECTIVES OF THE STUDY

Thus, the following goals are being pursued by the study described here:

1. To give an overview natural gas consumption and GDP in India for the years
   1990–2021.
2. To investigate the association and nature of causality between natural gas consumption and GDP in India.
3. To provide suggestions to policymakers about creating a natural gas domestic
   policy in India.

6. INFORMATION AND TECHNIQUES

6.1. Data Collection and Variables

For the years 1990 through 2021, we used annual statistics from the NGC and India's GDP. Fig. 1 shows a graphical representation of the data. The data have been taken from the World Bank Indicator. The natural gas is represented in billion cubic feet, while the GDP current is measured in US dollars. NGC has been employed as a variable for calculating the utilisation of natural gas, while GDP has been used to calculate GDP:

$$Y_t = m + b_e + u_t$$

where Y = GDP, measured as GDP at a constant price in this research study, e the natural gas domestic consumption, symbolised as NGC in the study, m the constant, u the error term and t the time trend.

Domestic natural gas use and GDP are related and interdependent. Using Eviews 7 software, Granger causality and Johansen Cointegration techniques are used to assess the hypothesis. A stationarity test for both research variables was done before the analysis. The Phillips–Perron and Augmented Dickey–Fuller procedures are used to achieve this. We also looked at the cointegration of the variables to check if there was a connection between the NGC and GDP before determining the direction of causation between NGC and GDP. The Johansen technique (Johansen, 1991; Johansen & Juselius, 1990) was employed as an improved cointegration test. The formula for figuring out each series' order of integration is given below:

$$DY_t = b0 + D_{Y_{t-1}} + F_1 D_{Y_{t-2}} + F_2 D_{Y_{t-2}} + \cdots + F_p D_{Y_{t-p}} \quad (1)$$

According to Phillips and Perron (1988) and Dickey and Fuller (1979), Y_t stands for series, while UT denotes an iid error term. Appropriate lags about DY_t are taken into account for whitening mistakes. The Schwarz Bayesian Criterion is used in the current article to calculate the lag length. Equation (1) should be used as a reference when testing the null hypothesis. According to the one-tailed option, d is not favourable; however, the truth is that d equals 0. If d is negative, the stationarity of Y_t cannot be disproved. It is a given that their variability may result in stationary when a model demonstrates linkages between the variables. Keeping long-term data in level variables is essential even while several economic long-term relationships are removed from their variations, preventing deceptive degradation of variables. A way to achieve both of the seemingly conflicting goals is provided by cointegration.

The cointegration approach examines whether there is a significant relationship between the research variables using series with the same integrated order. Johansen cointegration method used to check the cointegration that provides a likelihood test using the trace value and highest E-value. Cointegration results show that if more than two natural series trends are in the same direction over time and have a constant variance, they have a long-term relationship. Weak cointegration indicates no long-term connection between the listed variables.

7. ANALYSIS AND RESULT DISCUSSION

The Phillips–Perron and Augmented Dickey–Fuller approaches have been used to check the integration between GDP and NGC.

In this research, the following model has been considered:

$$Y_t = m + b_e + u_t$$

To check the hypothesis, whether a unit root test exists or not. The researcher sets the following hypothesis:

H0. $a = 1$ [existence of unit root]

H1. $a < 1$ [zero-order integration]

7.1. Unit Root Test Result

This fundamental time series analysis of natural gas and GDP is shown in Tables 5 and 6, respectively. Both tables summarised the test results of unit root and indicated series-on-1 differences. In the Phillips–Perron test, the length of lag is grounded on the Newey–West estimator, while the length for enhanced Dickey–Fuller analysis is grounded on the Akaike Criterion. If the integration series order is $I(0)$, the result should be disregarded, and it should then be modified to $I(1)$ to use the cointegration test. Tables 5–8 have demonstrated that the order of integration is stationary and that both terms are 1(1). The Johansen cointegration test can be used because the researcher discovered stationarity in the first stage.

Tables 5 and 6 show NGC unit root test results, and Tables 7 and 8 show GDP unit root test results. The ADF test, which has been selected on the Akaike

Table 5.   Unit Root Test Result for NGC.

Variables	ADF Test		
	At Level	**First Difference**	**OI**
NGC	−0.689305	−5.356076	
1% critical value	−3.689194	−3.689194	$I(1)$
5% critical value	−2.971853	−2.971853	$I(1)$

Source: Author's compilation.

Table 6.   Unit Root Test Result for NGC.

Variables	Phillips–Perron Test		
	At Level	**First Difference**	**OI**
NGC	−0.794831	−10.51670	
1% critical value	−3.661661	−3.670170	$I(1)$
5% critical value	−2.960411	−2.621007	$I(1)$

Source: Author's compilation.

Table 7. Unit Root Result for GDP.

| Variables | ADF Test | | OI |
	At Level	First Difference	
GDP	−5.208227	−5.895648	
1% critical value	−3.661661	−3.679322	$I(1)$
5% critical value	−2.960411	−2.967767	$I(1)$

Source: Author's compilation.

Table 8. Unit Root Test Result for GDP.

| Variables | Phillips–Perron Test | | OI |
	At Level	First Difference	
GDP	−5.191252	−9.906357	
1% critical value	−3.661661	−3.670170	$I(1)$
5% critical value	−2.960411	−2.963972	$I(1)$

Source: Author's compilation.

Criterion, has all series shown on one different lag length, while Phillips–Perron tests consider its lag length based on Newey West into account. It should not be accepted if the order of integration shows the result 1(0). Results have shown that the order of integration for the test is 1(1), which shows that they are stationary. When the variables are discovered to be stationary, the Johansen cointegration approach can be used as a further step (Cismaş et al., 2023; Yadav et al., 2023).

7.2. Result of Johansen Cointegration Test

The Johansen cointegration approach can be used where all the study variables combined have the same order of stationarity. This section analyses whether the variables of the study are cointegrated or not. Johansen cointegration is one of the superior and primary tests for finding the cointegration between the variables. Trace value and Maximum Eigenvalue have shown in Table 9 that no cointegration exists between variables. This result reflects that a long-term association does not exist between NGC and GDP in India.

Table 9. Result of Cointegration Test.

| Hypothesised | Eigen Value | CR Test | | CR Test (Maximum Eigen Value) | |
		T-Value	*C*-Value	*T*-Value	*C*-Value
None	0.356	12.91975	14.49471	12.22144	13.27360
At Most 1	0.023008	0.698305	3.941465	0.698305	3.941465

Source: Author's compilation.

Table 10.   Result of Causality Test.

Research Hypothesis	Observation	Lags	F-Test	p-Value	Research Hypothesis Rejected or Accepted	Result
NGC does not Granger cause GDP	30	2	0.13213	0.8768	Rejected	NGC does not Granger cause GDP
GDP does not Granger cause NGC		2	0.07752	0.9256	Rejected	GDP does not Granger cause NGC

Source: Author's compilation.

7.3 Results of Granger Test

Table 10 shows the results of the causality test. It gives evidence that no causality exists or runs from NGC to GDP as it has been statistically proved by *p*-value, that is, 0.8768, which is more than 0.05, so the first hypothesis is accepted. It means a decrease or increase in NGC does not affect GDP. As a result of the second hypothesis, the *p*-value result is 0.9256, which is more than 5%; the second hypothesis is also accepted. It shows that no causality exists between GDP and NGC. It signifies that a decrease or increase in GDP may not affect the natural gas domestic consumption in India. It shows that the GDP of India does not depend on natural gas domestic consumption.

8. CONCLUSION AND RESEARCH IMPLICATION

The result evaluates the relationship and direction between NGC and GDP for the study period 1990–2021 in India by utilising yearly data from World Development Indicators. Johansen's cointegration test has shown that no correlation existed between NGC and GDP. The empirical result of Granger causality has not found causality between NGC and GDP. The test showed that no causality exists between NGC to GDP and vice versa. Based on the research, the Government of India can create different policies for substituting natural gas for other energy sources to make a healthier impact on a sustainable environment in the short and long term. In the future, researchers can work on environmental degradation and GDP.

REFERENCES

Abid, M., & Mraihi, R. (2015). Energy consumption and industrial production: Evidence from Tunisia at both aggregated and disaggregated levels. *Journal of the Knowledge Economy*, 6(4), 1123–1137.
Adeniran, A. A., Adebayo, A. R., Salami, H. O., Yahaya, M. O., & Abdulraheem, A. (2019). A competitive ensemble model for permeability prediction in heterogeneous oil and gas reservoirs. *Applied Computing and Geosciences*, 1, 100004.

Ahmad, W. N. K. W., Rezaei, J., Tavasszy, L. A., & de Brito, M. P. (2016). Commitment to and preparedness for sustainable supply chain management in the oil and gas industry. *Journal of Environmental Management, 180*, 202–213.

Apergis, N., & Payne, J. E. (2010). Renewable energy consumption and economic growth: Evidence from a panel of OECD countries. *Energy Policy, 38*(1), 656–660.

Asghar, Z. (2008). Energy-GDP relationship: A causal analysis for the five countries of South Asia. *Applied Econometrics and International Development, 8*(1), 167–180.

Bartoli, A., Hamelin, L., Rozakis, S., Borzęcka, M., & Brandão, M. (2019). Coupling economic and GHG emission accounting models to evaluate the sustainability of biogas policies. *Renewable and Sustainable Energy Reviews, 106*, 133–148.

Chen, S., Conejo, A. J., Sioshansi, R., & Wei, Z. (2019). Unit commitment with an enhanced natural gas-flow model. *IEEE Transactions on Power Systems, 34*(5), 3729–3738.

Cismaș, L. M., Boţoteanu, G. I., Cojocaru, T. M., & Gruescu, R. M. (2023). Significance of corporate non-financial information disclosure for sustainable economic growth. *Journal of Green Economy and Low-Carbon Development, 2*(1), 1–10.

Dangwal, A., Kukreti, M., Angurala, M., Sarangal, R., Mehta, M., & Chauhan, P. (2023, March). A Review on the role of artificial intelligence in tourism. In M. Yamin & A.k. Saini (Eds.), *2023 10th international conference on computing for sustainable global development (INDIACom)* (pp. 164–168). IEEE.

Das, A., McFarlane, A. A., & Chowdhury, M. (2013). The dynamics of natural gas consumption and GDP in Bangladesh. *Renewable and Sustainable Energy Reviews, 22*, 269–274.

Destek, M. A. (2016). Natural gas consumption and economic growth: Panel evidence from OECD countries. *Energy, 114*, 1007–1015.

Dickey, D. A., & Fuller, W. A. (1979). Distribution of the estimators for autoregressive time series with a unit root. *Journal of the American Statistical Association, 74*(366a), 427–431.

Du Can, S. D. L. R., Khandekar, A., Abhyankar, N., Phadke, A., Khanna, N. Z., Fridley, D., & Zhou, N. (2019). Modeling India's energy future using a bottom-up approach. *Applied Energy, 238*, 1108–1125.

Energy outlook. (2018). Retrieved on 10th March 2023 from https://www.iea.org/countries/india

Ewing, B. T., & Thompson, M. A. (2007). Dynamic cyclical comovements of oil prices with industrial production, consumer prices, unemployment, and stock prices. *Energy Policy, 35*(11), 5535–5540.

Fadiran, G., Adebusuyi, A. T., & Fadiran, D. (2019). Natural gas consumption and economic growth: Evidence from selected natural gas vehicle markets in Europe. *Energy, 169*, 467–477.

Farhani, S., Chaibi, A., & Rault, C. (2014). CO_2 emissions, output, energy consumption, and trade in Tunisia. *Economic Modelling, 38*, 426–434.

Fatai, K., Oxley, L., & Scrimgeour, F. G. (2004). Modeling the causal relationship between energy consumption and GDP in New Zealand, Australia, India, Indonesia, the Philippines, and Thailand. *Mathematics and Computers in Simulation, 64*, 431–445.

Furuoka, F. (2016). Natural gas consumption and economic development in China and Japan: An empirical examination of the Asian context. *Renewable and Sustainable Energy Reviews, 56*, 100–115.

Galadima, M. D., & Aminu, A. W. (2020). Nonlinear unit root and nonlinear causality in natural gas-economic growth nexus: Evidence from Nigeria. *Energy, 190*, 116415.

Ghandat, S. (2015, November). *Indian natural gas scenario and analysis of shale gas with porter's five forces model.* https://ssrn.com/abstract=2692338

GOI. (2015). Retrieved on 12th January 2023 https://texmin.nic.in/annual-report2015-2016

Hossein, A., Yazdan, G. F., & Ehsan, A. G. (2012). The relationship between energy consumption, energy prices and economic growth: Case study (OPEC countries). *OPEC Energy Review, 36*(3), 272–286.

https://www.iea.org/reports/world-energy-outlook-2020 retrieved data in 12 August 2022

https://www.tnn.ltd/https://www.bp.com/content/dam/bp/businesssites/en/global/corporate/pdfs/energy-economics/energy-outlook/bp-energy-outlook-2018.pdf

Hu, J. L., & Lin, C. H. (2008). Disaggregated energy consumption and GDP in Taiwan: A threshold cointegration analysis. *Energy Economics, 30*, 2342–2358.

Ighodaro, C. A. (2010). Co-integration and causality relationship between energy consumption and economic growth: Further empirical evidence for Nigeria. *Journal of Business Economics and Management, 11*(1), 97–111.

India Natural Gas. (2017). https://www.worldometers.info/gas/india-natural-gas

Işik, C. (2010). Natural gas consumption and economic growth in Turkey: A bound test approach. *Energy Systems, 1*(4), 441–456.

Johansen, S. (1991). Estimation and hypothesis testing of cointegration vectors in Gaussian vector autoregressive models. *Econometrica: Journal of the Econometric Society, 59*(6), 1551–1580.

Johansen, S., & Juselius, K. (1990). Maximum likelihood estimation and inference on cointegration— With applications to the demand for money. *Oxford Bulletin of Economics and statistics, 52*(2), 169–210.

Kar, S. K., & Gupta, A. (Eds.). (2017). *Natural gas markets in India: Opportunities and challenges* (pp. 167–196). Springer Nature.

Kaur, A., Tanwar, A., Kaur, H., & Singh, J. (2023, February). A study on linkage between global warming indicators and climate change expenditure. *IOP Conference Series: Earth and Environmental Science, 1110*(1), 012059.

Khan, M. A., & Ahmad, U. (2008). Energy demand in Pakistan: A disaggregate analysis. *The Pakistan Development Review, 47*(4), 437–455.

Kong, Z., Lu, X., Jiang, Q., Dong, X., Liu, G., Elbot, N., & Chen, S. (2019). Assessment of import risks for natural gas and its implication for optimal importing strategies: A case study of China. *Energy Policy, 127*, 11–18.

Kum, H., Ocal, O., & Aslan, A. (2012). The relationship among natural gas energy consumption, capital and economic growth: Bootstrap-corrected causality tests from G-7 countries. *Renewable and Sustainable Energy Reviews, 16*(5), 2361–2365.

Kumar, V. V., Shastri, Y., & Hoadley, A. (2020). A consequence analysis study of natural gas consumption in a developing country: Case of India. *Energy Policy, 145*, 111675.

Laini, A., Bartoli, M., Castaldi, S., Viaroli, P., Capri, E., & Trevisan, M. (2011). Greenhouse gases (CO_2, CH_4 and N_2O) in lowland springs within an agricultural impacted watershed (Po River Plain, northern Italy). *Chemistry and Ecology, 27*(2), 177–187.

Leather, D. T., Bahadori, A., Nwaoha, C., & Wood, D. A. (2013). A review of Australia's natural gas resources and their exploitation. *Journal of Natural Gas Science and Engineering, 10*, 68–88.

Lee, C. C., & Chang, C. P. (2005). Structural breaks, energy consumption, and economic growth revisited: evidence from Taiwan. *Energy Economics, 27*(6), 857–872.

Li, Z. G., Cheng, H., & Gu, T. Y. (2019). Research on dynamic relationship between natural gas consumption and economic growth in China. *Structural Change and Economic Dynamics, 49*, 334–339.

Lotfalipour, M. R., Falahi, M. A., & Ashena, M. (2010). Economic growth, CO_2 emissions, and fossil fuels consumption in Iran. *Energy, 35*(12), 5115–5120.

Money control. (2013). Retrieved on 24 February 2023 from https://www.moneycontrol.com/stocks/marketinfo/bonus/index.php?sel_year=2013

Ozturk, I., & Al-Mulali, U. (2015). Investigating the validity of the environmental Kuznets curve hypothesis in Cambodia. *Ecological Indicators, 57*, 324–330.

Ozturk, I., Aslan, A., & Kalyoncu, H. (2010). Energy consumption and economic growth relationship: Evidence from panel data for low and middle income countries. *Energy Policy, 38*, 4422–4428.

Payne, J. E. (2011). US disaggregate fossil fuel consumption and real GDP: An empirical note. *Energy Sources, Part B: Economics, Planning, and Policy, 6*(1), 63–68.

Phillips, P. C., & Perron, P. (1988). Testing for a unit root in time series regression. *Biometrika, 75*(2), 335–346.

Rahman, M. J., Wahab, M. A., Nahiduzzaman, M., Haque, A. B. M. M., & Cohen, P. (2020). Hilsa fishery management in Bangladesh. *IOP Conference Series: Earth and Environmental Science, 414*(1), 012018.

Saboori, B., & Sulaiman, J. (2013). CO_2 emissions, energy consumption and economic growth in Association of Southeast Asian Nations (ASEAN) countries: A cointegration approach. *Energy, 55*, 813–822.

Saint Akadiri, S., Bekun, F. V., & Sarkodie, S. A. (2019). Contemporaneous interaction between energy consumption, economic growth and environmental sustainability in South Africa: What drives what? *Science of the Total Environment, 686*, 468–475.

Sari, R., Ewing, B. T., & Soytas, U. (2008). The relationship between disaggregate energy consumption and industrial production in the United States: An ARDL approach. *Energy Economics, 30*(5), 2302–2313.

Sen, A. (2015). Gas pricing reform in India – Implications for the Indian gas landscape. *NG 96, OIES paper.*

Shahbaz, M., Khan, S., & Tahir, M. I. (2013). The dynamic links between energy consumption, economic growth, financial development and trade in China: Fresh evidence from multivariate framework analysis. *Energy Economics, 40*, 8–21.

Shahbaz, M., Solarin, S. A., Sbia, R., & Bibi, S. (2015). Does energy intensity contribute to CO_2 emissions? A trivariate analysis in selected African countries. *Ecological Indicators, 50*, 215–224.

Shahiduzzaman, M., & Alam, K. (2014). A reassessment of energy and GDP relationship: The case of Australia. *Environment, Development and Sustainability, 16*(2), 323–344.

Solarin, S. A., & Ozturk, I. (2016). The relationship between natural gas consumption and economic growth in OPEC members. *Renewable and Sustainable Energy Reviews, 58*, 1348–1356.

Solarin, S. A., & Shahbaz, M. (2015). Natural gas consumption and economic growth: The role of foreign direct investment, capital formation and trade openness in Malaysia. *Renewable and Sustainable Energy Reviews, 42*, 835–845.

Tyagi, P., Grima, S., Sood, K., Balamurugan, B., Özen, E., & Eleftherios, T. (Eds.). (2023). *Smart analytics, artificial intelligence and sustainable performance management in a global digitalised economy.* Emerald Publishing Limited.

UNCTAD. (2012, April 21–26). *Natural gas as an engine of growth.* https://unctad.org/system/files/official-document/uxiiicn2012d6_en.pdf

Vivoda, V. (2012). Japan's energy security predicament post-Fukushima. *Energy Policy, 46*, 135–143.

Wang, S., Su, H., Chen, C., Tao, W., Streets, D. G., Lu, Z., & Cheng, Y. (2020). Natural gas shortages during the "coal-to-gas" transition in China have caused a large redistribution of air pollution in winter 2017. *Proceedings of the National Academy of Sciences, 117*(49), 31018–31025.

Weijermars, R., Sorek, N., Sen, D., & Ayers, W. B. (2017). Eagle ford shale play economics: Us versus Mexico. *Journal of Natural Gas Science and Engineering, 38*, 345–372.

World Bank. (2022). Retrieved on 17th March 2023 from https://data.worldbank.org/indicator/NY.GDP.MKTP.CD

Xie, B. C., Shang, L. F., Yang, S. B., & Yi, B. W. (2014). Dynamic environmental efficiency evaluation of electric power industries: Evidence from OECD (Organization for Economic Cooperation and Development) and BRIC (Brazil, Russia, India and China) countries. *Energy, 74*, 147–157.

Yang, Z., & Zhao, Y. (2014). Energy consumption, carbon emissions, and economic growth in India: Evidence from directed acyclic graphs. *Economic Modelling, 38*, 533–540.

Yadav, U. S., Sood, K., Tripathi, R., Grima, S., & Yadav, N. (2023). Entrepreneurship in India's handicraft industry with the support of digital technology and innovation during natural calamities. *International Journal of Sustainable Development & Planning, 18*(6), 1777–1791.

Ye, Z. (2020, June). Study on the natural gas consumption and its change prediction. *Journal of Physics: Conference Series, 1549*(4) 042103.

Zamani, M. (2007). Energy consumption and economic activities in Iran. *Energy Economics, 29*, 1135–1140.

Zhao, W., Cheng, Y., Pan, Z., Wang, K., & Liu, S. (2019). Gas diffusion in coal particles: A review of mathematical models and their applications. *Fuel, 252*, 77–100.

CHAPTER 8

ADOPTING ONLINE EDUCATION FOR SUSTAINABLE AND ECONOMIC DEVELOPMENT: A STRUCTURAL EQUATION MODEL

Rashi Jain[a,b] and Broto R. Bhardwaj[a,b]

[a]Bharati Vidyapeeth (Deemed to be University), Pune, India
[b]Institute of Management and Research, New Delhi, India

ABSTRACT

Purpose: *The purpose of this chapter is to identify various factors that may influence the adoption of online education by students in higher education institutions (HEIs) and contribute to the achievement of sustainable development goals (SDGs) post-COVID-19.*

Need for the Study: *The study addresses the need to ensure inclusive and equitable quality education, as emphasised by SDG4. It focuses on lifelong learning opportunities and aims to understand the impact of online education on students in HEIs. By identifying the factors that influence adoption, the study aims to contribute to the development of effective strategies for promoting online education.*

Methodology: *The study utilises a framework incorporating the use of Statistical Package for the Social Sciences (SPSS) and Analysis of Moment Structures (AMOS) software. The framework allows for the analysis of the collected data's reliability, validity and adequacy.*

Sustainable Development Goals: The Impact of Sustainability Measures on Wellbeing
Contemporary Studies in Economic and Financial Analysis, Volume 113B, 107–122
Copyright © 2024 by Rashi Jain and Broto R. Bhardwaj
Published under exclusive licence by Emerald Publishing Limited
ISSN: 1569-3759/doi:10.1108/S1569-37592024000113B008

Findings: *The study's findings indicate that providing students with afford-able online higher education can facilitate skill enhancement and create job opportunities. These findings highlight the potential of online education in contributing to the achievement of SDGs, particularly SDG4.*

Practical Implications: *The practical implications of the study suggest that promoting affordable online higher Education can have a positive impact on students, enabling them to acquire new skills and access job opportunities. By embracing online education, institutions can contribute to the advancement of SDGs and ensure inclusive and equitable quality education for all.*

Keywords: Online education; SD goals; higher education; quality education; COVID-19; SEM model; economic development

JEL Classifications: I25; I21; I23

INTRODUCTION

A new international development strategy was approved by participating countries, 'Changing our World: The 2030 Agenda for SD (SD)', at the United Nations (UN) General Assembly's 70th session in September 2015. SD is a worldwide development organising concept that promotes the well-being of both people and the earth (UNESCO, 2016). The sustainable development goals (SDGs) are a new, unified set of goals, targets and indicators that nations who are members of the UN will be required to utilise to define their programs and political actions for the next 15 years. There are 17 SDGs in total, with Goal 4 on Education serving as its central tenet because it is the only one that emphasises universal education, ensures quality education that is equitable and inclusive and fosters opportunities for lifelong learning for all. The UN Population Fund's 'State of Population' reports (UNFPA, 2009, 2011, 2019) consistently highlight the imperative of investing in activities empowering girls and women. The Millennium Development Goals, which were adopted by countries in 2001 and are due to expire at the end of this year, are expanded upon by the SDGs (Ford, 2015). The appropriate integration of Information and Communication Technology (ICT) is a critical strategy for improving education and developing and improving learners' performance and abilities. Several higher education institutions (HEIs) alter their teaching tactics to meet the various demands of these broad class of pupils and provide flexible learning routes through the use of e-learning hostile environments (Ghanem, 2020).

The 2030 development plan, on the other hand, views continuous education as an ongoing process that starts shortly after birth and persists through all phases of life. This approach includes numerous flexible learning pathways, entry and re-entry points for all ages (Brotherhood et al., 2020) and strengthened ties respectively formal and non-formal frameworks, including formal recognition of non-formal and informal focus on students, skills and proficiencies (Owens, 2017). Online learning, also referred to as online or adaptable learning, enables students to advance their skills and knowledge at a lower price (Farid et al., 2018). Al-Samarraie et al. (2016) and Altinay et al. (2018) are two references.

Chankseliani and McCowan (2020) stated as the essentialist dogma of development via higher education that fosters human capital growth and societal modernisation. Unfortunately, the rise of online learning, particularly in underdeveloped nations, remains slow (Hadullo et al., 2017). Most HEIs use a mixed learning strategy, utilising various learning management systems (LMS) (Al-Ammary et al., 2016); nonetheless, local institutions do not offer entirely online higher education degrees, minimising exposure to locals as well as those who may afford to pay for higher education (Owens, 2017).

The COVID-19 epidemic has caused significant interruptions in educational activity. Teachers in and under situations have found it difficult to provide learning to homes since access, availability and usage of educational technology are not ubiquitous (Hamaniuk et al., 2020; Khan et al., 2012). The shift to online instruction in underdeveloped nations was not smoother than in rich countries (Saeed, 2020). Because of the current COVID-19 epidemic, most educational institutions throughout the world have been closed since March 2020, and e-learning has been used internationally as an alternate teaching and learning strategy to maintain the educational process (Owens, 2017). As per a few late examinations, nations that do not offer completely online degrees are utilising brief applications, for example, Microsoft Groups and Zoom to give live talks and classes, with the backing of the LMS that was initially used to divide course material and tasks and for correspondence among teachers and students (Basilaia et al., 2020; Hamaniuk et al., 2020). According to Becker (2017) and Waghid and Waghid (2016), flexible learning, e-learning and mixed learning have now turned into the norm and a choice to eye education and learning in advanced education. Well-designed online learning at HEIs provides potential benefits such as accessibility, affordability and flexibility (Castro & Tumibay, 2021; Dhawan, 2020), which might have added to the rising enrolment in web-based classes and projects across HEIs. SDG4 is additionally upheld by e-learning as far as equivalent learning opens valuable doors for young men and young ladies with the capacity to finish their postsecondary instruction. According to Trakru and Jha (2019), e-learning gave young ladies in India opportunities for advanced education.

The motivation behind this study is to feature the important influential element in the adoption of online education and the attainment of economic growth via the adoption of online education by students of HEIs. It intends to contribute to the body of evidence and conceptualisation of online higher education's ability to contribute to the SDGs. It will analyse how online higher education leads to economic development in the country, fulfilling SDGs. SDG4 is additionally upheld by e-learning as far as equivalent learning opens valuable doors for young men and young ladies with the capacity to finish their postsecondary training. According to Trakru and Jha (2019), e-learning provided girls in India with chances for graduate degrees.

LITERATURE REVIEW

Online learning has emerged as a method that utilises information and Internet technologies to accelerate learning. It encompasses several vital attributes, represented by the letters 'e', such as electronic, practical, exploratory, experienced, extended, user-friendly and improved learning (Zhou et al., 2020). Online learning is adaptable and considers the inclusion of diverse students, aiming to promote lifelong learning and cater to individuals with limited social resources (Andrade & Alden-Rivers, 2019), disabilities (Altinay et al., 2018) and varying age and social status (González, 2019). Improving the online learning experiences of students has been the subject of research across multiple disciplines in the field of online education (Al-Samarraie et al., 2018). Furthermore, ongoing studies focus on understanding students' perspectives on internet-based learning and its correlation with academic achievement (Ke & Kwak, 2013; Wei & Chou, 2020). Sahin and Shelley (2008) suggest that student satisfaction with online classes can be enhanced by providing access to online resources and fostering a realistic and adaptive learning environment for effective knowledge exchange and communication.

Numerous review articles have highlighted the advantages of online learning, which are believed to be beneficial in achieving SDG 4. These advantages include adaptability, inclusivity, lifelong learning, equity, access to higher education and improved economic capabilities (Ghanem, 2020). Developing countries are increasingly embracing blended and fully online programs to enhance students' knowledge, skills and competencies (Barclay et al., 2018). Such programs create a collaborative and interactive atmosphere, students' abilities (Al-Ammary et al., 2016), promote internationalisation (Barclay et al., 2018) and facilitate exposure to diverse perspectives, thereby nurturing a culture of scientific conversation (Komochkova & Ikonnikova, 2019).

Before the COVID-19 pandemic, the United Nations predicted that by 2030, over 200 million children would be out of school, and only 60% of teenagers would complete upper secondary education. Although the dropout rates for primary and secondary education have decreased over the years, with a decline from 26% in 2000 to 17% in 2018, there is still a significant education crisis, especially in Sub-Saharan Africa, where more than 50% of children are not attending school or receiving the necessary education (Bahrain, 2020). To address this, governments of developing nations are integrating online education and ICT into their educational systems, However, these investments are unequal due to infrastructure deficits and limited budgets (Oxford Business Group. 2020).

The efficient use of e-learning can contribute to the sustainability of education, as emphasised by SDG 4.4. By 2030, there is a need to significantly increase the number of adults and young people equipped with the skills required for employment, decent jobs and entrepreneurial spirit, including technical and vocational skills, which in turn drive economic growth (SDG 4.4). According to Barclay et al. (2018) and ENQA (European Association for Quality Assurance) (2018), one of the main advantages of e-learning is the flexibility of time, location and speed. The effectiveness of the system and the happiness of the learners are both influenced by an intuitive interactive system (Ahmed et al., 2018; Kanwal & Rehman, 2017), high-quality material (Makokha & Mutisya, 2016) and high-quality technology (Saeid & Goodarzi, 2019). Teachers saw that students were more focused, engaged, autonomous and independent. Teachers have also noted an improvement in students' accomplishment in terms of transferrable abilities like critical thinking. What's more, SDG 4.7 states that all students should gain the abilities and information important to progress manageable turn of events, for example, in addition to other things, through guidance in practical development and harmless to the ecosystem ways of life, common liberties, orientation uniformity, the advancement of a culture of harmony and peacefulness, worldwide citizenship and a comprehension of social variety and the contribution that culture plays in supportable turn of events. The possibility of SD puts profound emphasis on the monetary and social pieces of reasonability. Given the above literature the following hypotheses have been framed:

H1. Technology influences the adoption of online education significantly.

H2. Interaction influences the adoption of online education significantly.

H3. Cost influences the adoption of online education significantly.

H4. Time influences the adoption of online education significantly.

H5. Quality influences the adoption of online education significantly.

H6. Adoption of online education influences economic development in the country significantly hence achieving SDG.

THE OBJECTIVE OF THE STUDY

To accomplish economic growth through the adoption of online education by students of HEIs, the chapter tries to identify the important influencing elements. It intends to increase the body of research and conceptualisation on the possible impact of higher education delivered online on the SDGs. It will evaluate how the country's economic growth eventually contributed to the achievement of the SDG.

RESEARCH METHODOLOGY

The review has embraced experimental review to find the connection between online education factors and their effect on accomplishing SDG. It is exploratory and descriptive research. Three hundred and seventeen college students were chosen as a sample from a variety of universities. To determine the most important influencing elements in the adoption of online education and to investigate the link between the attainment of economic development via the adoption of online education, data were gathered from higher education students using a questionnaire. To accomplish the goal and get definitive conclusions, a variety of methods and strategies have been used. SPSS and AMOS are the software utilised.

DATA ANALYSIS

Following data collection, factor analysis was performed, and seven factors were chosen from the total variance explained in Table A2. As the expected result is anything above 0.60 or 60%, the total variance is explained in Table A2 roughly 86%, regarded as good in the social sciences (Hair et al., 2007). For each variable, the ensuing codes are provided (Table 1). The number larger than 0.60, regarded as acceptable, was also shown in KMO test (Table A4). A significant value of 6030.221 ($p = 0.000$, $df = 210$) is provided by Bartlett's test of sphericity (Table A4). The sample was good enough according to the KMO sampling adequacy value, which was discovered to be 0.752. The communalities (Table A1) for all the elements larger than 0.5 are shown in Tables 1 and A1.

According to the rotated component matrix (Table A3), only the items with factor loading values greater than or equal to 0.50 were kept on the schedule. Seven components totalling all the statements have been combined. Interaction with statements I1 to I6 has been recognised as the first component. Cost incorporating statements from C1 to C6 have been determined as the second component. The third component, which includes statements 1 from TE1 through TE5, has been characterised as technology. The fourth element, which includes statements A1 through A5, has been recognised as adopting online education. The economic development component, which includes statements from ED1 through ED5, has been designated the fifth component. Time-containing statements from T1 to T5 have been recognised as the sixth component. The seventh and final component, quality, has been recognised as encompassing statements from Q1 to Q5.

Table 1. Code to Variables.

S.No.	Codes	Variables
1	TE	Technology
2	I	Interaction
3	C	Cost
4	T	Time
5	Q	Quality
6	A	Adoption
7	ED	Economic development

Source: Authors' compilation.

RELIABILITY OF INDIVIDUAL VARIABLES

The reliability of each variable was examined, and the following codes were assigned to each statement of the variables (Table 2). The reliability of each variable was adequate as Cronbach's α reliability coefficient α for all factors is above 0.8 which is considered to be excellent for the study.

Table 2. Codes for Each Statement.

S.No.	Statements	Cronbach's α Coefficient	Reliability Results
TE1	I have the appropriate digital equipment to access the university's digital environment.		
TE2	I believe that the technology we use in online education mode is up to the mark.	0.992	Excellent
TE4	High bandwidth speed is a must for the success of the online education system.		
TE5	Tools and media used to support the achievement of learning objectives.		
I1	I can easily interact with faculty in the online classroom.		
I2	I am comfortable discussing my doubts and queries in online education mode.		
I3	I can maintain a close relationship with classmates for quick and easy responses.	0.975	Excellent
I4	I can get quick feedback from the instructor in online mode.		
I5	Interaction is very easy in online education mode.		
C1	I believe that the online education system is more economical than the offline education system.		
C2	I believe that transportation cost is nil/ zero in the online education system.		
C3	I believe that most of the internet is a little high in the online education system.	0.928	Excellent
C4	I believe that the infrastructure cost of online education is a little high.		
C6	I believe that the fees charged in the online education system are very low.		
T1	I believe that transportation time can be easily saved in the online education system.		
T2	I can easily adjust the time according to my requirements.	0.930	Excellent
T3	I believe that online classes can be available 24*7 (flexible timing).		
T5	Time management is very easy in the online education system.		
Q1	The online mode of education enhanced my skills.		
Q2	I believe that very little documentation is required in the online education system.	0.841	Good
Q3	I believe that the faculty I get in online mode is highly qualified and experienced.		
Q5	The study material I get in online mode is of good quality.		
A1	Since there is no geographical barrier to online education, it increases its adoption.		
A2	I adopt the online mode because it is economical.	0.990	Excellent
A3	I adopted the online mode because it provides me with easy access to skills and training programs.		
A5	Since online mode saves my time, it increases its adoption.		
ED1	Taking online courses helped in develop my skills.		
ED2	Online education may help to increase per capita income.		
ED3	Taking online courses increased my pay scale.		
ED4	Taking online courses helped me in my promotion.	0.915	Excellent
ED5	Online education will help to increase the literacy rate of the country.		

Source: Authors' compilation.

STRUCTURAL EQUATION MODEL

The model fit metrics for Fig. 1 are shown in Table 3. According to Table A5, every index is inside the range (Appendices). As a result, the model is thought to be fit. Additionally, $p = 0.000$ was used to determine the significance of the components. The 'average variance extracted' (AVE) estimate is more significant than 0.5, as depicted in Table 4, and the 'convergent validity' (CR) for each item's ideal standardised loading is higher than 0.7, as depicted in Table 4. CR is also higher than

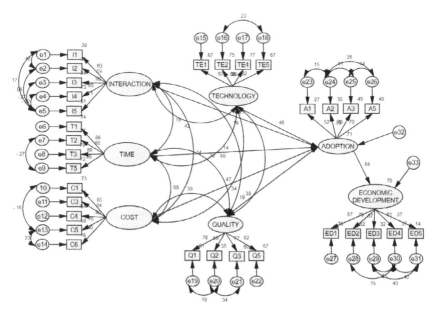

Fig. 1.   SEM Model. *Source*: Authors' compilation.

Table 3.   Model Fit Indices for Fig. 1.

MODEL FIT INDICES				
CMIN/DF	CFI	GFI	RMSEA	SRMR
3.457	0.913	0.864	0.066	0.0538

Table 4.   Convergent and Discriminant Validity for Fig. 1.

	CR	AVE	MSV	ASV
QUALITY	0.832	0.557	0.149	0.105
INTERACTION	0.861	0.562	0.177	0.067
COST	0.859	0.562	0.461	0.213
TIME	0.870	0.609	0.461	0.235
TECHNOLOGY	0.884	0.614	0.348	0.222

Source: Author's compilation.

AVE (Hair et al., 2007). Maximum shared variance and average shared variance, two measures of discriminant validity, are likewise less than AVE (Hair, 2006). As a result, the model achieves both convergent and discriminant validity.

CONCLUSION

The above special episode of Adoption Online Education revolves primarily around higher education and the SDGs. All countries, not just those typically categorised as 'developing' or 'emerging', must adhere to the 17 SDGs, which 2015 were upheld by all UN member states. They address a wide range of social, economic, environmental and innovation development-related challenges (Chankseliani & McCowan, 2021). The review discoveries show that every one of the elements was vital for the adoption of online education, and online education helps in the economic development of the country. 'Ensuring inclusive and equitable quality education and development can help for lifelong learning for all', read the fourth SDG. Numerous investigations have shown that advanced education advances knowledge and skills through instruction and research, which fosters economic growth (Bloom et al., 2014; Oketch et al., 2014). Higher education is beneficial for modernising societies (Rungfamai, 2019). Education focuses on the larger goal of sustainable growth, which takes precedence over economic efforts to decrease poverty and improve health (Kopnina, 2020). Because of this, other SDGs may be accomplished in addition to achieving SDG 4. The dominant paradigm of advancement and higher education's contributions to progression must be overcome for a sufficiently broadened vision and quest for knowledge that incorporates the privileges-based, abilities-based and liberation ways to deal with improvement (Chankseliani & McCowan, 2021). Because more educated workers appear to be better equipped to complete tasks that require reading and basic analysis, a nation's economy grows more productive as the number of educated workers increases. A higher level of knowledge does have a cost. A country can promote basic literacy initiatives while still experiencing economic growth without having to fund a sizeable network of educational facilities. The pandemic could severely limit the operations of institutions of higher learning due to the possibility of their being forced to close as well as looming financial risks and resource shortages. It jeopardises implementing the 2030 blueprint (UN, 2020). Even though the epidemic has been a challenge, it may offer a once-in-a-lifetime opportunity to re-evaluate higher education as a public good. In countries where more people enrol in and complete their education, economic growth is more rapid than in countries where the workforce is less educated. Many nations support primary and secondary education to improve economic performance. This makes investing in education comparable to investing in new equipment or other tangible assets. The results showed that 84% of respondents believed the adoption of online academic achievement had a significant impact on economic growth (Fig. 1). In order to help children receive a better education, raise per capita income, eradicate poverty, improve living standards and increase the country's literacy rate, all of which help to achieve the goals for SD set forth by the United Nations, online education, therefore, contributes to economic development. The quality, inter-action, cost, time and new tech of online education are additional factors that affect its acceptance.

Hence,

H1: Technology influences the adoption of Online education significantly. **Accepted**

H2: Interaction influences the adoption of Online education significantly. **Accepted**

H3: Cost influences the adoption of Online education significantly. **Accepted**

H4: Time influences the adoption of Online education significantly. **Accepted**

H5: Quality influences the adoption of Online education significantly. **Accepted**

H6: Adoption of Online education influences economic development in the country significantly hence achieving SDG. **Accepted**

IMPLICATIONS OF THE STUDY

Online learning is an adaptable learning pathway that empowers the considera-tion of different students and works on the idea of long-lasting learning. As of late, online learning is turning into a basic procedure that builds the entrance of valuable open doors for all individuals to higher education. Education for SD promotes the development of the knowledge, skills, understanding, attitudes and actions required to create a world that is sustainable in terms of natural insurance and protection, social value and economic manageability. HEIs are critical to long-term viability. It takes on a new role in the framework of sustainable development. It plays an important role in achieving Goal 4 on education, which calls for com-prehensive, impartial and high-quality education for all. In addition to encourag-ing entrepreneurship and technical advancements, education frequently increases productivity and creativity. Each degree of education earned increases personal income and lowers the likelihood of unemployment. To put it another way, every degree of education attained lowers the cost of unemployment benefits, generates more taxable revenue and boosts our economy. The authors analyse how higher education can address the issues of gender equality and women's empowerment, access to justice, promoting inclusive societies, and building effective, accountable and inclusive institutions. They additionally examine how advanced education can uphold comprehensive and feasible monetary development, full and useful business, and respectable work (Chankseliani & McCowan, 2021). Quality educa-tion is essential for energising strength and promoting social harmony because it enables people to overcome a pattern of destitution, reduces uneven character development and allows them to continue with a better and more effective presence. This study was done in Delhi NCR only.

Higher education as a common good presents an optimistic outlook for the future, post-pandemic higher education, and builds on the ideals that we all share, such as social justice and solidarity. The larger goal of sustainable development, which prioritises economic measures to reduce poverty and enhance health, is the foundation for education (Kopnina, 2020). One of the key elements of progress is education in many senses. No country can achieve sustainable economic growth without making significant investments in its human capital. Education helps people gain a better understanding of the world and of who they are. Their lifestyle is improved, which benefits them as well as society as a whole. Education fosters entrepreneurship, boosts productivity and creativity, and advances technology. Furthermore, it is crucial for ensuring societal and economic advancement and improving income distribution. As a result, in addition to fulfilling SDG 4, additional SDGs can also be reached. Out of the 10 SDG 4 objectives, SDG 4.3 can be achieved with the aid of online education since it guarantees equitable access at a reasonable price. To address the issues of sustainable development, higher education is crucial. However, the industry can do far more than provide sophisticated education. It can inform, enlighten and link communities with services and ground-breaking research (Owens, 2017). To achieve a knowledge-based economy, higher education is essential. Making sure that education is affordable and that everyone in developing countries has an equal opportunity to pursue higher education is crucial. The findings support the assertion that the viability of e-learning in higher education is highly correlated with its quality and that it offers a significant opportunity to achieve SDG4. E-learning also improves students' knowledge and abilities, increasing their chances of finding better work possibilities. Therefore, economic growth is impossible without education. Without a vital education, no economic progress is conceivable. A well-rounded educational system fosters not just productivity but also economic growth and increases per-capita income. At the micro-level of a single family, it is discernible.

REFERENCES

Ahmed, M. U., Hussain, S., & Farid, S. (2018). Factors influencing the adoption of e-learning in an open and distance learning institution of Pakistan. *Electronic Journal of e-Learning*, *16*(2), 148–158.

Al-Ammary, J., Mohammed, Z., & Omran, F. (2016). e-Learning capability maturity level in the Kingdom of Bahrain. *Turkish Online Journal of Educational Technology-TOJET*, *15*(2), 47–60.

Al-Samarraie, H., Selim, H., & Zaqout, F. (2016). The effect of content representation design principles on users' intuitive beliefs and use of e-learning systems. *Interactive Learning Environments*, *24*(8), 1758–1777.

Al-Samarraie, H., Teng, B. K., Alzahrani, A. I., & Alalwan, N. (2018). E-learning continuance satisfaction in Higher Education: A unified perspective from instructors and students. *Studies in Higher Education*, *43*(11), 2003–2019.

Altinay, Z., Altinay, F., Ossianilsson, E., & Aydin, C. H. (2018). Open education practices for learners with disabilities. *BRAIN. Broad Research in Artificial Intelligence and Neuroscience*, *9*(4), 171–176.

Andrade, M. S., & Alden-Rivers, B. (2019). Developing a framework for sustainable growth of flexible learning opportunities. *Higher Education Pedagogies*, *4*(1), 1–16.

Barclay, C., Donalds, C., & Osei-Bryson, K. M. (2018). Investigating critical success factors in online learning environments in higher education systems in the Caribbean. *Information Technology for Development*, *24*(3), 582–611.

Basilaia, G., Dgebuadze, M., Kantaria, M., & Chokhonelidze, G. (2020). Replacing the classic learning form at universities as an immediate response to the COVID-19 virus infection in Georgia. *International Journal for Research in Applied Science & Engineering Technology (IJRASET)*, *8*, 101–108.

Becker, A. (2017). Rage, loss and other footpaths: Subjectification, decolonisation and transformation in higher Education. *Transformation in Higher Education*, *2*(1), 1–7.

Bloom, D. E., Canning, D., Chan, K. J., & Luca, D. L. (2014). *Higher education and economic growth in Africa* [SSRN Scholarly Paper No. ID 2540166]. Social Science Research Network.

Brotherhood, T., Yang, L., & Chankseliani, M. (2020, 10 September). COVID-19 and higher education: Implications for equity, and a return to the common good. *The Post-Pandemic University*, *2*(1), 1–22.

Castro, M. D. B., & Tumibay, G. M. (2021). A literature review: Efficacy of online learning courses for higher education institution using meta-analysis. *Education and Information Technologies*, *26*, 1367–1385.

Chankseliani, M., & McCowan, T. (2021). Higher education and the SD goals. *Higher Education*, *81*(1), 1–8.

Dhawan, S. (2020). Online learning: A panacea in the time of COVID-19 crisis. *Journal of Educational Technology Systems*, *49*(1), 5–22.

ENQA. (2018). *Considerations for quality assurance of e-learning provisions* (pp. 222–230). [Occasional Papers, No. 26]. European Association for Quality Assurance in Higher Education AISBL 2018, Brussels,.

Farid, S., Qadir, M., Ahmed, M. U., & Khattak, M. D. (2018). Critical success factors of e-learning systems: A quality perspective. *Pakistan Journal of Distance & Online Learning*, *IV*(I), 1–20.

Ford, L. (2015, 21 April). SD goals: All you need to know. *The Guardian*, *19*. http://www.theguardian.com/global-development/2015/jan/19/sustainable-development-goals-united-nations

Ghanem, S. (2020, November). E-learning in higher Education to achieve SDG 4: Benefits and challenges. In *2020 Second international sustainability and resilience conference: Technology and innovation in building designs* (pp. 1–6). IEEE.

González, M. F. (2019). Research on virtual education, inclusion, and diversity. *The International Review of Research in Open and Distributed Learning*, *20*(5), 146–167.

Hadullo, K., Oboko, R., & Omwenga, E. (2017). A model for evaluating e-learning systems quality in higher education in developing countries. *International Journal of Education and Development Using ICT*, *13*(2), 185–204.

Hair, E., Halle, T., Terry-Humen, E., Lavelle, B., & Calkins, J. (2006). Children's school readiness in the ECLS-K: Predictions to academic, health, and social outcomes in first grade. *Early Childhood Research Quarterly*, *21*(4), 431–454.

Hair, J. F., Money, A. H., Samouel, P., & Page, M. (2007). Research methods for business. *Education+ Training*, *49*(4), 336–337.

Hamaniuk, V., Semerikov, S., & Shramko, Y. (2020). ICHTML 2020 – How learning technology wins coronavirus. In *SHS web of conferences* (Vol. 75, p. 00001). EDP Sciences.

Kanwal, F., & Rehman, M. (2017). Factors affecting e-learning adoption in developing countries – Empirical evidence from Pakistan's higher education sector. Factors affecting e-learning adoption in developing countries – Empirical evidence from Pakistan's higher education sector. *IEEE Access*, *5*(1), 10968–10978.

Ke, F., & Kwak, D. (2013). Online learning across ethnicity and age: A study on learning interaction participation, perception, and learning satisfaction. *Computers & Education*, *61*, 43–51.

Khan, M. H. S., Hasan, M., & Clement, C. K. (2012). Barriers to the introduction of ICT into Education in developing countries: The example of Bangladesh. *International Journal of Instruction*, *5*(2), 61–80.

Komochkova, O. O., & Ikonnikova, M. V. (2019). Modern online platforms and digital technologies in teaching linguistics in us higher education practice. *Information Technologies and Learning Tools*, *73*(5), 1–11, 125–134.

Kopnina, H. (2020). Education for SDG (ESDG): What is wrong with ESDGs, and what can we do better? *Education Sciences*, *10*(10), 261.

Makokha, G. L., & Mutisya, D. N. (2016). Status of e-learning in public universities in Kenya. *International Review of Research in Open and Distributed Learning*, *17*(3), 341–359.

Mohammed, M. N., Al-Zubaidi, S., Bahrain, S. H. K., Zaenudin, M., & Abdullah, M. I. (2020). Design and development of river cleaning robot using IoT technology. In 2020 *16th IEEE International Colloquium on Signal Processing & Its Applications* (CSPA) (pp. 84–87). IEEE.

Oketch, M., McCowan, T., & Schendel, R. (2014). The impact of tertiary education on development: A rigorous literature review. *DFID, 1*(1), 111–129.

Owens, T. L. (2017). Higher education in the SDG framework. *European Journal of Education, 52*(4), 414–420.

Oxford Business Group. (2020). *The report: Bahrain 2020.* https://oxfordbusinessgroup.com/bahrain-2020

Rungfamai, K. (2019). State, university, and Society: Higher Educational Development and university functions in shaping modern Thailand. *Higher Education, 78*(1), 149–164.

Saeed, S. (2020, October 24). *COVID-19 has exacerbated inequality in higher education.* University World News: The Global Window on Higher Education.

Saeid, N., & Goodarzi, M. (2019). Applying path analysis model in explaining the factors affecting the quality and usefulness of eLearning: The students' perspective. *Interdisciplinary Journal of Virtual Learning in Medical Sciences, 10*(3), 11–22.

Sahin, I., & Shelley, M. (2008). Considering students' perceptions: The distance education student satisfaction model. *Journal of Educational Technology & Society, 11*(3), 216–223.

Trakru, M., & Jha, T. K. (2019). e-Learning effectiveness in higher education. *International Research Journal of Engineering and Technology, 6*(5), 96–101.

UNESCO. (2016). *Education for people and planet: Creating sustainable futures for all* [Global Education Monitoring Report 2016]. UNESCO.

United Nations. (2020). *The SDG report 2020.* United Nations.

Waghid, Z., & Waghid, F. (2016). Examining digital technology for (higher) education through action research and critical discourse analysis. *South African Journal of Higher Education, 30*(1), 265–284.

Wei, H. C., & Chou, C. (2020). Online learning performance and satisfaction: Do perceptions and readiness matter? *Distance Education, 41*(1), 48–69.

Zhou, T., Huang, S., Cheng, J., & Xiao, Y. (2020). The distance teaching practice of combined mode of massive open online course micro-video for interns in the emergency department during the COVID-19 epidemic period. *Telemedicine and e-Health, 26*(5), 584–588.

APPENDIX

Table A1. Communalities.

	Initial	Extraction		Initial	Extraction
	Communalities				
TE1	1.000	0.977	T3	1.000	0.870
TE2	1.000	0.975	T5	1.000	0.776
TE4	1.000	0.984	Q1	1.000	0.682
TE5	1.000	0.978	Q2	1.000	0.518
I1	1.000	0.959	Q3	1.000	0.867
I2	1.000	0.934	Q5	1.000	0.836
I3	1.000	0.965	A1	1.000	0.963
I4	1.000	0.942	A2	1.000	0.971
I5	1.000	0.788	A3	1.000	0.979
C1	1.000	0.883	A5	1.000	0.970
C3	1.000	0.827	ED1	1.000	0.673
C4	1.000	0.856	ED2	1.000	0.801
C5	1.000	0.849	ED3	1.000	0.804
C6	1.000	0.899	ED4	1.000	0.758
T1	1.000	0.834	ED5	1.000	0.765
T2	1.000	0.855			

Extraction Method: Principal Component Analysis.

Source: Authors' compilation.

Table A2. Total Variance Explained.

Component	Initial Eigenvalues			Extraction Sums of Squared Loadings			Rotation Sums of Squared Loadings		
	Total	% of Variance	Cumulative %	Total	% of Variance	Cumulative %	Total	% of Variance	Cumulative %
1	5.559	17.931	17.931	5.559	17.931	17.931	4.615	14.886	14.886
2	5.105	16.467	34.398	5.105	16.467	34.398	4.278	13.798	28.684
3	4.547	14.666	49.064	4.547	14.666	49.064	3.942	12.718	41.402
4	3.565	11.500	60.564	3.565	11.500	60.564	3.869	12.482	53.884
5	3.123	10.075	70.639	3.123	10.075	70.639	3.801	12.263	66.146
6	2.438	7.864	78.503	2.438	7.864	78.503	3.425	11.050	77.196
7	2.403	7.753	86.256	2.403	7.753	86.256	2.808	9.060	86.256
8	0.682	2.201	88.457						
9	0.569	1.836	90.293						

Extraction Method: Principal Component Analysis.

Source: Authors' compilation.

Table A3.   Rotated Component Matrix.

	Component						
	1	**2**	**3**	**4**	**5**	**6**	**7**
I3	0.975						
I1	0.973						
I4	0.963						
I2	0.958						
I5	0.875						
C6		0.940					
C1		0.925					
C5		0.915					
C4		0.905					
C3		0.889					
TE4			0.981				
TE1			0.980				
TE2			0.980				
TE5			0.978				
A3				0.974			
A2				0.968			
A5				0.965			
A1				0.961			
ED3					0.882		
ED2					0.876		
ED5					0.860		
ED4					0.840		
ED1					0.798		
T3						0.925	
T2						0.920	
T1						0.909	
T5						0.874	
Q3							0.906
Q5							0.894
Q1							0.804
Q2							0.687

Source: Authors' compilation.

Table A4.   KMO and Barlett's Test.

Kaiser-Meyer-Olkin Measure of Sampling Adequacy		0.752
Bartlett's Test of Sphericity	Approx. Chi-Square	6030.221
	Df	210
	Sig.	0.000

Source: Authors' compilation.

Table A5.   Model Fit Indices.

Model Fit Indices	Author	Recommended Value
CMIN/DF	Marsh and Hocevar (1985)	<5 indicating a reasonable fit
	Kline (1998)	<3 indicates an acceptable fit
GFI	Byrne (2001), Hair et al. (2006)	>0.7 indicates an acceptable fit
CFI	Bentler (1990)	close to 0.9, which indicates a relatively good fit
	Hu and Bentler (1999)	>0.80 is permissible, >0.90 indicates a good fit, >0.95 indicates a great fit
RMSEA	Bentler (1990)	<0.05 indicates a good fit, 0.05-0.10 indicates a moderate fit
SRMR	Sharif and Nia (2018), Bentler (1990)	<0.09 acceptable fit

Source: Authors' compilation.

CHAPTER 9

INCREASING FINANCIAL INCLUSION IN INDIA FOR SUSTAINABLE ECONOMIC GROWTH AND DEVELOPMENT – A SEM APPROACH

Jitender Kumar Goyal[a,b] and Yamini Agarwal[a,b]

[a]Bharati Vidyapeeth (Deemed to be University), Pune, India
[b]Institute of Management and Research, New Delhi, India

ABSTRACT

Purpose: *The purpose of this study is to identify the elements that can enhance financial inclusion (FI) in a nation, which in turn promotes economic development and growth.*

Need for the Study: *FI is crucial in providing people with the skills and resources to manage their money effectively and make informed financial decisions. Accessible, reliable and secure financial services play a significant role in achieving sustainable development goals (SDGs) and fostering economic progress.*

Methodology: *Data from 571 respondents were collected for analysis. The study utilises Statistical Package for Social Sciences SPSS and Analysis of Moment Structures AMOS software to analyse data and achieve the study's objectives. The researchers employ these tools to obtain substantial results.*

Sustainable Development Goals: The Impact of Sustainability Measures on Wellbeing
Contemporary Studies in Economic and Financial Analysis, Volume 113B, 123–141
Copyright © 2024 by Jitender Kumar Goyal and Yamini Agarwal
Published under exclusive licence by Emerald Publishing Limited
ISSN: 1569-3759/doi:10.1108/S1569-37592024000113B009

Findings: *The findings indicate that FI contributes to economic growth (84%) and helps in accomplishing SDGs. Access, usage, affordability, technology, availability and technology adoption all play a vital role in increasing FI in the nation.*

Practical Implications: *The study's outcomes have practical implications for policymakers and stakeholders, emphasising the importance of promoting FI through various measures such as enhancing access, affordability and technological advancements in financial services.*

Keywords: Digital financial inclusion; SDGs; financial system; COVID-19; economic growth and development; banking; financial services

JEL Codes: G21; G53; G23; G28; F65

INTRODUCTION

The 2030 Sustainable Development Plan was embraced at the United Nations (UN) Development Summit in September 2015, demonstrating the vision to pursue win participation and acknowledge normal development under all circumstances and highlighting the scope and aspirations of this new global plan. The 2030 Sustainable Development Plan includes 17 goals for sustainable development that represent the collective aspiration of all people. Although it is not specifically mentioned in the UN sustainable development goals (SDGs), FI is a necessary condition for achieving all of the goals (Jia et al., 2021).

FI is the most common way of guaranteeing that everybody in an economy has simple admittance to, utilisation of, and cooperation in the formal monetary framework. It makes it simpler to find reasonable assets, potentially bringing down the cost of capital (Sarma & Pais, 2011). Even though it is not expressly stated in the UN SDGs, FI is critical to the advancement of both the objectives and the financial system (Jia et al., 2021). Improving the nation's economic status is critical for assuring long-term economic growth (EG) and development. According to Beck et al. (2009) and Brune et al. (2011), FI works on the limit of impeded families to retain monetary shocks, smooth utilisation, amass resources, put resources into human asset parts like prosperity and schooling, as well as exploit promising venture valuable open doors in their economies.

In many economies, digital FI has become a key development strategy, and related research is growing. Increasing EG and environmental quality are the primary goals of promoting digital FI (Ozturk & Ullah, 2022). According to inclusive digital FS, those in need can build up their savings, prepare for unforeseen economic shocks, use social benefits more effectively and make investments in opportunities that will help them escape poverty.

The pandemic's effects – a health crisis, as well as a devastating social and economic crisis over time and in the years to come – put developing nations most at risk. According to UNDP, income losses in developing nations are expected to exceed $220 billion and an estimated 55% (UNDP – United Nations Development Programme) of people worldwide lack access to social assurance. These losses will affect education, civil liberties and in the worst cases, basic food security and subsistence. Sustainable development requires promoting healthy lives and prosperity for all ages. There has never been a global health crisis like the one the world is currently going through. Coronavirus is causing millions of people to suffer, disrupting the global economy and upsetting their lives on a massive scale (UN, 2020).

There is relatively little empirical study into the connection between FI and the reduction of poverty (Tita & Aziakpono, 2017). However, the evidence suggests that FI has a positive impact on neediness. According to Beck et al. (2007), the impact of financial development (FD) on overall EG was responsible for 60% of income (Beck et al., 2007) growth, and the long-term impact of financial innovation on the income growth of the lowest households as a result of decreased income inequality was responsible for about 40% of income growth (Klapper & Singer, 2017).

The coronavirus has wrecked the lives of billions of people and put the world economy in jeopardy. The International Monetary Fund predicts a worldwide recession at least as severe as the one experienced in 2009. According to the International Work Association, over half of the world's workforce is at risk of losing their employment as job losses increase. Infrastructure and innovation, as well as inclusive and sustainable industrialisation, have the potential to unleash competitive economic forces that drive EG. They are critical in the introduction and progress of new technologies, in fostering global interaction and in enabling resource efficiency.

However, the majority of the composing on FD and social stratification assumes that by concentrating on increasing the income of the poorest people, financial growth may be able to reduce income inequality (Beck et al., 2007; Galor & Moav, 2004). Inconsistencies in finance can cause income disparity to increase as well (Claessens & Perotti, 2007; Seven & Coskun, 2016). The model developed by Greenwood and Jovanovic predicts an inverted U-shaped connection between EG and income inequality (Greenwood & Jovanovic, 1990). The least fortunate and most susceptible groups have been disproportionately affected by the coronavirus, which has exacerbated existing inequities. It has drawn attention to the weak social safety nets and economic inequality that make vulnerable groups suffer the greatest impact of the crisis. Simultaneously, social, political and monetary disparities have heightened the effects of the pandemic. On the monetary front, the COVID pandemic has essentially expanded overall joblessness and conclusively sliced specialists' earnings. The modest advancements in women's rights and orientation uniformity over the past few decades are also at risk due to coronavirus. For women and girls, the quality of their sex alone exacerbates the effects of the coronavirus in every area, including health, the economy, security and social assurance. Access to credit may directly affect the achievement SDGs of the UN, which include eradicating poverty, enhancing well-being and education, and reducing inequality (Kara et al., 2021). One of the significant cycles inside this cooperative structure is the monetary framework, which fills in as the vehicle that gives families admittance to formal monetary administrations, for example, bank accounts, customer credit or home loans. FI, or admittance to monetary administrations, is considered an essential prerequisite (Demirgüç-Kunt & Klapper, 2013; World Bank, 2014).

According to the World Bank, an inclusive financial system helps to allocate financial resources efficiently and allows individuals access to the channels they need to overcome hurdles to stability and growth, impartial resource distribution, poverty reduction and attaining sustainable development (Global Financial Development Report, 2014). Including excluded groups in informal FS such as security savings, credit and instalment, insurance and pension, and other financial goods can successfully enhance long-term EG (Jia et al., 2021).

LITERATURE REVIEW

FD might help monetary advancement monetarily, and the market-based movement of monetary organisations can upgrade the asset part and lift the adequacy of FD. Financial markets and institutions in the economy have central obligations to support capital efficiency, gather reserve funds, lead the development of new capital, control gambles and speed up exchanges. A solid monetary framework ought to empower financial turn of events and diminish dependence by reducing data and exchange expenses (Beck & Levine, 2004). Moreover, it has been guaranteed that rising admittance to monetary administrations might support capable yet unfortunate business visionaries to begin their organisations, for example, microenterprises. At the point when little organisation proprietors' fortunes improve, they will wish to grow their organisations by reinvesting a piece of their benefits, turning out secure revenue for both themselves and their representatives (Klapper et al., 2006). At the point when monetary business sectors and monetary organisations run appropriately, all market players might make judicious ventures by guiding cash to other valuable purposes, which can help financial turn of events and limit pay dissimilarity and need. However, monetary advancement may not decrease imbalance and destitution on the off chance that monetary business sectors are not working as expected and those in need have confined admittance to monetary administrations (Liu et al., 2021).

The importance of offering affordable FS to all segments of society is highlighted by FI. It was often believed that improving the poor's access to FS efficiently reduced their need and income inequality. Therefore, increasing FI would unquestionably aid in lowering income inequality and reducing need. The realisation of sustainable EG and the reduction of potential risks through FI significantly advanced financial stability. In general, FI is seen as a basic perspective in achieving development consideration. Access to finance allows economic monetary elements to go with vast decisions regarding spending and effective money management, partake in productive things and answer unforeseen momentary shocks, limiting the frequency of need and advancing pay parallelism (Jia et al., 2021). The UN SDG demonstrate how financial technology (FinTech) is a crucial facilitator of FI, which in turn enables sustainable development (SDGs). The genuine limit of FinTech to advance the SDGs might be perceived as a ground-breaking system for managing the making of supporting foundations to empower the online payments transformation (Arner et al., 2020). Burgess and Pande (2005), Brune et al. (2011), Allen et al. (2012) and Erlando et al. (2010) focus on giving validation that FI has brought down neediness and pay imbalance by expanding provincial financial destinations and further developing admittance to supporting for country regions, in light of encounters from India, Malawi, Kenya and Indonesia, separately.

SDG AND THE ROLE OF FI

In the 2030 SDGs, where it is highlighted as a target in 8 of the 17 goals, FI is depicted prevalently as an empowering agent of other aspirations. SDG 1 seeks to eradicate poverty; SDG 2 seeks to eradicate hunger; SDG 3 seeks to advance well-being and prosperity; SDG 5 seeks to advance gender equality and the economic empowerment of women; SDG 8 seeks to advance EG and jobs; SDG 9 seeks to advance industry, innovation and infrastructure; and SDG 10 seeks to eradicate inequality. Scholarly research has shown that FI strategies can boost the overall economic World Bank (2014) growth and the achievement of more challenging objectives. Table 1 depicts the role of financial inclusion (FI) in achieving these SDGs.

Given the undeniably clear connection between FI and advancement, states ought to keep on elevating for expanded admittance to and use of FS. Putting FS initially does not subvert assets from other essential SDG targets. The examination remembered for this paper gives influential proof that FI assists 19 with making the conditions that permit many SDGs to be accomplished. Access to financial institutions is required to accomplish everyday duties; yet, while this appears straightforward, it is only sometimes met in some remote communities of the country (Yue et al., 2019). FI aims to ensure that everyone has appropriate access to FS (Buszko et al., 2019). The recent rapid drop in bank branches has raised the danger of financial exclusion for some rural consumers (Náñez et al., 2020). Given the above literature following hypotheses have been framed:

H1. Access to financial services influences FI significantly.

H2. Usage of financial services influences FI significantly.

H3. Technology influences FI significantly.

H4. Availability of financial services influences FI significantly.

H5. Affordability of financial services influences FI significantly.

H6. FI influence EG and development in the country significantly hence achieving SDG.

Table 1.   SDG and Role of Financial Inclusion.

S. No.	SDG	Role of Financial Inclusion
1	NO POVERTY: End poverty in all its forms everywhere	When people are included in the financial system, they are better able to climb out of poverty by investing in business or education. By providing poor people with services, they need to make investments and manage unexpected expenses, financial inclusion facilitates the first SDG.
2	ZERO HUNGER: End hunger, achieve food security and improved nutrition and promote sustainable agriculture (SDG 2)	Farmers who have access to financial services often produce more generous harvests, leading to progress on the second SDG. Lack of access to credit and insurance inhibits farmers from making investments that could increase crop yields and strengthen food security. Financial services can help farmers increase their production to meet the food needs of growing populations.
3	GOOD HEALTH AND WELL-BEING: Ensure healthy lives and promote well-being for all at all ages (SDG 3)	Financial inclusion improves health by allowing people to manage medical expenses and better rebound from a health crisis. Research suggests that out-of-pocket payments on health care in developing countries are the main reason people remain in poverty. Financial services like medical insurance can provide a formal channel for mitigating the risks of health emergencies. Women especially have a high demand for health insurance products to address the common health concerns of pregnancy and childbirth, including greater susceptibility to infection.
4	GENDER EQUALITY: Achieve gender equality and empower all women and girls (SDG 5)	Financial inclusion of women contributes to gender equality by giving them greater control over their finances and their role within the family and society in general (Aker et al., 2014; Ashraf et al., 2010). Financial services help women assert their economic power, which is critical to promoting gender equality. Digital financial services also support women-owned businesses by reducing the risks of theft and lowering administrative and disbursement costs.
5	DECENT WORK AND ECONOMIC GROWTH: Promote sustained, inclusive and sustainable economic growth, full and productive employment, and decent work for all (SDG 8)	Including poor people in the formal financial system is a prerequisite for shared economic growth. When poor people are excluded from the formal financial system, the foundations of shared economic growth are weak. Access to financial institutions and products allows people to gain higher returns on capital. This leads to increases in their income and consequently affects economic growth.
6	INDUSTRY, INNOVATION AND INFRASTRUCTURE: Expanding Small Industry through digital financial inclusion (SDG 9)	Digital finance enables small businesses to grow, innovate, build infrastructure and reach new markets, bringing more people into the digital economy. Digital financial services can help MSMEs build payment histories and credit scores that can serve as collateral, resulting in greater access to finance. Digitising supply chain payments can lead to significant efficiency gains and increased revenue for MSMEs.

(Continued)

Table 1. (*Continued*)

S. No.	SDG	Role of Financial Inclusion
7	REDUCING INEQUALITY: (SDG 10)	People with access to financial services are better positioned to succeed economically and build a decent life, ultimately making it easier to reduce inequality. Digital finance can be a powerful equalising force, giving low-income households new tools to increase their incomes, improve financial resilience and access new economic and social opportunities. Digital financial services can increase productivity and income for rural households by connecting them to economic opportunities beyond their rural communities.

Source: Authors' compilation.

OBJECTIVE OF THE STUDY

To achieve sustainable EG and development through FI, the chapter aims to identify the key influencing factors in raising the level of FI in the nation. It aims to increase the body of knowledge and conceptualisation of FI's potential to advance the SDGs. It will evaluate how FI ultimately contributed to the nation's sustainable EG and development, achieving SDG.

RESEARCH METHODOLOGY

The study's methodology is empirical. Five hundred seventy-one respondents were chosen as a sample from various institutions. To identify the key influencing factors in raising the level of FI in the country and investigate the relationship between ensuring sustainable EG and the development of FI. The data were gathered through questionnaires from households, business people, Gig-workers, industrialists, daily-wage workers, working professionals, non-working individuals, and college students and teachers. Various tools and techniques have been used to accomplish the goal and reach definite conclusions. SPSS and AMOS are the programs used. The study employs an empirical methodology involving 571 respondents drawn from diverse institutions, that is, households, entrepreneurs, gig-workers, industrialists, daily-wage labourers, working professionals, non-working individuals, college students and teachers. The primary objective is to discern the pivotal factors influencing FI enhancement within the country and to explore the correlation between sustaining EG and FI development. Data collection was executed through questionnaires distributed among a broad spectrum of respondents residing in India. Respondent includes people from all segments, whether rich or poor, male or female, young or old, as FI means including every person in the financial ecosystem irrespective of caste, region, background, gender, etc. It does not discriminate against people on any parameters. In order to achieve the research objectives and derive conclusive results, a comprehensive array of tools and techniques have been employed. The study leveraged the software programs SPSS and AMOS for data analysis and statistical modelling. This approach ensures a robust and systematic investigation into the dynamics of FI and its relationship with sustainable EG and development.

DATA ANALYSIS

Factor analysis was performed to explore the factors, and seven variables were taken from the total Variance explained in Table A3. As anything above 0.60 or 60% is desired, the Total Variance Explained was approximately 71.01%, considered satisfactory in the social sciences (Hair et al., 2007). For each variable, the ensuing codes are provided (Table 2). A value greater than 0.60, considered acceptable, was also shown in KMO test (Table A1). Bartlett's sphericity test provides a significant value of 14,710.655 ($p = 0.000$, $df = 528$). According to the KMO sampling adequacy value, the sample was good enough, which was determined to be 0.901. The commonalities for all the items more significant than 0.5 are shown in Table A2.

According to Rotated Component Matrix (Table A4), only the items with factor loading values greater than or equal to 0.50 were kept on the schedule. Seven components totalling all the statements have been combined. Affordability, including statements from AF1 to AF5, has been identified as the first component. Technology statements from T1 to T5 have been identified as the second component. Access, including statements from A1 to A5, has been named the third component. The fourth element, which includes statements U1 through U5, has been identified as Usage. FI, which includes statements from FI1 to FI5, has been named the fifth component. The sixth element, which includes statements from AV1 to AV5, has been identified as availability. The seventh and final component is EG and development, including statements from EDG1 to EDG8.

RELIABILITY OF INDIVIDUAL VARIABLES

After examining each variable's dependability, the following codes are assigned to each variable's statement (Table 3). Since Cronbach's α reliability coefficient for all factors is above 0.8, which is regarded as excellent for the study, the reliability of each variable was adequate.

Table 2. Name of the Variable and Their Codes.

S.No.	Codes	Variables
1	A	Access to financial service
2	U	Usage of financial service
3	T	Technology
4	AV	Availability
5	AF	Affordability
6	FI	Financial inclusion
7	EDG	Economic development and growth

Source: Authors' compilation.

Table 3. Codes to Each Statement.

S. No.	Statements	Cronbach's α Coefficient	Reliability Results
T2	I think technology plays a crucial role in boosting DFI.	0.941	Acceptable
T3	I believe that law or regulation setting standards for complaints resolution is not adequate.		
T4	There is a need to implement user-friendly technology.		
T5	ICT helps me to use banking services from anywhere and anytime.		
A1	I have easy access to borrowing.	0.950	Excellent
A2	I have access to the Saving/Current/FD/RD account.		
A3	I can easily access insurance services.		
A4	I have access to mobile money.		
A5	I can access my Debit/Credit Card.		
U1	I use my account for depositing and withdrawing money only.	0.870	Good
U2	I regularly save money in banks.		
U4	I regularly use a debit card.		
U5	I feel that mobile money is easy to use.		
U6	I pay my bills over the internet.		
AF1	Banking services are too expensive.	0.856	Good
AF3	Overdraft/credit card facilities are too expensive.		
AF4	Using a debit card/ATM is too expensive.		
AF5	I can't afford the minimum maintenance of the bank account.		
AV2	I can easily avail of credit services from banks in case of emergency.	0.897	Good
AV3	IDs are crucial to avail of all banking services.		
AV4	ATMs of my bank are easily available to me.		
AV5	I can easily contact and avail services from bank agents.		
FI1	I believe increased access to FS will lead to FI	0.906	Good
FI2	I believe increased usage of FS will lead to FI.		
FI3	I believe the increased quality of FS will lead to FI.		
FI6	FI helps improve the country's economic development.		
EDG2	FI has enabled us to enjoy better economic status.	0.841	Acceptable
EDG3	FI has enabled your children to get a better education.		
EDG4	FI has helped to increase per capita income.		
EDG7	FI will help to eradicate poverty.		
EDG8	FI will help to increase the standard of living of people.		

Source: Authors' compilation.

STRUCTURAL EQUATION MODEL

The model fit metrics for Fig. 1 are shown in Table 4. According to Table A5, every index is within the range (Appendices). As a result, the model is thought to be fit. Additionally, $p = 0.000$ was used to determine the significance of the 28 factors. The average variance extracted (AVE) estimate is more significant than 0.5, and the convergent validity (CR) for each item's ideal standardised loading is higher than 0.7. CR is also higher than AVE (Hair et al., 2007) (Table 5). Maximum shared variance (MSV) and average shared variance (ASV), two measures of discriminant validity, are also less than AVE (Hair, 2006). As a consequence, the

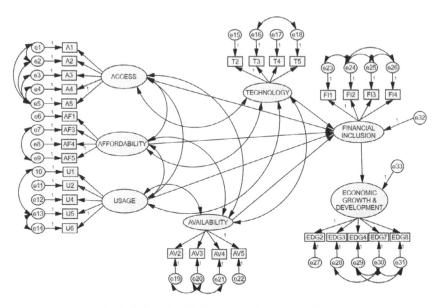

Fig. 1   SEM Model. *Source*: Authors' compilation.

Table 4.   Model Fit Indices for Fig. 1.

CMIN/DF	CFI	GFI	RMSEA	SRMR
3.578	0.909	0.861	0.067	0.0538

Source: Authors' compilation.

Table 5.   Convergent and Discriminant Validity for Fig. 1.

	CR	AVE	MSV	ASV
Access	0.832	0.557	0.149	0.105
Usage	0.861	0.562	0.177	0.067
Affordability	0.859	0.562	0.461	0.213
Technology	0.870	0.609	0.461	0.235
Availability	0.884	0.614	0.348	0.222

Source: Authors' compilation.

model has convergent as well as discriminant validity. All of the components are determined to be significant; all of the values are within the permitted ranges, and the model is found to be fit. It has been noticed that access to and use of FS is vital in increasing FI since there is a positive and substantial association between access to FS and FI and the use 65 of FS and FI. Usage has been identified as a significant influencer in increasing FI in the country, as access to FS alone cannot help achieve maximum FI. Therefore, the usage of FS is significant. Providing FS at an affordable cost helps in the utilisation of services by the underprivileged section of society and hence helps in the inclusion of every individual in the financial system. Since technology allows widespread access and utilisation of services, it has become a critical component of digital FI and the transition to a digital economy. SDGs such as SDG1 (No Poverty), SDG2 (Zero Hunger), SDG3 (Good Health and Well-Being), SDG5 (Gender Equality), SDG8 (Decent Work and Economic Growth), SDG9 (Industry, innovation, and Infrastructures), SDG10 (Reduced inequality) and SDG17.

Partnership for the goals may all be realised through improving the country's degree of FI. FI promotes financial growth by providing individuals with banking and FS. FI can assist people with escaping destitution since it offers banking and financial assistance at a minimal cost. As a result, FI is a tool that facilitates and intensifies EG, encourages employment and improves financial wellness. The increase of FI promotes EG through capital accumulation and technological progress. Since people can access FS, they have access to monetary benefits, which help them increase their standard of living and access better education, providing them with better job opportunities and income. Hence increasing per capita income and enjoying better economic status. This, in turn, helps in developing an economy.

DISCUSSION

Many international organisations consider FI a priority goal, including the new UN Plan 2030. FI means establishing a banking market that individuals may readily access. The accessibility of FS was highlighted in one of the seven SDGs (hereafter SDGs) in the 2015 United Nations Plan 2030 (Demirgüç-Kunt & Singer, 2017). FI is a complex concept, however. Researchers have shown the causal connection between FI and economic development in recent years using a variety of FI metrics (Cumming et al., 2014; Demirgüç-Kunt & Klapper, 2013; El-Zhoghbi et al., 2019; Honohan, 2004; Klapper et al., 2016). According to a study conducted in India, growth was boosted between 2004 and 2013 by banking entrance, deposits and the availability and use of banking services (Sharma, 2016). Admittance to FS under ideal circumstances, as per hypothesis, makes it simpler to design use, screen utilisation propensities, handle well-being-related concerns and partake in great projects like preparation and schooling. Various creators have investigated the benefits of FI. By and large, analysing specific aspects in light of models and evaluations of specific projects is done everywhere. Klapper and Singer (2017) introduced experimental information on how FI could help accomplish the SDGs.

The findings demonstrated that FI has a significant impact on EG and development, with 84% of respondents agreeing (Fig. 1). Therefore, FI helps to achieve EG and development because it enables people to appreciate better economic status, pursue better education, increase per capita income, end destitution and raise standard of living, all of which help to advance the sustainable development objectives set forth by the UN. Additionally, access, usage, affordability, technology, availability and technology all contribute to the nation's increased FI. The Global System for Mobile Communications Association claims that 'for developing countries, mobile money has enabled a "leap" in financial infrastructure by replacing antiquated payment methods and putting FS in the hands of individuals who were previously barred'. Information asymmetry is addressed with portable cash, which boosts income activation. In response to the challenges posed by the Coronavirus pandemic, the adoption of portable currency has seen a notable surge in India. The undeniable necessity of flexible cash is particularly pronounced in developing nations, where it serves as a crucial remedy for the impediments faced in conducting business during these trying times.. FI is not a new policy in India. In an effort to provide credit and FS, banks were nationalised in 1969.

However, despite significant efforts, a sizable portion of the population (about 65% of the adult population) has continued to be cut off from the benefits provided by the integrated financial sector (Nagdev et al., 2021). It is well known that the Government of India has introduced several technology-based initiatives to make India a digitally active nation. Thus, by implementing successful measures for digital FI, the entry of cashless transactions is made possible, and FI in India would rise as a result.

Hence,

H1. Access influences FI significantly. **ACCEPTED**

H2. Usage influences FI significantly. **ACCEPTED**

H3. Technology influences FI significantly. **ACCEPTED**

H4. Availability influences FI significantly. **ACCEPTED**

H5. Affordability influences FI significantly. **ACCEPTED**

H6. FI influence EG and development in the country significantly hence achieving SDG. **ACCEPTED**

IMPLICATIONS OF THE STUDY

During the last 25 years, the globe has made significant progress towards decreasing severe poverty. Somewhere in the range of 1990 and 2015, the number of individuals living on under $1.90 each day, the worldwide model for outrageous destitution, fell by one billion, carrying us nearer to the UN SDGs. Yet, the benefits of economic advancement have been distributed differently among nations, regions and people. More than 700 million people globally remain impoverished, a startlingly enormous number and the situation is deteriorating in certain countries, particularly those plagued by brutal wars and weak institutions (Emara & Mohieldin, 2020). Financial access measures have a positive, measurably huge effect on decreasing outrageous neediness. The banking industry is a significant driver in the transition to completely sustainable growth. This is exhibited by the expansive variety of projects, organisations and sectoral groupings that bring joined monetary foundations from around the world (Náñez-Alonso et al., 2022). Understanding how the computerised economy is developing universally and in Africa is essential for the fourth modern transformation (4IR). The 4IR depends on the utilisation of innovation, process digitisation and other financial and business process digitalisation. Like the FS business, the arrangement of computerised FS is a piece of advanced change (Mhlanga, 2020). These administrations are gotten to and conveyed through versatile cell phones and advanced stages. Charge cards, Mastercards and telephone banking are only a few models. These administrations additionally consolidate state-of-the-art dispersed processing thoughts like internet-based stages, adaptable instalments and crypto resources. They are generally called fintech (Agur et al., 2020). The primary emphasis of this piece is the various currencies among these services. Flexible cash usage opens up access to financial services for previously unbanked population segments, integrating them more deeply into the conventional financial system. This enhances the possibility that those who are financially poor, work in the unorganised sector and require help will save (Ouma et al., 2017). The method of monetary inclusion, which strives to help people experiencing poverty, is still in progress. It is a big undertaking that needs collaborative efforts, partnerships, passionate participation, commitment and responsibility from all parties involved, such as the government, financial institutions, authorities, the commercial sector and the whole local community. FI plays an integral part in economic progress by fostering a culture of saving among a substantial percentage of the population and growing the productive capacity of financial institutions (Sarma, 2012). FI also protects the financial stability and other resources of low-income groups in emergencies by bringing them within the confines of the legal banking industry. FI decreases usurious lending to disadvantaged people by increasing easy access to formal credit.

CONCLUSION

The present study addresses the pivotal nexus between FI and sustainable EG and development, with a focus on aligning with UN SDGs. This investigation discerns critical determinants, encompassing accessibility, usage, affordability, technological integration and availability which exert substantial influence on augmenting FI within a nation. The comprehensive literature review underscores the pivotal role of FI in addressing challenges such as poverty and income inequality, thereby fostering overall economic development. FI is intrinsically related to FD because it promotes EG and development of the financial sector, and it is heavily dependent on the provision of financial services (Aniruddh & Kumar, 2021; Usman et al., 2021). It drives financial activity, which is dependent on the number of people who have access to financial services (Saleem et al., 2022). Notably, digital FI emerges as a pivotal strategy, especially amid the ongoing global health and economic challenges triggered by the COVID-19 pandemic. The study posits hypotheses pertaining to the impact of accessibility, usage, affordability, technological integration and availability of financial services on FI. Employing empirical analysis with a sample comprising 571 respondents from diverse sectors, the findings substantiate these hypotheses, elucidating the significant influence of these factors on FI. Furthermore, the study delves into the role of FI in realising specific SDGs, such as poverty alleviation, hunger mitigation, enhancement of health and well-being, promotion of gender equality, creation of decent work, stimulation of industry and innovation, and reduction of inequality.

Emphasising the pivotal role of FI, the study highlights its contribution to alleviating extreme poverty and fostering sustainable EG. Notably, it suggests that digital financial services, particularly mobile money, can serve as transformative tools to integrate unbanked populations into the formal financial system. Practical implications for policymakers and stakeholders underscore the imperative of policies promoting accessibility, affordability and technological advancements in financial services. Furthermore, the findings contribute a new dimension to the finance-growth relationship, emphasising the relevance of FI as a significant driver of economic development goals (EDGs). Governments and policymakers are urged to address regulatory challenges while concurrently fostering EG in financially inclusive countries through FI. Understanding the link between FI and EG is crucial for formulating and implementing policies that enhance access to financial services, ultimately reducing income inequality. To achieve these goals, the study advocates for social awareness campaigns and state-wide initiatives to educate people on the benefits of regular financial services use. Increased utilisation of financial services, especially among vulnerable groups, can lead to a reduction in informal transactions. The study also recommends addressing the increased cost of financial services by providing them online, leveraging mobile banking and internet banking platforms and insights into the intricate interplay between FI and sustainable development. By identifying pivotal influencers of FI and illustrating its impact on SDGs, the research underscores the indispensability of inclusive financial systems in constructing resilient and equitable economies. The findings serve as a foundational resource for policymakers, financial institutions and stakeholders, guiding the formulation of strategies that position FI as a catalyst for comprehensive economic development and the realisation of global sustainability objectives. Therefore, policymakers are urged to formulate comprehensive measures that tackle regulatory challenges while concurrently fostering EG through FI. This approach aims to contribute to the reduction of income inequality and the improvement of access to financial services.

REFERENCES

Arner, D. W., Buckley, R. P., Zetzsche, D. A., & Veidt, R. (2020). Sustainability, FinTech and FI. *European Business Organization Law Review, 21*(1), 7–35.

Agur, I., Peria, S. M., & Rochon, C. (2020). Digital FS and the pandemic: Opportunities and risks for emerging and developing economies. *International Monetary Fund Special Series on COVID-19, Transactions, 1*(1), 1–13.

Aker, J., Boumnijel, R., McClelland, A., & Tierney, N. (2014). Payment mechanisms and anti-poverty programs: Evidence from a mobile money cash transfer experiment in Niger. *Tufts University, 65*(1), 1–37.

Allen, F., Carletti, E., Cull, R., Qian, J., Senbet, L., & Valenzuela, P. (2012). Resolving the African financial development gap: Cross-country comparisons and a within-country study of Kenya. In S. Edwards, S. Johnson, & D. Weil (Eds.), *NBER volume on African economic successes.* University of Chicago Press (Forthcoming).

Aniruddh, S., & Kumar,R. (2021). A cross country study of financial inclusion and economic development with special emphasis on India. *Indian Journal of Economics and Development, 17*(1), 11–24.

Ashraf, N., Karlan, D., & Yin, W. (2010). Female empowerment: Further evidence from a commitment savings product in the Philippines. *World Development, 28*(3), 333–344.

Bank, W. (2014). *Global financial development report 2014: FI* (pp. 121–135).World Bank Publications.

Beck, T., & Levine, R. (2004). Stock markets, banks, and growth: Panel evidence. *Journal of Banking & Finance, 28*(3), 423–442.

Beck, T., Demirgüç-Kunt, A., & Honohan, P. (2009). Access to FS: Measurement, impact, and policies. *The World Bank Research Observer, 24*(1), 119e145.

Beck, T., Demirgüç-Kunt, A., & Levine, R. (2007). Finance, inequality, and the poor. *Journal of Economic Growth, 12*(1), 27e49.

Bentler, P. M. (1990). Comparative fit indexes in structural models. *Psychological bulletin, 107*(2), 238.

Brune, L., Gine, X., Goldberg, J., & Yang, D. (2011). *Commitments to save: A field experiment in rural Malawi.* [World Bank Policy Research Working Paper No. 5748].

Burgess, R., & Pande, R. (2005). Do rural banks matter? Evidence from the Indian social banking experiment. *American Economic Review, 95*(3), 780–795.

Buszko, M., Krupa, D., & Chojnacka, M. (2019). Why young people do not use bank products – The case of Poland. Zeszyty Naukowe. *Organizacja i Zarządzanie/Politechnika Śląska, 137*(1), 23–34.

Byrne, B. M. (2001). Structural equation modeling with AMOS, EQS, and LISREL: Comparative approaches to testing for the factorial validity of a measuring instrument. *International journal of testing, 1*(1), 55–86.

Claessens, S., & Perotti, E. (2007). Finance and inequality: Channels and evidence. *Journal of Comparative Economics, 35*(4), 748–773.

Cumming, D., Johan, S., & Zhang, M. (2014). The economic impact of entrepreneurship: Comparing international datasets.*Corporate Governance: An International Review, 22*(2), 162–178.

Demirguc-Kunt, A., & Klapper, L. (2013). Measuring FI: explaining variation in the use of FS across and within countries. In *Brookings Papers on Economic Activity* (pp. 279–321).

Demirgüç-Kunt, A., & Singer, D. (2017). *FI and inclusive growth: A review of recent empirical evidence.* [World Bank Policy Research Working Paper 8040].

Demirgüç-Kunt, A., Klapper, L., & Singer, D. (2013). *FI and legal discrimination against women* (pp. 279–340). [Policy research working paper 6416]. World Bank. Economic Activity .

El-Zoghbi, M., Holle, N., & Soursourian, M. (2019). *Emerging evidence on FI: Moving from black and white to color, CGAP.* World Bank.

Emara, N., & Mohieldin, M. (2020). FI and extreme poverty in the MENA region: A gap analysis approach. *Review of Economics and Political Science, 5*(3), 207–230.

Erlando, A., Riyanto, F. D., & Masakazu, S. (2020). FI, economic growth, and poverty alleviation: evidence from eastern Indonesia. *Heliyon, 6*(10), e05235.

Galor, O., & Moav, O. (2004). From physical to human capital accumulation: Inequality and the process of development. *The Review of Economic Studies, 71*(4), 1001–1026.

Greenwood, J., & Jovanovic, B. (1990). Financial development, growth, and the distribution of income. *Journal of Political Economy, 98*(5, Part 1), 1076–1107.

Hair, J. F., Black, W. C., Babin, B. J., Anderson, R. E., & Tatham, R. L. (2006). *Multivariate data analysis.*Pearson Prentice Hall.

Hair, J. F., Money, A. H., Samouel, P., & Page, M. (2007). Research methods for business. *Education Training, 49*(4), 336–337.

Honohan, P. (2004). *Financial development, growth and poverty: How close are the links?* [World Bank Policy Research Working Paper 3203].World Bank.

Hu, L. T., & Bentler, P. M. (1999). Cutoff criteria for fit indexes in covariance structure analysis: Conventional criteria versus new alternatives. *Structural equation modeling: a multidisciplinary journal, 6*(1), 1–55.

Jia, S., Qiu, Y., & Yang, C. (2021). SDGs, FI, and grain security efficiency. *Agronomy, 11*(12), 2542.

Kara, A., Zhou, H., & Zhou, Y. (2021). Achieving the United Nations' SDG through FI: A systematic literature review of access to finance across the globe. *International Review of Financial Analysis, 77*(1), 1–9.

Klapper, L., Laeven, L., & Rajan, R. (2006). Entry regulation as a barrier to entrepreneurship. *Journal of Financial Economics*, *82*(3), 591–629.

Klapper, L., & Singer, D. (2017). The opportunities and challenges of digitizing government-to-person payments. *The World Bank Research Observer*, *32*(2), 211–226.

Kline, R. B. (1998). Software review: Software programs for structural equation modeling: Amos, EQS, and LISREL. *Journal of psychoeducational assessment*, *16*(4), 343–364.

Liu, G., Huang, Y., & Huang, Z. (2021). Determinants and mechanisms of digital FI development: Based on urban-rural differences. *Agronomy*, *11*(9), 18–33.

Marsh, H. W., & Hocevar, D. (1985). Application of confirmatory factor analysis to the study of self-concept: First-and higher order factor models and their invariance across groups. *Psychological bulletin*, *97*(3), 562.

Mhlanga, D. (2020). Industry 4.0 in finance: The impact of artificial intelligence (AI) on digital FI. *International Journal of Financial Studies*, *8*(3), 45.

Nagdev, K., Rajesh, A., & Misra, R. (2021). The mediating impact of demonetisation on customer acceptance for IT-enabled banking services. *International Journal of Emerging Markets*, *16*(2), 222–233.

Náñez-Alonso, S. L., Jorge-Vazquez, J., & Reier Forradellas, R. F. (2020). Detection of FI vulnerable rural areas through access to cash index: Solutions based on the pharmacy network and a CBDC. Evidence based on Ávila (Spain). *Sustainability*, *12*(18), 74–80.

Náñez-Alonso, S. L., Jorge-Vazquez, J., Echarte Fernández, M. Á., Kolegowicz, K., & Szymla, W. (2022). Financial exclusion in rural and urban contexts in Poland: A threat to achieving SDG eight? *Land*, *11*(4), 539.

Ouma, S. A., Odongo, T. M., & Were, M. (2017). Mobile FS and FI: Is it a boon for savings mobilization? *Review of Development Finance*, *7*(1), 29–35.

Ozturk, I., & Ullah, S. (2022). Does digital FI matter for economic growth and environmental sustainability in OBRI economies? An empirical analysis. *Resources, Conservation and Recycling*, *185*, 106489.

Saleem, R. ,Nasreen, S., & Azam, S. (2022). Role of financial inclusion and export diversification in determining green growth: Evidence from SAARC economies. *Environmental Science and Pollution Research*, *10*(2), 1–14.

Sarma, M., & Pais, J. (2011). FI and development. *Journal of International Development*, *23*(5), 613–628.

Seven, U., & Coskun, Y. (2016). Does financial development reduce income inequality and poverty? Evidence from emerging countries. *Emerging Markets Review*, *26*, 34–63.

Sharif, S. P., & Nia, H. S. (2018). *Structural equation modeling with AMOS*. Artin Teb.

Sharma, D. (2016). Nexus between FI and economic growth: Evidence from the emerging Indian economy.*Journal of Financial Economic Policy*, *8*(1), 13–36.

Tita, A. F., & Aziakpono, M. J. (2017). *The effect of FI on welfare in sub-Saharan Africa: Evidence from disaggregated data.* [Working paper 679]. *Economic Research Southern Africa* (ERSA). *Economic Research Southern Africa* (ERSA).

UNDP. (2020). *COVID-19: Looming crisis in developing countries threatens to devastate economies and ramp up inequality. Report.*

Usman, M., Makhdum, M. S. A.,& Kousar, R. (2021). Does financial inclusion, renewable and non-renewable energy utilization accelerate ecological footprints and economic growth? Fresh evidence from 15 high estemitting countries. *Sustainable Cities and Society*, *65* Article 102590.

World Bank. (2014). *Global financial development report.*World Bank.

World Health Organisation. (2011). *World report on disability*. https://www. who.int/disabilities/world_report/2011/report/en/

Yue, X. G., Cao, Y., Duarte, N., Shao, X. F., & Manta, O. (2019). Social and FI through nonbanking institutions: A model for rural Romania. *Journal of Risk and Financial Management*, *12*(4), 166.

APPENDIX

Table A1. KMO and Bartlett's Test.

Kaiser–Meyer–Olkin Measure of Sampling Adequacy		0.905
Bartlett's Test of Sphericity	Approx. Chi-Square	9722.107
	Df	351
	Sig.	0.000

Source: Authors' compilation.

Table A2. Communalities.

	Initial	Extraction		Initial	Extraction
A1	1.000	0.770	T4	1.000	0.984
A2	1.000	0.771	T5	1.000	0.975
A3	1.000	0.769	AV2	1.000	0.912
A4	1.000	0.694	AV3	1.000	0.971
A5	1.000	0.810	AV4	1.000	0.871
U1	1.000	0.895	AV5	1.000	0.933
U2	1.000	0.836	FI1	1.000	0.963
U4	1.000	0.875	FI2	1.000	0.970
U5	1.000	0.475	FI3	1.000	0.978
U6	1.000	0.893	FI4	1.000	0.969
AF1	1.000	0.897	EDG2	1.000	0.886
AF3	1.000	0.800	EDG3	1.000	0.886
AF4	1.000	0.892	EDG4	1.000	0.794
AF5	1.000	0.849	EDG7	1.000	0.734
T2	1.000	0.976	EDG8	1.000	0.776
T3	1.000	0.973			

Extraction Method: Principal Component Analysis.

Source: Authors' compilation.

Table A3. Total Variance Explained.

Component	Initial Eigenvalues			Extraction Sums of Squared Loadings			Rotation Sums of Squared Loadings		
	Total	% of Variance	Cumulative %	Total	% of Variance	Cumulative %	Total	% of Variance	Cumulative %
1	9.943	32.076	32.076	9.943	32.076	32.076	3.534	11.401	11.401
2	3.512	11.330	43.406	3.512	11.330	43.406	3.463	11.170	22.570
3	2.499	8.060	51.465	2.499	8.060	51.465	3.395	10.953	33.523
4	2.016	6.504	57.969	2.016	6.504	57.969	3.093	9.979	43.501
5	1.597	5.151	63.120	1.597	5.151	63.120	3.009	9.706	53.207
6	1.319	4.254	67.374	1.319	4.254	67.374	2.911	9.392	62.599
7	1.146	3.696	71.070	1.146	3.696	71.070	2.626	8.471	71.070
8	0.818	2.639	73.709						
9	0.713	2.301	76.010						

Extraction Method: Principal Component Analysis.

Source: Authors' compilation.

Table A4. Rotated Component Matrix.

	Component						
	1	2	3	4	5	6	7
AF4	0.822						
AF5	0.807						
AF1	0.798						
AF3	0.790						
T3		0.812					
T5		0.810					
T4		0.796					
T2		0.719					
A1			0.819				
A4			0.815				
A3			0.808				
A5			0.775				
A2			0.749				
U2				0.749			
U1				0.735			
U4				0.731			
U5				0.696			
U6				0.630			
FI2					0.790		
FI3					0.775		
FI4					0.740		
FI1					0.608		
AV4						0.863	
AV3						0.819	
AV2						0.788	
AV5						0.748	
EDG8							0.781
EDG4							0.759
EDG7							0.741
EDG3							0.724
EDG2							0.721

Extraction Method: Principal Component Analysis.
Rotation Method: Varimax with Kaiser Normalisation.

Source: Authors' compilation.
[a]Rotation converged in seven iterations.

Table A5. Model Fit Indices.

Model Fit Indices	Author	Recommended Value
CMIN/DF	Marsh and Hocevar (1985)	<5 indicating a reasonable fit
	Kline (1998)	<3 indicates an acceptable fit
GFI	Byrne (2001); Hair et al. (2006)	>0.7 indicates an acceptable fit
CFI	Bentler (1990)	Close to 0.9, which indicates a relatively good fit
	Hu and Bentler (1999)	>0.80 is permissible, >0.90 indicates a good fit, >0.95 indicates a great fit
RMSEA	Bentler (1990)	<0.05 indicates a good fit, 0.05–0.10 indicates a moderate fit
SRMR	Sharif and Nia (2018); Bentler (1990)	<0.09 acceptable fit

Source: Authors' compilation.

CHAPTER 10

A SYSTEMATIC LITERATURE REVIEW ON CORPORATE GOVERNANCE IN INDIA

Anuj Aggarwal[a], Sparsh Agarwal[a], Vedant Jaiswal[a] and Poonam Sethi[b]

[a]VSBS, VIPS-TC, Delhi, India
[b]Hindu College, University of Delhi, India

ABSTRACT

Introduction: *Historically, the corporate governance (CG) framework was designed primarily to safeguard the economic interests of shareholders, as a result of political and legal interventions, developing into an effective instrument for stakeholders and society in general.*

Purpose: *The core objectives of the study include: identifying journals/publications responsible for publishing CG studies in India, key CG issues covered by CG researchers, the amount of high-impact CG literature across different time periods, sectors/industries covered by CG researchers and different research instruments (quantitative or qualitative) used in CG studies in India.*

Design/methodology: *The chapter used a sample of 130 corporate governance studies that fulfil the selection criteria, drawn from the repository of over 100 reputed journals that are either recognised by the Australian Business Deans Council (ABDC) or indexed by SCOPUS. A systematic literature review has been carried out pertaining to CG issues in India, based on various statistical tools, data, industries, research outlets & citations, etc.*

Sustainable Development Goals: The Impact of Sustainability Measures on Wellbeing
Contemporary Studies in Economic and Financial Analysis, Volume 113B, 143–165
Copyright © 2024 by Anuj Aggarwal, Sparsh Agarwal, Vedant Jaiswal and Poonam Sethi
Published under exclusive licence by Emerald Publishing Limited
ISSN: 1569-3759/doi:10.1108/S1569-37592024000113B010

Findings: *The results show an overwhelming number of studies have assessed the relationship between CG variables and firm performance, which could be measured through a variety of performance metrics such as ROA and ROI. Apart from empirical analysis, many conceptual studies use repetitive basic statistical tools like descriptive statistics or regression analysis. The chapter offers insights into current achievements and future development.*

Originality/value: *This bibliometric study is a useful guide for policymakers, corporate leaders, research organisations and management faculty to draw insights from work produced by eminent researchers in GC in India.*

Keywords: Corporate governance; CG practices; CG framework; CG reporting; systematic literature review; board independence; board size; audit committee; ownership structure

JEL Codes: G14; G40; D53; M14

INTRODUCTION

According to OECD (1999 cited in Sale, 2004), good corporate governance 'ensures that corporations take into account the interests of a wide range of con-stituencies, as well as of the communities within which they operate, and that their boards are accountable to the company and the shareholders'. It basically means that the managers and directors have proper incentives to perform tasks to the best of their abilities on behalf of the shareholders, and the latter is well-communicated about the activities of the organisation (Sale, 2004). Hence, it can be said that corporate governance provides a meaningful response to the agency problems, arising out of the separation of ownership and management, as share-holders are often 'inactive' to hold the 'powerful' managers accountable for their actions carried out in their name (Wells, 2010).

There are a host of internal and external drivers that can determine the CG framework prevalent in the industry. The internal components include the nature and independence of the board of directors, ownership structure, debt struc-ture, managerial compensation, audit committee and audit quality. The external components are as follows: dynamic labour markets, legal compliance matters, regulatory framework, etc. There has been a paradigm shift in India's corporate governance architecture as the regulatory bodies continue to shape India's finan-cial landscape in light of new global challenges.

LITERATURE REVIEW

There is a vast set of themes being discussed across various areas such as earnings management, board of directors' independence, shareholders' ownership, firm performance, firm valuation, etc. A whole array of studies has discussed at length important issues concerning the overall corporate governance framework in India such as corporate scandals (Kaur, 2017; Narayanaswamy et al., 2015); quality of disclosures with respect to internal controls, financial information (Ashfaq & Rui, 2019; Haldar & Raithatha, 2017; Hundal, 2016); competitiveness and value creation (Haldar et al., 2016); and ownership structure (Gollakota & Gupta, 2006).

A lot of CG research studies have established a correlation among corporate governance variables and the performance of a firm (Singla & Singh, 2019), although the findings have been inconsistent and even conflicted as some research scholars have found a strong correlation between CG variables and financial performance, while others have found statistically insignificant association between major CG variables like board composition, board size, audit committee attributes, frequency of meetings, gender diversity, and firm performance (Bansal & Sharma, 2016; Kagzi & Guha, 2018; Mishra & Mohanty, 2014).

For the purpose of this study, the selected research papers have been divided into three broad streams: (1) research papers based on primary data; (2) research papers based on secondary data; and (3) research papers based on strategic literature review or conceptual analysis.

OBJECTIVES OF THE STUDY

The underlying objective of the study is to comprehensively review the existing corporate governance literature in India to know:

- Which journal publications/outlets have been primarily responsible for publishing corporate governance studies in India?
- How has research studies in India covered the key issues associated with corporate governance?
- Which are the qualitative and quantitative instruments applied in the prior CG research in India?
- How much of the seminal CG literature generated across different time frames?
- Which sectors or industries have been at the forefront of corporate governance research in India?

RESEARCH METHODOLOGY

This study has used prior corporate governance studies that have been undertaken in the Indian context. According to Tranfield et al. (2003) 'traditional or narrative reviews frequently thoroughness, and in many cases are not undertaken as a genuine piece of investigation'. It advocated that systematic reviews enhance the quality of study as it encompasses the broad investigation of research work carried out by scholars across different time periods. It involves three stages with nine different phases. However, the present study has employed the methodology devised by Ahmad and Omar (2016), which customised corporate governance research into a five-step process:

1. Framing of research questions;
2. Identification of keywords and databases;

3. Selection and assessment;
4. Data extraction; and
5. Data synthesis

IDENTIFICATION OF KEYWORDS AND DATABASES

There have been different keywords used to extract research papers published in the area of corporate governance in India. To begin with, the general phrase 'Corporate governance' has been used to generate search results. As a result, a lot of research papers were identified that matched the general keyword/phrase, some were found to be useful, while others were ignored. Furthermore, different terminologies were used to extract more relevant studies including CG framework, CG structure, CG practices, CG mechanism, CG attributes, board of directors, ownership, audit committee, etc.

Several databases or research outlets that contain corporate governance studies were shortlisted. These include: Inderscience, Emerald, Wiley Online Library, Sage Publications, ScienceDirect, Springer, Taylor and Francis, etc. All these selected databases prohibit the publication of predatory or commercial journals; contain peer-reviewed studies that are also well-cited by other researchers in their respective studies. This study has made sincere efforts to analyse the corporate governance literature from 2000 onwards till 2022. The voluntary 'Desirable Corporate Governance Code' was published by the Confederation of Indian Industry (CII) in 1998; followed by Clause 49 of the Listing Agreement issued by SEBI between 2000 and 2004.

Hence, the selection criteria adopted for the inclusion of high-quality and relevant research studies from a pool of shortlisted studies are as follows:

1. Studies that are published in peer-reviewed journals;
2. Studies that contain empirical evidence or observations with respect to CG in India;
3. Studies that are published in the specific time-frame, that is, 2000–2021.

Initially, a general search of the term 'Corporate Governance in India' yielded 330 studies. Furthermore, the selection criterion was applied, which brought the number of studies down to 195, which are to be screened further for selection. Then, a final quality assessment was carried out, which resulted in the exclusion of 65 research papers, hence, in total, 130 research papers have been used to fulfil the objectives of the study.

RESULTS AND INTERPRETATION

The necessary literature has been retrieved from relevant databases to fulfil the research objectives of the study. The following are Tables 1–8 that have summarised the sampled studies, to be carefully analysed for the purpose of data interpretation.

Table 1. CG Studies Based on Primary Data.

S.No.	Author(s)	Findings
1	Khanna and Palepu (2004)	In India's IT industry, the corporate governance framework has been impacted by the emergence of globalisation of product and talent markets.
2	Singla and Singh (2019)	It has been found that the firm value is negatively correlated with board independence, whereas it is positively correlated with audit committee independence.
3	Mishra and Kapil (2018a)	The appropriate board size and high degree of board independence affects firm performance positively. Further, the frequency of board meetings and separation of CEO and Chairman are linked with increased firm value.
4	Dossani (2012)	Due to the adoption of developed nation CG norms, companies that get private equity money are likely to demonstrate ethical standards of corporate governance as compared to those who don't have presence of PE players on board.
5	Subramanian and Reddy (2012)	Voluntarily disclosing more about their board practices allows firms to gain competitiveness in international markets, but market share reduces with ownership-related disclosures.
6	Singla and Singh (2018)	Private-sector firms are more responsive than public-sector firms when it comes to adherence to prescribed rules and regulations and regulatory compliances.
7	Arora and Bhandari (2017)	Good governance and a well-defined CSR mechanism ensures that firms are further motivated to enhance their CG practices, resulting into higher valuation of firm.
8	Singh and Kansil (2017)	It is found out that the corporate governance effectiveness is enhanced due to increased foreign investors' participation in the organisation as they appropriately exercise their ownership rights.
9	Bachmann and Pereira (2014)	The study has outlined the development of the idea of 'corporate human rights accountability' in consonance with the international laws.
10	Das and Pattanayak (2016)	The study has concluded that stakeholder forms of governance are most preferred in the higher education institutions in India.
11	Qurashi (2018)	In accordance with UN's CG guide, the CG codes of Pakistan and Bangladesh (issued by BEI) have a convergence rate of about 77 percent (40 out of 52); India (issued by BSEC) has a convergence rate of about 50 percent (26 out of 52); and Bangladesh (issued by BEI) has a convergence rate of about 41 percent (21 out of 52).
12	Srivastava et al. (2019)	Inverse relationship exists between the price of shares and corporate governance practices. Further, access to equity financing is convenient for well-run businesses.
13	Kansil and Singh (2018)	Based on fuzzy set theory, this study has identified five main governance issues: pattern of ownership, the code of best CG practices, the legal frameworks, which includes national monitoring organisations, false independence of independent directors in the judicial system and decision-making.

(Continued)

Table 1.   (*Continued*)

S.No.	Author(s)	Findings
14	Gupta and Sharma (2014)	Financial efficiency and stock performance are marginally affected by the corporate governance practices of a firm.
15	Haldar and Raithatha (2017)	The firm's financial disclosure policies are greatly improved by the composition of audit committee and stronger corporate governance standards.
16	Srivastava et al. (2018a, 2018b)	The results indicate that board size, board independence, and number of female directors may negatively affect the cost of equity; however, factors such as independent directors, increased and female participation significantly increase the ROA.
17	Chauhan et al. (2016)	The study has found that there is a positive correlation between CG practices and firm performance.
18	Gulati et al. (2020)	The effectiveness of the board, the function of the audit, executive compensation, risk management, shareholders' rights and information, standards of transparency and quality of disclosures are the six distinct dimensions that make up the indices created to encapsulate the state of corporate governance.
19	Marques et al. (2018)	The issuer's corporate governance practices typically contribute to the execution of its commitments. These businesses also score higher on the ECLAC Index.
20	Mishra and Mohanty (2014)	In contrast to legal compliance indicator, the board and proactive indicators have a substantial impact on the firm's success. The CG score is a reliable indicator of a company's performance.
21	Shahid (2019)	Strong corporate governance policies enhance both the degree of investment in the companies and the board members' monitoring role.
22	Abraham et. al. (2015)	Indian businesses adhere closely to the clause – 49 governance disclosure standards. Government-run businesses release much less information than privately run businesses.
23	Al-Mudhaki and Joshi (2004)	The higher the frequency of the meetings of AC, the greater is the effect on Internal Control. The representation and makeup of AC are not independent enough.
24	Amaladoss et Al. (2011)	TCS does not make use of the Web 2.0-enhanced content and design elements on its website.
25	Goel and McIver (2017)	Lower gearing is linked to the growth of the stock market, but higher gearing is linked to better institutional development in India.
26	Kandukuri et al. (2015)	Better corporate governance procedures also improve a company's financial performance.
27	Kang and Nanda (2018)	The transparency and compliance index of managerial compensation are strongly correlated with the existence of a pay committee.
28	Kohli and Saha (2008)	Strong positive correlation between corporate governance and a firm's market value.

(*Continued*)

Table 1. (*Continued*)

S.No.	Author(s)	Findings
29	Puri and Kumar (2018)	In case of listed enterprises in India, size of the firm, ownership concentration, degree of financial leverage, type of industry, foreign listing, quality of external auditors, and performance of the audit committee, all have a substantial impact on their voluntary corporate governance practices (VCGP).

Source: Authors' own compilation.

Table 2. CG Studies Based on Secondary Data.

S.No.	Author(s)	Findings
1	Shikha and Mishra (2019)	The paper discusses the separation of powers between the promoters and the board and introduces a slew of new measures for better governance.
2	Chatterjee (2011)	Despite the disclosure of information on governance reporting, the information remains inconclusive with a high degree of variation between companies.
3	Bose (2009)	The paper suggests a code of conduct for board members, additional independent directors on boards, an expanded role for the Audit Committee, and thorough risk assessments to meet the global CG standards.
4	Goel (2018)	The Indian companies have shown great improvement in their Corporate Governance structure despite the fall in the number of board inductions of independent directors. No direct correlation between CG reforms and financial linkages.
5	Sidhu and Kaur (2019)	The financial reporting mechanism can be monitored more effectively with an active audit committee, resulting in higher stock market liquidity.
6	Haldar et al. (2016)	International competitiveness is greatly impacted by the degree of flexibility in corporate governance, alongside other factors.
7	Masud et al. (2018)	The 'Environmental sustainability reporting performance' (ESRP) is positively correlated with board size, board independence, foreign and institutional ownership, in the context of South Asian countries.
8	Dwivedi and Jain (2005)	A greater percentage of international ownership in the firm is linked to a rise in the firm's valuation.
9	Kiranmai and Mishra (2019)	The firm's CG variables do not directly impact its performance; rather the size of the board has a higher correlation with respect to performance.
10	Prasad, Sankaran and Prabhu (2019)	CEO duality, along with other factors, contributes towards improving the working capital management of the firm.
11	Shankar and Cordeiro (2016)	Firm's performance is enhanced by social capital, the quality of independent directors and industry-level expertise.
12	Prasanna (2013)	Stock market volatility has been substantially reduced as a result of the promulgation of Clause 49 of the listing agreement.

(*Continued*)

Table 2. (*Continued*)

S.No.	Author(s)	Findings
13	Saravanan et al. (2016)	The non-executive compensation is significantly correlated with CG variables such as board size, proportion of non-executive directors on the board and CEO duality.
14	Mishra and Mohanty (2018)	The study has found a significant positive association between firm's CG practices and its financial performance.
15	Vig and Datta (2018)	Value creation, or EVA, of organisations have a favourable link with the quality of corporate governance. However, it is determined that the influence is negligible.
16	Jaiswall and Firth (2009)	The CEO's compensation is significantly linked to the independence and functioning of remuneration committees.
17	Nagar and Raithatha (2016)	An increase in controlling ownership is likely to result in more cash flow manipulation. Better auditing and board scrutiny are unable to stop this deception. Such manipulation, nevertheless, has decreased recently.
18	Chahal and Kumari (2013)	The firm's financial performance is positively correlated with the quality of audit committee and ownership structure; on the other hand, boardroom features have a little impact.
19	Kumari and Pattanayak (2017)	CG standards in terms of quality of audit procedures, board composition, and performance-based pay are the variables that influence firms' earnings management.
20	Katarachia et al. (2018)	Indian corporations need to do a better job of disclosing their corporate governance practices.
21	Palaniappan (2017)	A negative correlation exists between board qualities including board size and the firms' financial performance metrics such as ROA and ROE.
22	Arora and Sharma (2016)	Larger boards are linked to increased intellectual depth, which in turn aids in decision-making and improves performance. On the contrary side, the findings show that profitability and return on equity have little connection to measures of corporate governance.
23	Saravanan et al. (2017)	The average executive salary has a strong favourable impact on both the family and non-family enterprises.
24	Gill (2013)	Central public-sector enterprises that do not follow CG guidelines with respect to the overall board composition do not necessarily have to face significant financial implications.
25	Saggar and Singh (2017)	In contrast to family ownership, 'Board size and gender diversity have positively significant effects on risk disclosure, while identification of the largest shareholder with ownership concentration has a detrimental effect on disclosure of risk information in the case of Indian promoter body corporate, foreign promoter body corporate, and non-institutions'.
26	Kaur and Singh (2018)	Assessment of a firm's goodwill is impacted by the ownership structure and the board's strength in numbers.

(Continued)

Table 2. (*Continued*)

S.No.	Author(s)	Findings
27	Mishra (2016)	According to the findings of the study, quality of profits is dependent on three major factors: size of audit committee, the number of directorships held by audit committee members, and the frequency of audit committee meetings.
28	Mohapatra (2016)	The company's valuation is strongly linked with the Board's independence, but it has no discernible effect on operating performance, according to the study.
29	Hundal (2016)	Audit committee members who are less (more) busy produce better (worse) financial reporting for their companies.
30	Islam (2016)	A strong positive correlation exists between the firm's CG practices and its performance.
31	Kavitha et al. (2019)	The firm's financial disclosures are favourably impacted by the proportion of independent directors, negatively by dual boards and the director's workload.
32	Ashfaq and Rui (2019)	Characteristics of the board and audit committee and government ownership have a favourable, considerable impact on the disclosure of internal controls.
33	Kang and Nanda (2018)	The disclosure and compliance index of executive compensation is considerably and favourably correlated with the size of the company and the existence of a pay committee.
34	Kang and Nanda (2017)	As a company's accounting performance improves, managerial compensation rises. Additionally, managerial compensation is considerably and favourably correlated with foreign institutional shareholding.
35	Kagzi and Guha (2018)	The study has established a positive correlation between the firm performance and board's gender ratio, age, length of service and educational background. All these factors are part of 'demographic diversity index'.
36	Mayur and Saravanan (2017)	A larger board is associated with better business performance. Further, there is very little association found between board meeting frequency and board composition with firm performance.
37	Kaur (2017)	When independent directors make up a sizeable portion of the boards, that is, fewer number of people are sitting on boards of a significantly larger number of companies, as a result, violating SEBI's guidelines.
38	Subramanian (2017)	The number of 'Vote Against' suggestions varies significantly depending on the sort of 'controlling ownership' of the businesses.
39	Singla and Singh (2019)	The firm value is positively correlated with audit committee independence, but negatively correlated with board independence.
40	Mishra and Kapil (2018b)	There is a positive relationship between firm performance and board's characteristics including Board size and Board Independence. Furthermore, frequency of board meetings and separation of CEO and Chairman are linked with increased firm value.

(*Continued*)

Table 2. (*Continued*)

S.No.	Author(s)	Findings
41	Kapoor and Goel (2019)	The attentiveness of audit committee members and the independent directors have a bearing on the quality of financial reporting and earnings management procedures.
42	Haldar et al. (2018)	In the case of Indian companies, independent board directors have little impact on business performance.
43	Bhatt and Bhattacharya (2017)	When comparing family enterprises to non-family firms, board structure has a detrimental influence on firm performance.
44	Mishra and Kapil (2017)	CG practices have a greater effect on market-based measures than on accounting-based measures. There is a strong positive correlation between firm performance and promoters' ownership. Furthermore, firm performance is not significantly related to Board independence; however, it is positively correlated with return on assets (ROA).
45	Adnan et al. (2018)	The public-sector ownership affects the reporting quality of CSR, whereas the quality of CG enhances the social responsibility of the business.
46	Aggarwal et al. (2019)	The performance of standalone firms (measured by Tobin's Q) is positively correlated with the diversity of the board; however, this correlation is inverse for firms affiliated with a group.
47	Annamalai et al. (2010–2017)	This paper is concerned with calculating aggregate CG scores based on 13 firm-level attributes for the period 2010–2017 in the context of six Asian economies.
48	Aparna et al. (2022)	Upon analysing and evaluating ONGC and ITC based on the Board of Directors and governance, it was found that there is a negligible presence of women directors. Further, in direct violation of SEBI's regulations, a single person was occupying the position of Chairman and CEO in both the organisations.
49	Bansal and Sharma (2016)	On one hand, the firm's performance is positively impacted by board size, separation of CEO and Chairman of the Board, but factors like the frequency of meetings and audit committee's independence have no impact on the performance of Indian enterprises.
50	Chauhan and Dey (2017)	Most of the women directors on the boards of Indian companies belong to the founder's family and simply project founder's ideas and thus they do not have any significant impact on firm's performance.
51	Col and Sen (2019)	Emerging market companies adhere to the more stringent corporate governance norms of the developed markets via international acquisitions.
52	Helmers et al. (2017)	Board interlocks have a considerable favourable impact on both R&D and patenting.
53	Patibandla (2006)	On one hand, foreign investors contribute favourably towards operational performance in terms of profitability, whereas public financial institutions contribute unfavourably in the overall business performance.

Table 2. (*Continued*)

S.No.	Author(s)	Findings
54	Sarkar and Sarkar (2000)	Foreign stock participation enhances the value of the firm.
55	Sarkar and Sarkar (2009)	Multiple independent directorships are significantly associated with increased business value.
56	Shaw et al. (2016)	The extensive domain knowledge of the directors, particularly independent directors, as well as their accumulated connections, increase the likelihood of success of the company.
57	Al-ahdal et al. (2020)	The Indian firms outperform their Gulf counterparts in terms of practices of corporate governance and financial results.
58	Black and Khanna (2007)	When there is a specific corporate action by the firm, large firms on average earn 4.5 per cent more during the three-day window, from the date of announcement, as compared to small firms.
59	Aggarwal and Ghosh (2015)	The performance indicators showed no discernible connection between firm's performance and the increase in directors' compensation. However, there is a strong association between the two from an accounting perspective. Hence, while the directors' compensation does not considerably increase the firm's external worth, it does increase its intrinsic value.
60	Akbar et al. (2012)	The role of FI's as nominee directors is mainly namesake. They follow a conservative approach and their presence is only a formality despite being the largest shareholders.
61	Balasubramanian et al. (2010)	Favourable association between company market value and both a sub-index focusing on shareholder rights and the overall governance index.
62	Bhatt and Bhattacharya (2015)	Boards with a larger size were more effective for a company's performance. Board diligence and independent directors, however, do not impact. Family businesses outperformed other businesses to non-family businesses.
63	Das and Dey (2016)	There is an insignificant relationship between CG attributes such as CEO duality, board remuneration, promoters' involvement and firm's performance, while there is a positive relationship between board diversity and performance.
64	De Jonge (2014)	Comparatively speaking, state-owned businesses in China do better as compared to India, probably due to China's less progressed political empowerment of women and India's far more advanced economic involvement of women.
65	Dossani (2012)	Due to the adoption of developed nation CG norms, the study has found that companies that get private equity money exhibit stronger standards of corporate governance than those that do not.

(*Continued*)

Table 2.   (*Continued*)

S.No.	Author(s)	Findings
66	Jackling and Johl (2009)	The firm performance is positively impacted by board size but it is negatively impacted by outside directors with repeated appointments.
67	Jaiswall and Bhattacharyya (2016)	In both the public and private sectors, the CEO compensation dependent on ownership characteristics, as opposed to the board and CEO qualities, is positively associated with future business performance.
68	Jameson et al. (2014)	Tobin's Q has a strong negative correlation with controlling shareholder board membership.
69	Kota and Tomar (2010)	The research paper concludes that a significant number of independent non-executive directors have failed to maintain necessary oversight of the board's activities.
70	Kumar and Singh (2013)	It was discovered that promoter ownership level and corporate performance were positively correlated, while board size and company value were negatively correlated.
71	Mohapatra (2016)	The value of a company is positively impacted by board independence. Board independence did not directly affect operating performance, according to the study.
72	Muttakin and Subramaniam (2015)	Disclosure of corporate social responsibility is adversely correlated with CEO dualism and positively correlated with government ownership, international ownership and board independence.
73	Narayanaswamy et al. (2015)	The Satyam scandal's impact has been minimal on the Indian audit committees.
74	Prasad, Sankaran, et al. (2019)	The study demonstrated major differences in executive pay of senior corporate executives depending on the factors such as proximity to controlling shareholders' group, executive vs non-executive, independent vs non-independent, etc.
75	Prasanna (2014)	The study draws insights from the recent spate of corporate governance reforms that have been undertaken in India and provides positive evidence to validate its thesis.
76	Prasanna and Menon (2012)	Greater promoter ownership decreases stock liquidity.
77	Saravanan et al. (2017)	Board size has a significant negative impact on family and non-family enterprises while the average executive salary has a positive impact on the performance.
78	Sehgal and Mulraj (2008)	This research has claimed that India has a long way to go in terms of laying the regulatory framework that increases the corporate compliance and improves the quality of disclosures.
79	Yameen et al. (2019)	For the hotel sector to be regarded as a competent corporate governance practitioner, corporate governance processes must be greatly enhanced.

Source: Authors' own compilation.

Table 3. CG Studies Based on Systematic Literature Review or Conceptual Analysis.

S.No.	Author(s)	Findings
1	Bharathi Kamath (2019)	The CG characteristics only impact large-cap companies with respect to intellectual capital performance.
2	Sarkar et al. (2012)	The findings validate the claim that Indian capital markets reward companies with efficient CG processes, governance standards and procedures.
3	Dash (2012)	The majority of research work covering the role of media in influencing corporate governance has already been completed.
4	Estrin and Prevezer (2011)	The study claims that informal institutions could replace formal institutions to enhance the level of investments, especially in emerging markets.
5	Kimber et al. (2005)	The paper argues that it is the primary job of HRM practitioners to spell out the firms' vision, mission, values and philosophy to the stakeholders including customers, suppliers, employees, bankers, auditors, etc. to ensure highest levels of transparency and integrity.
6	Shikha (2017)	The evolution of CG with respect to the new economic order is extensively discussed and deliberated upon.
7	Machold and Vasudevan (2004)	There has been a lot of pressure to transition towards 'Anglo-Americanisation' of governance, but this study has revealed the diversity of governance structures across different set-ups.
8	Lakhani (2012)	The study has found the cultural similarity between otherwise rivals: China and India, who are likely to benefit immensely from the implementation of a stakeholder model of corporate governance.
9	Patra (2013)	Infosys has established new guidelines for engaging with stock exchanges, shareholders and the general public.
10	Muniapan and Shaikh (2007)	Numerous ideas from Kautilya's Arthashastra are still relevant to modern company administration.
11	Kavitha and Nandagopal (2013)	The study has elaborated upon a hybrid model based on India's socio-economic, political and legal systems, which will be most suitable for India instead of transitioning into the 'Anglo-American model of corporate governance'.
12	Uzma (2018)	The paper has carried out a rigorous theoretical examination of many CG codes and regulations adopted in the Indian context.
13	Gollakota and Gupta (2006)	Different types of business ownership emerged as a result of changes in institutional and legal frameworks that were brought about by changes in value systems. However, the final product is an amalgamation of various co-existing ownership structures.
14	Guha et al. (2019)	Changes in CG practices that prioritise shareholders have little impact on India's financial markets expansion.
15	Balasubramanian and George (2012)	The paper has reviewed the fundamental internal corporate governance procedures, along with institutional frameworks, board structures and designated roles, as enshrined in the Clause 49 of the listing agreement.

(Continued)

Table 3.   (*Continued*)

S.No.	Author(s)	Findings
16	Rajagopalan and Zhang (2008)	The study has analysed the corporate governance changes in emerging markets. It has concluded that foreign companies are more likely to implement CG regulations appropriately and adopt significant forms of participation in the governing of the enterprises.
17	Singh et al. (2011)	In light of CG regulatory developments in India, the study has analysed the concerns and issues in two different time periods – from 1950–1990 (pre-liberalisation) to 1991–2011 (post-liberalisation).
18	Gupta and Singh (2018)	The ability of the country's powerful, dominating shareholders to rig the system could jeopardise the progress made to the adoption of best corporate governance practices in India.
19	Gopinath (2008)	Historically, the banking industry of India has been mostly stable, and there have not been any significant threats that could jeopardise the superstructures of the economy or the financial system.
20	Gupta and Shallu (2014)	Recent studies demonstrate that global investors prioritise corporate governance when making investment decisions, particularly given the volatile environment of the securities market.
21	Lakshman and Akhter (2013)	The article discusses the key success criteria in IPL as well as reveals the many violations of SEBI's Corporate Governance Code via its questionable practices.
22	Ravi (2012)	The study has identified the CG weaknesses and has recommended strategic measures to fix the current CG framework.
23	Reed (2002)	Focuses on the implications of 'Anglo-American' CG model, especially in view of the instability in financial markets.
24	Sanan (2016)	The firm performance is significantly impacted by independent women directors.
25	Srivastava et al. (2018a)	In the contemporary world, corporate governance emphasises a firm's necessity for survival over protecting shareholders' rights.

Source: Authors' own compilation.

Table 4.   Corporate Governance Studies Based on Application of Quantitative or Qualitative Tools.

S.No.	Tool Used	No. of Papers (Frequency)
1	Descriptive analysis	55
2	Panel data analysis	40
3	Regression/correlation	74
4	Other	12

Source: Authors' own compilation.

Table 5. Corporate Governance Studies Based on Sector or Industry Type.

S.No.	Type of Industry	No. of Papers (Frequency)
1	Financial services	37
2	Non-financial services	46
3	Manufacturing	30
4	Conceptual and review	17
Total		130

Source: Authors' own compilation.

Table 6. Corporate Governance Studies Based on Time Period.

S.No.	Time Period	No. of Papers (Frequency)
1	Up to 2000	0
2	2000–2005	7
3	2005–2010	13
4	2010–2015	29
5	2015–2022	81
Total		130

Source: Authors' own compilation.

Table 7. CG Studies Based on Publishers and Journal Citations.

S.No.	Name of the Publisher	No. of Papers (Frequency)	Citations
1	Emerald	44	2,624
2	Elsevier	21	2,363
3	Springer	20	1,833
4	Inderscience	26	2,086
5	Other publishers	19	1,190
Total		130	

Source: Authors' own compilation.

Table 8. Corporate Governance Studies Based on Key Issues or Attributes.

S.No.	Key Issues/Attributes	No. of Papers (Frequency)
1	Board of directors' issues	78
2	Audit committee/quality issues	37
3	Ownership issues	33
4	Other issues	35

Source: Authors' own compilation.

In Table 1, there are 29 studies that have adopted a qualitative approach to analyse various issues of corporate governance. There are 19 studies that have either used a questionnaire design or interview method to ascertain findings, while the remaining 10 studies have devised a corporate governance index to ascertain a particular score to arrive at meaningful results.

In Table 2, there are 79 studies that have used secondary data of companies or indices extracted from annual reports or recognised databases such as Reuters, Bloomberg, Prowess, etc. The majority of these studies have obtained financial data to be used for quantitative research to draw meaningful inferences pertaining to different corporate governance areas such as firm performance, earnings management, firm value, capital markets volatility & performance, etc.

In Table 3, there are 25 studies that have used the review approach or conceptual analysis to discuss the range of corporate governance issues including governance reforms, governance regulations, corporate governance in India vis-à-vis global context, role of media & institutions, corporate scandals, corporate governance reporting, shareholders' activism, corporate human rights responsibility, etc.

In Table 4, the studies are categorised on the basis of the usage of quantitative instruments. Most of the CG studies (74) in India have used multiple regression/correlation technique; while 40 studies have employed sophisticated panel data models (fixed or random effects); 55 studies have drawn results using descriptive statistics and frequency distributions; and 12 studies have used other techniques such as non-parametric tests, event analysis, GARCH analysis, etc.

In Table 5, the studies have been segregated based on broad-based industries that it has analysed or deliberated upon. Out of 130 sampled studies, 17 studies are conceptual or review-based, hence they cannot be categorised based on sector. The remaining 103 studies have been classified into three industries: Financial services, Non-financial services and Manufacturing. The highest number of studies are based on non-financial services (46) which include travel, tourism and hospitality, health and ed'ucation, transportation and logistics, ICT, trade, etc.; followed by financial services (37) including banking, NBFC's, insurance, asset management, etc.; and finally manufacturing sector (30).

In Tables 6 and 7, the research studies have been classified based on the number of published papers and their citations in well-known journals across different time periods. These two tables have attempted to answer the research question about the research outlets that have published major bodies of work in the area of corporate governance in India. The numbers are as follows: Emerald journals (44 studies), followed by Inderscience (26 studies), Elsevier (21), Springer (20) and the remaining 19 studies in other publishers including Wiley online library, ScienceDirect, Taylor & Francis, Sage Publications, etc. Furthermore, the results show the studies published in Emerald journals (2,624); Elsevier (2,363); Inderscience (2,086); Springer (1,833) and remaining in the other publishers (1,190). This indicates that Emerald is the leading and influential research outlet for publishing peer-reviewed studies in matters of corporate governance in India.

Moreover, most of the corporate governance studies (81) have been undertaken recently between 2015 and 2022, while there are no studies of value before the year 2000, as there was very little awareness about corporate governance then in India. Furthermore, 29 studies were published between the period 2010–2015; 13 studies in 2005–2010 and 7 studies in 2000–2005.

In Table 8, the research papers are classified on the basis of CG attributes or key issues it discussed. The findings have indicated that 78 studies have predominantly studied Board of Directors' issues (size, composition, remuneration, independence, etc.); 37 studies have investigated ownership structure of companies (promoters, foreign & institutional, minority ownership, etc.); 33 studies have discussed attributes pertaining to audit committee and audit quality, while 35 studies have focused on other issues like corporate governance reporting (including social and environmental sustainability), CG's evolution and multi-decade reforms in India, cross-cultural differences among emerging markets in terms of their legal and regulatory framework, role of institutions in boosting CG's effectiveness, role of CG in facilitating M&A's, role of CG in academic ecosystem, role of effective CG communications & media, CG scandals in the history of India Inc., advent of shareholders' activism in the 21st century, corporate human rights responsibility and influence of ancient India's texts on present corporate governance paradigm.

CONCLUSION AND FUTURE SCOPE OF STUDY

The study clearly shows that an overwhelming amount of prior research in India is concerned with establishing the link between CG variables and corporate performance, which could be measured through a variety of performance metrics such as ROA, ROI, ROCE and Tobin's q. Furthermore, the results show that apart from empirical analysis, a lot of conceptual studies have been published using basic statistical tools like descriptive statistics or regression analysis, but the problem with them is they are often repetitive. Finally, the chapter offers profound insights into what has already been done and what can be done. The bibliometric approach adds tremendously to the existing literature and can be a useful guide for policymakers, regulatory bodies, research organisations, academicians and corporate executives.

There is enormous scope for future researchers, as there are a lot of gap areas related to corporate governance in India including IT governance, sustainability reporting, green governance, quality of financial disclosures and compliance practices in the post-Covid world, convergence of domestic and global corporate governance standards, board expertise, etc.

REFERENCES

Abraham, S., Marston, C., & Jones, E. (2015). Disclosure by Indian companies following corporate governance reform. *Journal of Applied Accounting Research, 16*(1), 114–137.

Adnan, S. M., Hay, D., & van Staden, C. J. (2018). The influence of culture and corporate governance on corporate social responsibility disclosure: A cross country analysis. *Journal of Cleaner Production, 198*, 820–832.

Aggarwal, R., & Ghosh, A. (2015). Director's remuneration and correlation on firm's performance: A study from the Indian corporate. *International Journal of Law and Management, 57*(5), 373–399.

Aggarwal, R., Jindal, V., & Seth, R. (2019). Board diversity and firm performance: The role of business group affiliation. *International Business Review, 28*(6), 1–17.

Ahmad, S., & Omar, R. (2016). Basic corporate governance models: A systematic review. *International Journal of Law and Management, 58*(1), 73–107.

Akbar, M., Khan, S. A., & Khan, F. (2012). The relationship of stock prices and macroeconomic variables revisited: Evidence from Karachi stock exchange. *African Journal of Business Management, 6*(4), 1315–1322.

Al-ahdal, W. M., Alsamhi, M. H., Tabash, M. I., & Farhan, N. H. (2020). The impact of corporate governance on financial performance of Indian and GCC listed firms: An empirical investigation. *Research in International Business and Finance*, *51*, 101083.

Al-Mudhaki, J., & Joshi, P. L. (2004). The role and functions of audit committees in the Indian corporate governance: Empirical findings. *International Journal of Auditing*, *8*(1), 33–47.

Amaladoss, M. X., Manohar, H. L., & Jacob, F. (2011). Communicating corporate governance through websites: A case study from India. *International Journal of Business Governance and Ethics*, *6*(4), 311–339.

Aparna, K., & Amilan, S. (2022). Customers' response to mandatory corporate social responsibility in India: an empirical evidence. *Social Responsibility Journal* (ahead-of-print).

Arora, A., & Bhandari, V. (2017). Do firm-level variables affect corporate governance quality and performance? Evidence from India. *International Journal of Corporate Governance*, *8*(1), 1–24.

Ashfaq, K., & Rui, Z. (2019). The effect of board and audit committee effectiveness on internal control disclosure under different regulatory environments in South Asia. *Journal of Financial Reporting and Accounting*, *17*(2), 170–200.

Bachmann, S. D., & Pereira, V. (2014). Corporate human rights responsibility and multi-nationality in emerging markets – A legal perspective for corporate governance and responsibility. *International Journal of Business Governance and Ethics*, *9*(1), 52–67.

Balasubramanian, N., Black, B. S., & Khanna, V. (2010). The relation between firm-level corporate governance and market value: A case study of India. *Emerging Markets Review*, *11*(4), 319–340.

Balasubramanian, N., & George, R. (2012). Corporate governance and the Indian institutional context: Emerging mechanisms and challenges: In conversation with K V Kamath, Chairman, Infosys and ICICI Bank. *IIMB Management Review*, *24*(4), 215–233.

Bansal, N., & Sharma, A. K. (2016). Audit committee, corporate governance, and firm performance: Empirical evidence from India. *International Journal of Economics and Finance*, *8*(3), 103.

Bhatt, R. R., & Bhattacharya, S. (2015). Board structure and firm performance in Indian IT firms. *Journal of Advances in Management Research*, *12*(3), 232–248.

Bhatt, R. R., & Bhattacharya, S. (2017). Family firms, board structure and firm performance: Evidence from top Indian firms. *International Journal of Law and Management*, *59*(5), 699–717.

Black, B. S., & Khanna, V. S. (2007). Can corporate governance reforms increase firm market values? Event study evidence from India. *Journal of Empirical Legal Studies*, *4*(4), 749–796.

Bose, I. (2009). Corporate governance and law-role of independent directors: Theory and practice in India. *Social Responsibility Journal*, *5*, 94–111.

Chahal, H., & Kumari, A. (2013). Examining talent management using CG as proxy measure: A case study of State Bank of India. *Corporate Governance: The International Journal of Business in Society*, *13*(2), 198–207.

Chatterjee, D. (2011). A content analysis study on corporate governance reporting by Indian companies. *Corporate Reputation Review*, *14*(3), 234–246.

Chauhan, Y., & Dey, D. K. (2017). Do female directors really add value in Indian firms? *Journal of Multinational Financial Management*, *42*, 24–36.

Chauhan, Y., Lakshmi, K. R., & Dey, D. K. (2016). Corporate governance practices, self-dealings, and firm performance: Evidence from India. *Journal of Contemporary Accounting & Economics*, *12*(3), 274–289.

Col, B., & Sen, K. (2019). The role of corporate governance for acquisitions by the emerging market multinationals: Evidence from India. *Journal of Corporate Finance*, *59*, 239–254.

Das, A., & Dey, S. (2016). Role of corporate governance on firm performance: A study on large Indian corporations after implementation of Companies' Act 2013. *Asian Journal of Business Ethics*, *5*(1), 149–164.

Das, N., & Pattanayak, J. K. (2016). Corporate governance mechanism for academic institutions imparting higher education in India. *International Journal of Management in Education*, *10*(2), 204–217.

Dash, A. K. (2012). Media impact on corporate governance in India: A research agenda. *Corporate Governance: The International Journal of Business in Society*, *12*(1), 89–100.

De Jonge, A. (2014, November). The glass ceiling that refuses to break: Women directors on the boards of listed firms in China and India. In *Women's studies international forum* (Vol. 47, pp. 326–338). Pergamon.

Dossani, R. (2012). Private equity and corporate governance in India. *Journal of Asia Business Studies*, *6*(2), 223–238.

Dwivedi, N., & Jain, A. K. (2005). Corporate governance and performance of Indian firms: The effect of board size and ownership. *Employee Responsibilities and Rights Journal*, *17*(3), 161–172.

Estrin, S., & Prevezer, M. (2011). The role of informal institutions in corporate governance: Brazil, Russia, India, and China compared. *Asia Pacific Journal of Management*, *28*(1), 41–67.

Gill, S. (2013). Rethinking the primacy of board efficacy for governance: Evidence from India. *Corporate Governance: The International Journal of Business in Society*, *13*(1), 99–129.

Goel, K., & McIver, R. (2017). India's corporate governance reforms and listed corporations' capital structures. *Delhi Business Review*, *16*(2), 7–18.

Goel, P. (2018). Implications of corporate governance on financial performance: An analytical review of governance and social reporting reforms in India. *Asian Journal of Sustainability and Social Responsibility*, *3*(1), 1–21.

Gollakota, K., & Gupta, V. (2006). History, ownership forms and corporate governance in India. *Journal of Management History*, *12*(2), 185–198.

Gopinath, S. (2008). Corporate governance in the Indian banking industry. *International Journal of Disclosure and Governance*, *5*(3), 186–204.

Guha, S. K., Samanta, N., Majumdar, A., Singh, M., & Bharadwaj, A. (2019). Evolution of corporate governance in India and its impact on the growth of the financial market: An empirical analysis (1995-2014). *Corporate Governance: The International Journal of Business in Society*, *19*(5), 945–984.

Gulati, R., Kattumuri, R., & Kumar, S. (2020). A non-parametric index of corporate governance in the banking industry: An application to Indian data. *Socio-Economic Planning Sciences*, *70*, 100702.

Gupta, P., & Sharma, A. M. (2014). A study of the impact of corporate governance practices on firm performance in Indian and South Korean companies. *Procedia-Social and Behavioral Sciences*, *133*, 4–11.

Gupta, P. K., & Shallu, S. (2014). Evolving legal framework of corporate governance in India – Issues and challenges. *Juridical Tribune*, *4*, 239.

Gupta, P. K., & Singh, S. (2018). Corporate governance structures in transition economies–issues and concerns for India. *Acta Universitatis Agriculturae et Silviculturae Mendelianae Brunensis*, *66*(6), 1459–1467.

Haldar, A., & Raithatha, M. (2017). Do compositions of board and audit committee improve financial disclosures? *International Journal of Organizational Analysis*, *25*(2), 251–269.

Haldar, A., Rao, S. V. D., & Momaya, K. S. (2016). Can flexibility in corporate governance enhance international competitiveness? Evidence from knowledge-based industries in India. *Global Journal of Flexible Systems Management*, *17*(4), 389–402.

Haldar, A., Shah, R., Rao, S. N., Stokes, P., Demirbas, D., & Dardour, A. (2018). Corporate performance: Does board independence matter? Indian evidence. *International Journal of Organizational Analysis*, *26*, 185–200.

Helmers, C., Patnam, M., & Rau, P. R. (2017). Do board interlocks increase innovation? Evidence from a corporate governance reform in India. *Journal of Banking & Finance*, *80*, 51–70.

Hundal, S. (2016). Busyness of audit committee directors and quality of financial information in India. *International Journal of Business Governance and Ethics*, *11*(4), 335.

Islam, A. U. (2016). Corporate governance performance of publicly listed companies in India: A cross-sectional industry analysis of BSE 200. *International Journal of Corporate Governance*, *7*(4), 306–324.

Jackling, B., & Johl, S. (2009). Board structure and firm performance: Evidence from India's top companies. *Corporate Governance: An International Review*, *17*(4), 492–509.

Jaiswall, S. S. K., & Bhattacharyya, A. K. (2016). Corporate governance and CEO compensation in Indian firms. *Journal of Contemporary Accounting & Economics*, *12*(2), 159–175.

Jaiswall, M., & Firth, M. (2009). CEO pay, firm performance, and corporate governance in India's listed firms. *International Journal of Corporate Governance*, *1*(3), 227–240.

Jameson, M., Prevost, A., & Puthenpurackal, J. (2014). Controlling shareholders, board structure, and firm performance: Evidence from India. *Journal of Corporate Finance*, *27*, 1–20.

Kagzi, M., & Guha, M. (2018). Does board demographic diversity influence firm performance? Evidence from Indian-knowledge intensive firms. *Benchmarking: An International Journal*, *25*(3), 1028–1058.

Kamath, B. (2019). Impact of corporate governance characteristics on intellectual capital performance of firms in India. *International Journal of Disclosure and Governance*, *16*(1), 20–36.

Kandukuri, R. L., Memdani, L., & Babu, P. R. (2015). Effect of corporate governance on firm performance–a study of selected Indian listed companies. In *Overlaps of private sector with public sector around the globe* (Vol. 31, pp. 47–64). Emerald Group Publishing Limited.

Kang, L. S., & Nanda, P. (2017). How is managerial remuneration determined in India?*Journal of Accounting in Emerging Economies*, *7*(2), 154–172.

Kang, L. S., & Nanda, P. (2018). What determines the disclosure of managerial remuneration in India?*Journal of Financial Reporting and Accounting*, *16*(1), 2–23.

Kansil, R., & Singh, A. (2018). Institutional ownership and firm performance: evidence from Indian panel data. *International Journal of Business and Emerging Markets*, *10*(3), 250–269.

Kapoor, N., & Goel, S. (2019). Do diligent independent directors restrain earnings management practices? Indian lessons for the global world. *Asian Journal of Accounting Research*, *4*(1), 52–69.

Katarachia, A., Pitoska, E., Giannarakis, G., & Poutoglidou, E. (2018). The drivers of corporate governance disclosure: The case of Nifty 500 index. *International Journal of Law and Management*, *60*(3), 681–700.

Kaur, G. (2017). The influence of board characteristics on corporate illegality. *Journal of Financial Regulation and Compliance*, *25*(2), 133–148.

Kaur, A., & Singh, B. (2018). Corporate reputation: Do board characteristics matter? Indian evidence. *Indian Journal of Corporate Governance*, *11*(2), 122–134.

Kavitha, D., & Nandagopal, R. (2013). Changing perspectives of corporate governance in India. *International Journal of Indian Culture and Business Management*, *7*(1), 72–89.

Kavitha, D., & Nandagopal, R. (2019). Impact of the busyness and board independence on the discretionary disclosures of Indian firms. *International Journal of Law and Management*, *61*(2), 250–266.

Khanna, T., & Palepu, K. G. (2004). Globalization and convergence in corporate governance: Evidence from Infosys and the Indian software industry. *Journal of International Business Studies*, *35*(6), 484–507.

Kimber, D., Lipton, P., & O'Neill, G. (2005). Corporate governance in the Asia Pacific region: A selective review of developments in Australia, China, India and Singapore. *Asia Pacific Journal of Human Resources*, *43*(2), 180–197.

Kiranmai, J., & Mishra, R. K. (2019). Corporate governance practices in listed state-owned enterprises in India: An empirical research. *Indian Journal of Corporate Governance*, *12*(1), 94–121.

Kohli, N., & Saha, G. C. (2008). Corporate governance and valuations: Evidence from selected Indian companies. *International Journal of Disclosure and Governance*, *5*(3), 236–251.

Kota, H. B., & Tomar, S. (2010). Corporate governance practices in Indian firms. *Journal of Management & Organization*, *16*(2), 266–279.

Kumar, N., & Singh, J. P. (2013). Effect of board size and promoter ownership on firm value: Some empirical findings from India. *Corporate Governance*, *13*(1), 88–98.

Kumari, P., & Pattanayak, J. K. (2017). Linking earnings management practices and corporate governance system with the firms' financial performance: A study of Indian commercial banks. *Journal of Financial Crime*, *24*(2), 223–241.

Lakhani, A. (2012). Cross-cultural implications on the legal requirements for corporate governance in China and India. *International Journal of Private Law*, *5*(2), 136–156.

Lakshman, C., & Akhter, M. (2013). Corporate governance scandals in the Indian Premier League (IPL): Implications for labour. *Labour & Industry: A Journal of the Social and Economic Relations of Work*, *23*(1), 89–106.

Machold, S., & Vasudevan, A. K. (2004). Corporate governance models in emerging markets: The case of India. *International Journal of Business Governance and Ethics*, *1*(1), 56–77.

Marques, T. A., De Sousa Ribeiro, K. C., & Barboza, F. (2018, October). Corporate governance and debt securities issued in Brazil and India: A multi-case study. *Research in International Business and Finance*, *45*, 257–270.

Masud, M., Kaium, A., Nurunnabi, M., & Bae, S. M. (2018). The effects of corporate governance on environmental sustainability reporting: Empirical evidence from South Asian countries. *Asian Journal of Sustainability and Social Responsibility*, 3(1), 1–26.

Mayur, M., & Saravanan, P. (2017). Performance implications of board size, composition and activity: Empirical evidence from the Indian banking sector. *Corporate Governance: The International Journal of business in Society*, 17(3), 466–489.

Mishra, M. (2016). Audit committee characteristics and earnings management: Evidence from India. *International Journal of Accounting and Financial Reporting*, 6(2), 247–273.

Mishra, R., & Kapil, S. (2017). Effect of ownership structure and board structure on firm value: evidence from India. *Corporate Governance: The International Journal of Business in Society*, 17(4), 700–726.

Mishra, R. K., & Kapil, S. (2018a). Effect of board characteristics on firm value: evidence from India. *South Asian Journal of Business Studies*, 7(1), 41–72.

Mishra, R. K., & Kapil, S. (2018b). Board characteristics and firm value for Indian companies. *Journal of Indian Business Research*, 10(1), 2–32.

Mishra, S., & Mohanty, P. (2014). Corporate governance as a value driver for firm performance: Evidence from India. *Corporate Governance*, 14(2), 256–280.

Mishra, S., & Mohanty, P. (2018). Does good governance lead to better financial performance? *International Journal of Corporate Governance*, 9(4), 462–480.

Mohapatra, P. (2016). Board independence and firm performance in India. *International Journal of Management Practice*, 9(3), 317–332.

Muniapan, B., & Shaikh, J. M. (2007). Lessons in corporate governance from Kautilya's Arthashastra in ancient India. *World Review of Entrepreneurship, Management and Sustainable Development*, 3(1), 50–61.

Muttakin, M. B., & Subramaniam, N. (2015). Firm ownership and board characteristics: Do they matter for corporate social responsibility disclosure of Indian companies? *Sustainability Accounting, Management and Policy Journal*, 6(2), 138–165.

Nagar, N., & Raithatha, M. (2016, September 14). Does good corporate governance constrain cash flow manipulation? Evidence from India. *Managerial Finance*, 42(11), 1034–1053.

Narayanaswamy, R., Raghunandan, K., & Rama, D. V. (2015). Satyam failure and changes in Indian audit committees. *Journal of Accounting, Auditing & Finance*, 30(4), 529–540.

Palaniappan, G. (2017). Determinants of corporate financial performance relating to board characteristics of corporate governance in Indian manufacturing industry: An empirical study. *European Journal of Management and Business Economics*, 26(1), 67–85.

Patibandla, M. (2006). Equity pattern, corporate governance, and performance: A study of India's corporate sector. *Journal of Economic Behavior & Organization*, 59(1), 29–44.

Patra, K. K. (2013). Opportunities and challenges of corporate governance reforms in India: A study on Infosys Technologies. *International Journal of Indian Culture and Business Management*, 7(3), 430–440.

Prasad, K., Sankaran, K., & Prabhu, N. (2019). Relationship between gray directors and executive compensation in Indian firms. *European Journal of Management and Business Economics*, 28(3), 239–265.

Prasad, P., Sivasankaran, N., Saravanan, P., & Kannadhasan, M. (2019). Does corporate governance influence the working capital management of firms: Evidence from India. *International Journal of Corporate Governance*, 10(1), 42–80.

Prasanna, P. K. (2011, April 28 and 29). Corporate governance and stock market liquidity in India. In *Finance and corporate governance conference*, Melbourne, Australia.

Prasanna, P. K. (2014). Firm-level governance quality and dividend decisions: Evidence from India. *International Journal of Corporate Governance*, 5(3/4), 197–222.

Prasanna, P. K., & Menon, A. S. (2012). Corporate governance and stock market liquidity in India. *International Journal of Behavioural Accounting and Finance*, 3(1-2), 24–45.

Puri, V., & Kumar, M. (2018). Factors influencing adoption and disclosure of voluntary corporate governance practices by the Indian listed firms. *International Journal of Corporate Governance*, 9(1), 91–126.

Qurashi, M. H. (2018). Corporate governance code comparison for South Asian emerging economies. *International Journal of Law and Management*, *60*(2), 250–266.

Rajagopalan, N., & Zhang, Y. (2008). Corporate governance reforms in China and India: Challenges and opportunities. *Business Horizons*, *51*(1), 55–64.

Ravi, S. P. (2012). Strategic change management: Corporate governance failures in India and USA – A tale of two countries. *International Journal of Strategic Change Management*, *4*(3–4), 281–304.

Reed, A. M. (2002). Corporate governance reforms in India. *Journal of Business Ethics*, *37*(3), 249–268.

Saggar, R., & Singh, B. (2017). Corporate governance and risk reporting: Indian evidence. *Managerial Auditing Journal*, *32*, 378–405.

Sale, H. (2004) Delaware's good faith. *Cornell Law Review*, *89*, 456–460.

Sanan, N. K. (2016). Board gender diversity and firm performance: Evidence from India. *Asian Journal of Business Ethics*, *5*(1), 1–18.

Saravanan, P., Sivasankaran, N., Srikanth, M. A. R. A. M., & Shaw, T. S. (2017). Enhancing shareholder value through efficient working capital management: An empirical evidence from India. *Finance India*, *31*(3), 851–871.

Saravanan, P., Srikanth, M., & Avabruth, S. M. (2016). Executive compensation, corporate governance, and firm performance: Evidence from India. *International Journal of Corporate Governance*, *7*(4), 377–403.

Saravanan, P., Srikanth, M., & Avabruth, S. M. (2017). Compensation of top brass, corporate governance, and performance of the Indian family firms – An empirical study. *Social Responsibility Journal*, *13*(3), 529–551.

Sarkar, J., & Sarkar, S. (2000). Large shareholder activism in corporate governance in developing countries: Evidence from India. *International Review of Finance*, *1*(3), 161–194.

Sarkar, J., & Sarkar, S. (2009). Multiple board appointments and firm performance in emerging economies: Evidence from India. *Pacific-Basin Finance Journal*, *17*(2), 271–293.

Sarkar, J., Sarkar, S., & Sen, K. (2012, August). A corporate governance index for large listed companies in India. *Pace University Accounting Research Paper*. https://dx.doi.org/10.2139/ssrn.2055091

Sehgal, A., & Mulraj, J. (2008). Corporate governance in India: Moving gradually from a regulatory model to a market-driven model – A survey. *International Journal of Disclosure and Governance*, *5*(3), 205–235.

Shahid, M. (2019, September–October). Does corporate governance play any role in investor confidence, corporate investment decisions relationship? Evidence from Pakistan and India. *Journal of Economics and Business*, *105*, 1–11.

Shaw, T. S., Cordeiro, J. J., & Saravanan, P. (2016). Director network resources and firm performance: Evidence from Indian corporate governance reforms. *Asian Business & Management*, *15*(3), 165–200.

Shikha, N. (2017). Corporate governance in India – The paradigm shift. *International Journal of Corporate Governance*, *8*(2), 81–105.

Shikha, N., & Mishra, R. (2019). Corporate governance in India-battle of stakes. *International Journal of Corporate Governance*, *10*(1), 20–41.

Sidhu, M. K., & Kaur, P. (2019). Effect of corporate governance on stock market liquidity: Empirical evidence from Indian companies. *Decision*, *46*(3), 197–218.

Singh, A., & Kansil, R. (2017). Impact of foreign shareholdings on corporate governance score: Evidence from Bombay Stock Exchange, India. *International Journal of Business and Globalisation*, *19*(1), 93–110.

Singh, J. P., Kumar, N., & Uzma, S. H. (2011). The changing landscape of corporate governance framework in India. *International Journal of Indian Culture and Business Management*, *4*(5), 506–522.

Singla, M., & Singh, S. (2018). Impact of institutional set-up on the responsiveness to change in a firm's governance structure: A comparative study of public and private sector enterprises in India. *Global Journal of Flexible Systems Management*, *19*(2), 159–172.

Singla, M., & Singh, S. (2019). Board monitoring, product market competition and firm performance. *International Journal of Organizational Analysis*, *27*, 1036–1052.

Srivastava, V., Das, N., & Pattanayak, J. K. (2018a). Corporate governance: Mapping the change. *International Journal of Law and Management*, *60*(1), 19–33.

Srivastava, V., Das, N., & Pattanayak, J. K. (2018b). Women on boards in India: A need or tokenism? *Management Decision*, *56*(8), 1769–1786.

Srivastava, V., Das, N., & Pattanayak, J. K. (2019). Impact of corporate governance attributes on cost of equity: Evidence from an emerging economy. *Managerial Auditing Journal, 34*(2), 142–161.

Subramanian, S. (2017). Proxy advisory voting recommendations in India – An exploratory study. *Journal of Indian Business Research, 9*(4), 283–303.

Subramanian, S., & Reddy, V. N. (2012). Corporate governance disclosures and international competitiveness: A study of Indian firms. *Asian Business & Management, 11*(2), 195–218.

Tranfield, D., Denyer, D., & Smart, P. (2003). Towards a methodology for developing evidence-informed management knowledge by means of systematic review. *British Journal of Management, 14*(3), 207–222.

Uzma, S. H. (2018). Corporate governance practices: Global convergence and Indian perspective. *Qualitative Research in Financial Markets, 10*(3), 285–308.

Vig, S., & Datta, M. (2018). Corporate governance and value creation: A study of selected Indian companies. *International Journal of Indian Culture and Business Management, 17*(3), 259–282.

Wells, H. (2010). The birth of corporate governance.*Seattle University Law Review, 33*(4), 1247–1292.

Yameen, M., Farhan, N. H., & Tabash, M. I. (2019). The impact of corporate governance practices on firm's performance: An empirical evidence from Indian tourism sector. *Journal of International Studies, 12*(1), 208–228.

CHAPTER 11

ENHANCING SUSTAINABILITY THROUGH A QUALITY-CENTRIC APPROACH

Baljinder Kaur, Adarsh Rajput and Ayushi Garg

Chitkara Business School, Chitkara University, Rajpura, Punjab, India

ABSTRACT

Purpose: *The assessment of the linkage between quality and several SDGs is crucial due to the significant impact quality has on multiple dimensions. This study employs a comprehensive methodology to elucidate the various dimensions of quality. Additionally, it examines the relationship between quality and multiple SDGs, a topic that has not been previously investigated.*

Design/Methodology/Approach: *The question arises here that how maintaining quality leads to sustainability; well this question is answered in this study through a content analysis of previous studies and showing the importance of theme quality in various aspects of sustainability like TBL, sustainable development goals (SDGs), etc.*

Findings: *Quality has proven to be an admirable approach towards sustainability. The risen need for sustainability has brought many perspectives of the world. It can be environmental, social and economic and further these aspects have their own areas for improvement. The complexity of the structure of sustainability requires a basic common area to be focused on, and in this study, quality has proven to be one.*

Sustainable Development Goals: The Impact of Sustainability Measures on Wellbeing
Contemporary Studies in Economic and Financial Analysis, Volume 113B, 167–187
Copyright © 2024 by Baljinder Kaur, Adarsh Rajput and Ayushi Garg
Published under exclusive licence by Emerald Publishing Limited
ISSN: 1569-3759/doi:10.1108/S1569-37592024000113B011

Implications: *Through the SDGs it can be derived that each goal had an area where quality needed to be worked on. The several zones of quality are interlinked. Quality of life will automatically improve the education, health water and sanitation services. Therefore, the focus should be laid on attaining sustainability through quality. Quality is achieving excellence in something or a substance that satisfies the requirements needed from it or the resources are utilised effectively and efficiently.*

Originality/Value: *This study uses a holistic approach in which dimensions of quality have been explained and further the linkage of quality with different SDGs was assessed which has not yet been explored earlier.*

Keywords: Quality management; sustainable development; approach; TBL; sustainable development goals; industry

JEL Codes: F01; O11; Q01; Q20; P18

1. INTRODUCTION

The concept of 'sustainable development' gained significant recognition and is presently employed across various domains. In scholarly papers, conferences and the campaign slogans of environmental and development activists today, sustainable development is a recurrent topic. The sustainable development concept has a long history in our society and receives the kind of board-based attention that other development concepts lack (Scopelliti et al., 2018; Shepherd et al., 2016). In 1992's United Nations Earth Summit in Rio de Janeiro, the concept of SD was established and considered one of the most urgent subjects for international policy. The United Nations Framework 21, which was endorsed by 150 participating countries, encompasses a policy framework for sustainable development that prioritises the fulfilment of basic needs in impoverished nations. The concept of development was initially presented by the United States in 1976 through the Bariloche Model. Subsequently, in 1987, the Brundtland Commission put forth a proposition stating that 'sustainable development entails meeting the current needs while safeguarding the needs of future generations'. This proposal further propelled the notion of development.

The concept of quality is rather an approach to sustainability. The word quality in general means 'standard' or a degree of excellence in something; but how achieving excellence in something will lead to sustainability? In this research, this question will be answered by studying in depth the concept of quality and its contribution in areas like the three concerns: environment, economy and society (TBL) and in achieving the sustainable development goals (SDGs). The aspect of quality in sustainability is not considered a pre-eminent subject though it contributes a lot to maintaining sustainability. This chapter will discuss all the possible ways that how impeccably quality has led towards sustainability. The current study concentrates on talking about the idea of sustainability, quality and dimensions of quality and then linking quality with several SDGs.

1.1. Development

The concept of growth is multifaceted, encompassing several theories, interpretations and meanings. Development can be characterised as 'a progressive process in which the abilities of individuals expand in terms of their ability to create new systems, address challenges, adapt to continuous transformations, and actively and creatively pursue novel objectives' (Peet, 1999). According to Reyes (2001), a nation is considered to be in a state of development when it endeavours to fulfil the requirements of its population by employing rational and sustainable practises in the utilisation of its natural resources and systems. Development is often characterised as a complex process encompassing not only economic progress but also the modification of social structure, attitudes and institutions as well as the elimination of extreme poverty and the mitigation of inequality. Various theories, including modernisation, dependence, world systems and globalisation theories, are employed to conceptualise the notion of development (Todaro & Smith, 2006). According to Liebert et al. (1979) development is defined as 'the process of change in growth and capability over the period of time, as a function of maturation and interaction with the environment'.

1.2. Sustainability

As stated by Basiaga (1999), the concept of sustainability pertains to the capacity to maintain the longevity of an object, outcome or process. The concept of sustainability encompasses the effective and fair distribution of resources across multiple generations, while simultaneously engaging in socioeconomic activities, with the aim of preserving a limited ecosystem (Stoddart, 2011). Ben-Eli (2015) proposes that sustainability may be understood as a dynamic equilibrium wherein the population's interactions with the ecosystem's carrying capacity are carefully balanced with the extent to which the environment can be utilised by individuals without causing any adverse effects. The concept of sustainability pertains to the actions undertaken by individuals and their capacity to fulfil their needs and desires while minimising any negative impact on the available resources for production (Thomas, 2015). Given the inherent challenges in anticipating the needs and demands of future generations, it becomes imperative to consider the notion of cross-generational fairness when defining sustainability (Mensah & Enu-Kwesi, 2018). Contemporary sustainability theories strive to incorporate and give precedence to social, environmental and economic frameworks with the objective of effectively addressing human interests in a manner that is beneficial to the human population (Hussain et al., 2014; UNSD, 2018). The concept of sustainability was officially defined by the United Nations Brundtland Commission in 1987 as the act of satisfying the requirements of the current generation while ensuring that the capacity of future generations to fulfil their own needs remains intact.

1.3. Sustainable Development

The concept of 'sustainable development' is commonly employed in the discourse around development, and it has garnered several definitions, interpretations and connotations. Sustainable development, as commonly understood, refers to the process of achieving development that can be sustained eternally or for a specified duration (Dernbach, 1998, 2003; Lele, 1991; Stoddard, 2011). This idea can be summed up with a sentence that combines the words 'sustainable' and 'development'. The fact that SD has been characterised in so many different ways and that people interpret it in so many different ways has resulted in so many diverse definitions of SD. The Brundtland Commission Report, authored by Schaefer and Crane, presents a word that is widely employed with high frequency. This chapter elucidates the concept of sustainable development (SD) as a strategic approach to address current societal needs while ensuring the preservation of resources and opportunities for future generations.

Due to the accelerated population expansion and the decreasing availability of resources to meet human requirements, it has been noted that the significance of Sustainable Development grows with each new day. According to Hák et al. (2016), sustainable development contributes to preserving the harmony between social well-being, environmental integrity and economic growth. The concepts of sustainability and sustainable development are often treated as the same and are also considered synonyms by many but these are two distinguishable concepts. Sustainability is the main objective or end point of the process called sustainable development (Diesendorf, 2000). This was reinforced by arguing that while 'sustainability' refers to a state whereas SD refers to the process of attaining this state (Gray, 2010).

> 'Sustainable development is development that meets the needs of the present without compromising the needs of future generations to meet their own needs'.
>
> – Brundtland (1987)

> 'Sustainable development involves designing a social and economic system that ensures that these goals – real income growth, higher educational standards, improved national health, and improved overall quality of life – are sustained'.
>
> – Pearce et al. (1989)

The concept consists of two primary concepts: the first pertains to the notion of necessities, particularly the fundamental necessities of the impoverished populace, which should be accorded with utmost importance. The second concept relates to the environmental constraints imposed by the existing state of technology and social structure, which hinder its ability to fulfil the requirements of both present and future generations.

1.4. Evolution of Sustainable Development Goals

1972 – The first UN Conference on the Environment took place in Stockholm in 1972 as awareness of global politics grew. The inaugural assembly of global leaders convened by the United Nations aimed to address the emerging concern of 'human impact on the environment and its interconnection with economic development'. The primary aim of the conference was to ascertain common values and viewpoints that may effectively influence and guide the worldwide population in safeguarding the 'Human Environment'.

1987 – The Brundtland Report from 1987 provided the first formal definition of sustainable development by the United Nations through Oxford University Press.

> The phrase 'meeting the needs of the present without compromising the ability of future generations to meet their own needs' is used here.
>
> – Brundtland, Gro Harlem

Following this, the idea of sustainable development started to catch on. The Brundtland Report shed light on the necessity of combining social justice and inclusiveness, environmental preservation and economic development.

1992 – The United Nations Conference on Environment and Development was held in Rio de Janeiro, Brazil in 1992. This initiative was the inaugural global endeavour to formulate strategies and programmes aimed at steering development towards a more sustainable trajectory. The fundamental objective of the International Earth Summit was to effectively tackle urgent concerns pertaining to environmental preservation and social advancement.

1994 – The concept of Triple Bottom Line was introduced by John Elkington, the founder of a sustainability consultant firm, in the year 1994. In his statement, he emphasised the need for organisations not solely prioritising profit and loss accounts. He argued that all organisations should adhere to specific guidelines that take into account the three distinct bottom lines: society, economy and environment. Hence Triple Bottom Line is seen as an important premise which is the component of the foundation of sustainable development.

1997 – In order to mitigate the release of greenhouse gases, member nations of the United Nations entered into an agreement known as the Kyoto Protocol in the year 1997. The operationalisation of the United Nations Framework Convention on Climate Change necessitates the implementation of the Kyoto Protocol, which imposes a requirement on industrialised nations to reduce their greenhouse gas emissions to levels that are lower than those recorded in 1990. This worldwide endeavour was a pioneering effort in addressing the issue of climate change. The Kyoto Protocol was ratified by over 150 states in 1997.

2015 – In 2015, the 2030 Agenda for Sustainable Development was unanimously accepted by the 193 member nations of the United Nations (UN). The historical agenda delineates a set of 17 SDGs and corresponding targets aimed at promoting the well-being and advancement of both the planet and humanity. These objectives encompass various aspects, including the preservation of human dignity, the establishment of peace and the fostering of wealth. It is imperative that all of these goals are successfully attained within the timeframe of 2030. The proposed plan outlines many initiatives across multiple sectors, encompassing sanitation, poverty alleviation and economic development, with a focus on addressing the social needs and aspirations of the local population (National Geographic, 2022). The achievements of the millennium development goals

(MDGs), as established by the United Nations, laid the groundwork for the subsequent formulation of the SDGs.

2016 – The SDGs of the 2030 Agenda for Sustainable Development were officially ratified by global leaders during a momentous United Nations Summit in September 2015 and were implemented on 1 January 2016.

2019 – In order to achieve all 17 SDGs, this report focuses on a few key areas, including finance, flexibility, a sustainable and inclusive economy, more effective institutions, local activity, better data use and the application of science, technology and innovation with a stronger emphasis on digital transformation.

2022 – The World Summit on Sustainable Development is an annual event organised by the Energy and Natural Resources Institute (TERI). This year, the summit is being held virtually and centres around the overarching subject of 'Towards a Sustainable Planet: Ensuring a Sustainable and Just Future'.

2. METHODOLOGY

The primary goal of this study is to conduct a content analysis of existing literature. The data was obtained from secondary published sources. Various academic databases and search engines, such as EBSCO, Google Scholar, Proquest and K-Hub, as well as government publications and conference proceedings, were utilised to gather relevant studies for this research.

3. OBJECTIVE OF THE STUDY

Previous studies have indicated that the notion of sustainable development is rather nascent, with limited research undertaken thus far. Only a limited number of areas within the field of sustainable development have been previously investigated. The assessment of the linkage between quality and several SDGs is crucial due to the significant impact quality has on multiple dimensions. This study employs a comprehensive methodology to elucidate the various dimensions of quality. Additionally, it examines the relationship between quality and multiple SDGs, a topic that has not been previously investigated.

4. QUALITY

The study considers quality management (QM) as a wider concept that can be divided into numerous regions like quality of life, quality in product development, quality in health, educational sector, agricultural sector, infrastructure and the relationships among the organisation. Betterment in each area leads towards sustainable development. According to conceptual analysis, many assumptions regarding quality have been proposed by the managers, the first suggests 'quality means goodness' (Crosby, 1979). It was argued by Crosby that goodness cannot be measured but quality can be, as it is defined as 'conformance to requirements' (according to the requirements). However, Crosby here mingled two different concepts, that is, the meaning of quality with how to measure it; this mistake is made by several social and behavioural scientists (Greenwood, 1991). The approach that reflects the meaning of quality but not measurement efforts is known as 'transcendent approach' by Garvin (1984). To conclude this approach the following definition was presented: 'Quality is the goodness or excellence of something. It is assessed against accepted standards of merit for such things and against the interests/needs of users and other stakeholders'.

Conformance to specifications: The conventional definition of quality, which has drawn a lot of criticism, is 'conformance to specifications'. The manufacturing-based approach to quality product development relies on specifications and criteria as the standard for evaluating production performance and output (Gawin, 1984). A product is considered of high quality when it meets these benchmarks.

Fitness for use: The incorporation of user needs is a fundamental aspect of the prevalent concept of quality. The acquisition of quality in modern market economies is attributed to the assessment of consumer ratings for the goods being offered (Gamin, 1984). The concept of quality is elevated to a central position when considering the importance of consumers' purchasing decisions and the substantial influence that product quality has on those decisions. The utilisation of this concept in works of art is seen as less appropriate due to the absence of active engagement by its users.

4.1. Total Quality Management

Total quality is a strategic approach to conducting business operations, with the objective of enhancing the overall performance of an organisation's processes, individuals, surroundings and offerings, hence augmenting its competitiveness. Total quality management (TQM) comprises a set of 11 essential elements, as outlined by Goetsch and Davis (2016). These components encompass a strategic underpinning, a customer-centric approach, an unwavering dedication to quality, a scientific methodology, a sustained commitment over the long-term, collaborative teamwork, the ongoing enhancement of processes, investment in education and training, the establishment of freedom through control, the alignment of objectives, active employee participation and the empowerment of individuals. According to Benavides-Velasco et al. (2014), TQM is widely recognised and has sustained its popularity as a management principle. QM refers to a comprehensive framework comprising several principles and methodologies. Contemporary manufacturing organisations are recognising the necessity of adopting a comprehensive approach to gain a competitive edge in the market. It is becoming evident that making isolated modifications in specific business areas is no longer satisfactory. The implementation of comprehensive QM is necessary to address several aspects such as supplier and customer interactions, service and procedure development and customer delivery (Shan et al., 2013).

4.2. Dimensions of Quality

4.2.1. Quality of Life (QoL)

The prominence of quality of life (QoL) in local, national and European Union agendas has been extensively documented in various studies conducted over the past few decades (SELMA, 2004). This theory has a significant influence on various sectors, such as urban and regional planning, health promotion, disability studies, social indicators research and economic and mental health research, shaping the social and political trends observed in these fields. The implementation of a robust quality-of-life system facilitates comprehension of social and economic trends. The assessment of liveability, environmental quality, quality of life and sustainability serves as a foundation for making informed decisions on the enhancement of national, regional and local resources. The establishment, preservation and active promotion of sustainability can be facilitated by the use of quality-of-life research and the implementation of evidence-based policy. According to the United Nations Agenda 21 Report published in 1993, there is a recognised need for further study to substantiate the implementation of sustainable management practices. The report emphasises the imperative for nations to actively cultivate, adopt and effectively implement the requisite methodologies and strategies for achieving sustainable development.

4.2.2. Quality in Education

In addition to imparting students with the requisite knowledge and skills pertinent to their chosen professional domain, a high-quality education encompasses the essential task of equipping them with the capacity for continuous learning throughout their lives. The primary objective of education should be to provide students with the essential abilities to engage in critical thinking and take action for the betterment of mankind and society beyond the confines of the educational setting. When evaluating the efficacy of centre-based early childhood care and education (ECCE) services, both the structural and procedural elements have traditionally been considered. Structural quality encompasses various factors that contribute to the overall effectiveness of an educational setting. These factors include the academic and professional qualities possessed by instructors, the ratio of adults to children, the size of classes and the physical environment in which learning takes place. The significance of process quality in educational endeavours and the dynamics between educators and learners cannot be overstated. A prerequisite for achieving high process quality is the presence of good structural quality, which encompasses factors such as teacher qualifications and favourable teacher-to-child ratios. As to the Indian Quality Standards for Early Childhood Care and Education (Government of India, 2013), the physical environment, personnel qualifications and caregiver-to-child ratio are seen as essential indicators of quality in the field of ECCE.

4.2.3. Quality in Health Care

The market for medical equipment plays a crucial role in ensuring quality assurance for the effective diagnosis and treatment of patients. In order to arrive at optimal medical decisions, it is imperative to employ measurements that are both precise and accurate. Insufficient calibration of medical devices can lead to various issues such as malfunctions in medical equipment, erroneous diagnosis and potentially deadly errors. Continuous calibration of biomedical equipment is necessary to ensure the implementation of a National Quality Health Infrastructure in the Health Sector as well as to ensure the provision of accurate and precise measurements that can be linked back to national standards. The calibration services provided by the Indian National Metrological Institute, also known as CSIR-NPL, enable the traceability of medical equipment to national standards, hence enhancing quality control in this context.

4.2.4. Air Quality and Smart Cities
In order to improve the health and well-being of its residents, sustainable smart cities must embrace air quality monitoring as a crucial component. The data on air quality is important for creating significant datasets that include spatiotemporal data to aid city managers in making decisions about effective interventions for enhanced living environments as well as for the proper management of a sustainable city.

4.2.5. Agriculture Quality
Due to the increasing demand for food, encompassing both quantity and quality, there arises a heightened necessity for the industrialisation and intensification of the agricultural sector. The agriculture industry is currently being presented with a range of advanced solutions through the very promising Internet of things technology. Scientific organisations and research institutions are actively engaged in leveraging Internet technology to address diverse agricultural challenges and develop innovative products and services.

4.2.6. Water Quality
A variety of pollutants are putting the world' s water resources at greater risk, which is causing the water quality in rivers, lakes, aquifers and the oceans to decline. Water availability for diverse human applications and ecological functions is hampered by declining water quality.

4.2.7. Soil Quality
Maintaining soil quality is crucial to ensuring that future generations will be able to cultivate and feed themselves. Global agricultural resources are becoming more valuable as the world's population grows drastically and the demand for animals and their products rises (Delgado, 2003). Food cannot be grown to suit the needs of both animals and people without healthy soil. Therefore, it is crucial to concentrate on regional efforts to find and implement agricultural systems that can enhance livestock and provide people with sustainable food.

4.2.8. Infrastructure Quality

United Nations Industrial Development Organisation defines the quality infrastructure as

> the system comprising the organizations (public and private) together with the policies, relevant legal and regulatory framework, and practices needed to support and enhance the quality, safety and environmental soundness of goods, services and processes. The quality infrastructure is required for the effective operation of domestic markets, and its international recognition is important to enable access to foreign markets. It is a critical element in promoting and sustaining economic development, as well as environmental and social well-being. It relies on metrology, standardization, accreditation, conformity assessment, and market surveillance.

4.2.9. Product Quality

One of the main goals of the production process is to deliver high-quality items. Although the term 'good quality' is ambiguous, it can be interpreted as a product with few defects. Organisations want to increase output while maintaining a high standard of quality as demand rises. Increasing manufacturing operations could endanger the environment, though. The production companies are faced with two issues as a result of this situation: how to sustain production volume while achieving high quality with little environmental impact.

4.2.10. Relationship Quality

Understanding sport consumer-organisation relationships depends on relationship quality because it can

- give a platform for organising diverse relational constructs.
- offer insight into evaluating relationship-marketing efficacy.
- be used to organise wide-ranging relational conceptions.
- be crucial to understand sport consumer-organisation relationships.
- identify and address relationship issues.

4.3. Relationship Between Quality and Sustainability

Sustainability can be defined as the ability to persist and endure over a prolonged duration, whereas quality pertains to the capability of satisfying specified criteria or standards. The concept of sustainability pertains to the enduring well-being of an organisation over an extended period of time. The task involves understanding the strategies and mechanisms that will enable the business to sustain and thrive in the future.

5. TRIPLE BOTTOM LINE

The triple bottom line is a fundamental principle that underpins the concept of sustainable development. The initial utilisation of the concept was attributed to

John Elkington, who established a consultancy firm specialising in sustainability. In contrast to the prevalent emphasis on the income statement, which was prominent during that period and continues to be prevalent in numerous organisations, this proposition advocates for businesses to consider three prospective outcomes. Consequently, enterprises are required to evaluate the extent to which socially responsible practices are integrated into their value chain.

The triple bottom line is a fundamental principle that underpins the concept of sustainable development. The initial utilisation of the concept was attributed to John Elkington, who established a sustainability consultancy enterprise. In contrast to the prevailing emphasis on the income statement, which was widely favoured during that period and continues to be prevalent in numerous organisations, this proposition advocates for enterprises to consider three prospective outcomes. Consequently, enterprises are required to evaluate the extent to which socially responsible practices are integrated into their value chain.

5.1. Triple Bottom Line and Quality

Given the significant impact of quality of life on both economic and social welfare, issues pertaining to quality of life have emerged as prominent concerns on the political agenda. In alternative terms, individuals residing in industrialised nations are increasingly recognising that matters impacting human well-being extend beyond mere economic considerations, and that an individual's standard of living is not solely contingent upon their material wealth (Pacione, 1993). Dissert and Deller (2000) argue that objective measurements, commonly referred to as social indicators, are valuable tools for assessing the quality of life in various geographical contexts such as neighbourhoods, cities and rural areas. These measurements provide a comprehensive overview of an individual's well-being and encompass verifiable conditions that are associated with a specific cultural unit (Marans, 2003). Dissart and Deller (2000) propose that subjective quality of life pertains to the extent to which an individual's existence is perceived to align with internal standards, whether such standards are inferred or explicitly stated. One of the most debated aspects of the quality of life approach pertains to the utilisation of subjective indicators. Although physical, social and economic aspects exhibit interdependence, subjective quality of life pertains to the quality of life as indicated by an individual's psychological state of life satisfaction rather than objective situations and circumstances.

6. SUSTAINABLE DEVELOPMENT GOALS AND QUALITY

At the United Nations in New York, an open-ended working group established by the UN General Assembly proposed the global SDG, which include 17 goals and 169 targets. In addition, an initial set of 330 indicators was launched in March 2015 and was officially adopted by the UN's 193 member states on 25 September 2015. Under the heading 'transforming our world', the SDGs have outlined a broad and aspirational objective. To maintain the vertical consistency of policies and actions, the SDGs are anticipated to be monitored at the sub-national, national, regional and global levels. National governments are primarily responsible for monitoring the SDG indicators in terms of formal reporting (UN, 2017). One or more custodians are assigned to each SDG indicator, and they are in charge of (i) establishing the global methodology using the best available science, research and data knowledge and (ii) locating the data sources that can be used to support the SDG indicator.

6.1. Linkage of SDGs with Quality

6.1.1. Goal 1: No Poverty

Since the 1970s, bringing down the poverty has been a front-line topic in international debates. The United Nations' 193 member states adopted the SDGs in 2015. The first SDG, called No Poverty, aspires to 'end poverty in all its forms and everywhere' (UN, 2016). It was affirmed that 85% of the poor population belongs to rural areas (Alkire et al., 2014). The role of quality in achieving this goal stands in the area of improving quality of life. Quality of life has a wider scope and it covers various aspects like health, education and economy (employment opportunities), improving the standard of living or lifting up the agricultural sector, etc., in the context of eradicating the poverty concerns like education, agriculture, employment, standard of living. It is very important to focus on these areas of quality in order to achieve this goal.

Focusing on the educational sector: Education helps a person to develop skills learn new things and hence get opportunities for earning; therefore, it is a key tool to reduce poverty. According to Tsujita, a researcher at the Institute of Developing Economies, 'there may be a chance of escaping poverty through education'. The Indian government appears to have agreed with the aforementioned assertion and has taken action to support it. To this end, a project called Sarva Shiksha Abhyan was begun in 2002 with the goal of enrolling all 6–14-year-old children in basic education by the year 2010.

Focusing on agricultural sector: The major rural sector of India is dependent on the primary sector, that is, agriculture for their income. Therefore, it is necessary to lift this sector by adding quality by providing them with facilities or subsidies.

6.1.2. Goal 2: Zero Hunger

To achieve UN SDG 2, which calls for eradicating hunger by 2030, millions of people in the Global South must have access to basic food security. In the world, 135 million people experience acute food insecurity (FSIN, 2020), which affects about 2 billion people (FAO et al., 2019). African, Asian and Latin American countries make up the majority of nations experiencing food shortages (FAO et al., 2019). Since 2015, there have been more hungry individuals overall, particularly in South Asia and sub-Saharan Africa (FAO et al., 2017; WHO, 2018). Therefore, it will become increasingly challenging for many Global South nations to solve hunger by 2030.

For this quality to agricultural sector will help and also using the resources efficiently, that is, not wasting them. To serve the large number of population productivity has to be increased and also the crops grown should be able to meet the nutrient requirements of the people. For this high-quality products should be used for farming; the seeds, techniques and tools should be of premium quality and the use of harmful chemicals should be prohibited. The government should take initiatives by providing subsidies and lifting the agricultural sector for the fulfilment of this goal.

6.1.3. Goal 3: Good Health and Well-Being

The SDG 3 goal of good health and well-being places an emphasis on leading a healthy lifestyle and promoting well-being for all ages. It illustrates two key ideas:

1. Health is not only a fundamental human right but is also defined as an investment in national stability and sustainable development; and
2. Welfare is defined as a condition containing a variety of physical or psychological aspects that may be taken into account independently or together.

Physical well-being concentrates on general good health and fulfilment of body's fundamental needs. On the other hand, psychological well-being is an approach that involves personal evaluations and can be influenced by social or economic success, satisfaction and concord with oneself, other persons or the environment.

This goal can be attained by adding quality to the health sector. The health facility is something, which should be feasible, economical and of high quality, using new technology, advanced treatments and high-quality service. Further education should be emphasised. The education in the medical profession should be cost-effective and accurate. Also spiritual education should be made necessary for all students to keep mental health healthy.

6.1.4. Goal 4: Quality Education

The SDG 4 'Quality Education' targets providing fair education that includes everyone and ensures that there are chances for lifetime learning for everyone, which offers a new viewpoint on education for the next 15 years. The objective of this goal has been further subdivided into seven possible outcomes and three means. These are

(4.1)   quality in primary as well as secondary education;
(4.2)   taking care of the quality of pre-primary education;
(4.3)   proportionate admittance for higher education;
(4.4)   employability skills;
(4.5)   gender discrepancy and other vulnerable groups;
(4.6)   literacy and numeracy;
(4.7)   extensive education on sustainable development:
    (a)   comprehensive and safe education opportunities,
    (b)   scholarships for higher learning,
    (c)   qualification of teachers.

Education is a sector contributing to nearly all the sectors; it can be health, technology, development, etc. From the above context, the areas where quality can be included can be clearly sighted. Focusing on equitable, fair and inclusive education opportunities is necessary for the growth of the economy. Alongside considering qualifications of teachers and what is to be taught and in what manner it should be taught are great factors contributing to the quality of education.

6.1.5. Goal 5: Gender Equality

In alignment with SDG 5 pertaining to gender equality, the objective is to attain parity between genders and empower women and girls to thrive (UN 2015). Gender equality was included as one of the MDGs by the United Nations from 2000 to 2015. It has subsequently been included as SDG 5 in the 2030 Agenda (UN, 2015). SDG 5 aspires to empower women and girls around the world and achieve gender equality by eliminating gender inequities, discrimination and violence against women (UN, 2015). A case study of SDG 5 is particularly significant given that this year marks the 25th anniversary of the Beijing Declaration and Platform for Action, which stated that women's rights are human rights (UN Women, 1995). This can be achieved by quality education only as it gives a mindset to the person and develops ethics and responsibility towards the society.

6.1.6. Goal 6: Clean Water and Sanitation

Among the 17 SDGs, the sixth goal has a vision to 'warrant the availability and sustainable administration of water and sanitation for everyone'. The water is an essential resource required for development activities both in quantity as well as quality. The use and uses of water have seen a drift since the population is hiked and urbanisation is taking place. This has turned the water deficient and pollutant and this is affecting people, environment and economy. So, wastewater treatment should be taken into consideration for lifting water quality. The succession of this goal will be a great pleasure to humankind, socio-economic development and quality of life, counting health and environmental preservation.

Water and sanitation quality are an essential part to prevent many diseases. It is being observed that diarrhoeal disease has been a major cause for the deaths of 1.5 million people each year among which up to 3,60,000 were children under the age of five. This usually takes place in low-income developing countries (including India). Also, according to the data approx. 58% of diarrhoeal diseases are generated through unhygienic and unprotected water supply and sanitation (WHO, 2017). Maintaining water quality will constitute towards the health of the people and also enhance the quality of life.

6.1.7. Goal 7: Affordable and Green Energy

The objective of SDG 7 is to guarantee universal access to dependable, cost-effective, environmentally friendly and up-to-date energy sources for all individuals.

The establishment of Sustainable Energy for All as SDG 7 and the advancement of enhanced human well-being through the adoption of clean energy are both outcomes stemming from the importance of energy accessibility.

The notion of smart cities is prominent within this framework. The implementation of intelligent and cost-effective urban systems contributes to the achievement of sustainability objectives by utilising renewable energy sources and employing diverse treatment facilities to safeguard the environment.

6.1.8. Goal 8: Decent Work and Economic Growth

SDG 8 calls for sustained, inclusive and sustainable economic growth, full and productive employment, and decent work for everyone. SDG 8 has 12 goals, including innovation, diversification and technological advancement. The expansion of micro, small and medium-sized firms is also demanded, along with the decoupling of economic growth from environmental deterioration and access to financial services. Furthermore, it sets the 2030 target of 'full and productive work for all', 'equal work of equal value', the abolition of forced labour, modern slavery and human trafficking, the promotion of sustainable tourism and enhanced trade aid for developing countries.

Adding quality to all sectors of the economy increases efficiency and effectiveness and gets the best outcomes. Lifting the primary, secondary and tertiary sectors has different requirements and they bring different outcomes. The primary sector involves agriculture or extraction of natural resources, so its quality requirement is in the context of agricultural inputs and raw materials; the secondary sector is engaged in manufacturing, so quality may vary from advanced technology and high-quality standards and raw materials to be maintained for the making of the product; however, the third-sector tertiary sector has a wider scope. It includes services like transportation, communication, finance and administration; this sector calls on quality in the aspect of quality delivery of these services and this can be attained through quality education and working on skill development. All this will lead to economic growth.

6.1.9. Goal 9: Industry, Innovation and Infrastructure

Goal 9 of the SDG is supported by three basic pillars: industry, infrastructure and innovation. Without a doubt, SDG 9 will impact forests, livelihoods based on forests and economies based on forests in a number of ways.

The 2030 Agenda for Sustainable Development, which was adopted by the UN in 2015 to address these gaps and combat climate change, particularly asks for infrastructure and industrial investments in SDG 9. Under this agenda, developed countries have committed to assisting emerging and underdeveloped nations in their development. Developing and poor countries need long-lasting infrastructure investments, sustainable industrial innovations and creative approaches if they are to combat climate change, achieve sustainable economic growth and develop their social and grassroots sectors. Universities, businesses, non-governmental organisations and governments must collaborate to create solutions to these problems in this direction.

Here, product quality and infrastructure quality will be helpful. Product quality refers to the ability of a product to satisfy the consumer. A product may attain the level of quality required if it is regularly inspected against quality standards; it should be efficient and effective, that is, no wastage of resources; and it does not cause any harmful effect on people as well as to the environment and should economical.

Infrastructure quality calls for a framework that guarantees that goods and services are secure and of a high calibre known as quality infrastructure. It includes everything from accreditation, metrology and market surveillance to standardisation and conformity assessment (testing, inspection and certification).

6.1.10. Goal 10: Reduced Inequalities

The 10th SDG explicitly acknowledges the imperative to effectively tackle inequality both inside nations and beyond borders. This purpose encompasses various goals, including income disparity reduction, social and political empowerment, discrimination elimination, implementation of more egalitarian fiscal and wage policies, management of migration, establishment of effective financial regulation and promotion of democratic global economic governance. The goal of the Reduced Inequalities agenda is to promote equitable access to education, fair distribution of resources and equal financial prospects for all individuals. In addition, it also calls for a consistent and equitable allocation of resources among nations. This objective can be achieved through the provision of high-quality education and the cultivation of strong interpersonal connections among individuals, organisations and nations alike. Education, as previously discussed, fosters a sound mental outlook and appropriate conduct. Nurturing relationships will promote collaboration among individuals and mitigate the presence of any form of discrimination.

6.1.11. Goal 11: Sustainable Cities and Communities

SDG 11, sustainable cities and communities, aims to provide accessible public transport, reduce urban sprawl, involve local governments more in decision-making, better safeguard cultural assets and address climate change and urban resilience challenges. Inclusionary, secure, resilient and sustainable urban and human settlements are additional goals. The idea of 'smart cities' calls for a system that is accessible to all people, environmentally friendly and fair. Governments should therefore concentrate on implementing quality in cities.

6.1.12. Goal 12: Responsible Consumption and Production

SDG 12 calls for a decoupling of economic growth from unsustainable resource usage and emissions as well as improved waste and hazardous material management and promotes responsible consumption and production.

Efficiency and effectiveness are two main domains for maximising the outcomes and reducing the waste and making it cost-effective. Efficiency is the ability to accomplish more with the same amount of material, human and financial resources. It is production maximisation. Efficiency is the level of performance those resources provide. In order to ensure that the needs of future generations are not jeopardised, sustainable consumption and production refer to the 'use of services and related products that respond to basic needs and improve quality of life while minimising the use of natural resources and toxic materials as well as the emissions of waste and pollutants over the life cycle of the service or product'.

6.1.13. Goal 13: Climate Action

'Take urgent action to combat climate change and its impacts'. This broad objective is broken down into five distinct aims, each of which focuses on various solutions to difficulties brought on by climate change. Additionally, some 'non-climate' goals, notably those addressing various social and economic elements, incorporate targets and indicators pertinent to climate hotspots. The zones of quality such as environmental quality, air quality and water quality should be obtained using tools and techniques for achieving this goal and environmental exploitation should be stopped, and resources should be saved. Waste management, recycling water and reducing carbon emissions are some ways to increase quality in these sectors and add towards environment.

6.1.14. Goal 14: Life Below Water

SDG 14: life below water seeks to conserve the marine ecosystems. Thus, the preservation and sustainable use of marine ecosystem services is the main driving force behind this objective. SDG 14 also aims to abolish the kinds of fishery subsidies that contribute to overfishing in some areas by setting criteria for removing sea pollution, reducing sea acidity and regulating the fishing industry for sustainable fishing. Due to uncontrolled and supported fishing, several fish species are fast vanishing. Enhancing water quality and reducing trash discharges in the ocean. With the aid of water treatment, less trash is released into the ecosystem. The status of the ecosystem is considerably improved when wastewater is treated since less waste is released into the environment.

6.1.15. Goal 15: Life on Land

Goal 15 ('Life on Land') of the 17 SDGs states that protecting and restoring forest ecosystems is a major problem for nations all over the world. According to the 2015 Global Forest Resources Assessment (FRA), forests make up 30.6% of the Earth's surface area despite the fact that they have undergone severe deterioration as a result of numerous anthropogenic and natural processes. Consider how natural processes and human interaction have 'woven' the fabric of life on Earth over millions of years.

Due to the needs of an increasing population and per capita income during the 1970s, human influences on Earth's existence have sharply increased. While nature is currently providing more resources than ever before, the abundance and integrity of ecosystems, the uniqueness of local ecological communities, the number and abundance of wild species and the number of locally domesticated varieties have all declined to unprecedented levels on a global scale. The vital benefits that humans obtain from nature are diminished by these changes, which also jeopardise the environmental processes that support human health as well as the standard of living for current and future generations.

Quality of life of all living beings on earth by taking initiatives to lift the living standards. All the stakeholders of the earth should get an equal share in resources and exploitation of the natural habitat and animals should be prohibited. The health and ending of poverty should be focused while protecting the environment.

6.1.16. Goal 16: Piece Justice and Strong Institutions

The official title of Goal 16 of the 2030 Agenda for Sustainable Development is 'Promoting peaceful and inclusive communities for sustainable development, ensuring access to justice for all, and establishing effective, accountable, and inclusive institutions at all levels'. Sustainable development and sustained development are incompatible with each other in the absence of peace. SDG 16 is an instrument to encourage adaptability, safeguard development advancement and finally lead to a more enduring peace. To accomplish this, good relationships between nations, businesses, other groups and people are required.

6.1.17. Goal 17: Partnership for the Goals

The SDG Partnership aims to 'strengthen the means of implementation and revitalise the global partnership for sustainable development' by recognising multi-stakeholder partnerships as significant vehicles for mobilising and sharing knowledge, expertise, technologies and financial resources to support the achievement of the SDGs in all countries. According to Rühli et al. (2017), multi-stakeholder settings are institutional arrangements, where concerned actors from the public, private and not-for-profit sectors meet to negotiate integrative outcomes while supplying resources and capacities. Relationship quality will again help diverse sectors come together in collaboration and focus to attain sustainability in economic, social and environmental aspects of a country and economy to grow.

7. IMPLICATIONS OF THE STUDY

The SDGs report 2022 provides a comprehensive overview of the progress and future trajectory of the 2030 Agenda for Sustainable Development, including up-to-date data and estimates. Through comprehensive examinations of key indicators associated with each goal, this approach effectively monitors the advancement made at both regional and global levels in relation to the 17 goals. According to the report, the 2030 Agenda for Sustainable Development and the preservation of humankind are facing significant peril as a result of interrelated and cascading challenges. The report underscores the gravity and extent of the challenges we encounter. The confluence of crises, namely COVID-19, climate change and conflicts, is exerting a significant impact on all of the SDGs. The aforementioned crises are also exerting a ripple impact on several domains including food and nutrition, health, education, the environment, and peace and security. The report outlines the reversal of progress in various areas, including the eradication of hunger and poverty, improvement of health and education, provision of key services and other significant developments. Furthermore, it discerns the specific regions or aspects that necessitate prompt intervention in order to preserve the SDGs and achieve substantial advancements for both individuals and the ecosystem within the timeframe of 2030. The SDGs indicate that each target encompasses a specific domain in which improvements in quality are required. The various domains of quality are interconnected, such that improvements in one domain, such as education, health, water and sanitation services, can lead to enhancements in overall quality of life. Hence, it is imperative to prioritise the achievement of sustainability by emphasising the aspect of quality. Quality can be defined as the attainment of excellence in a particular entity or the fulfilment of the necessary criteria or standards. It also encompasses the efficient and effective utilisation of resources.

8. CONCLUSION

So in wholesome, we can say that quality has proven to be an admirable approach towards sustainability. The rising need of sustainability has brought many perspectives to the world. It can be environmental, social and economic aspects and further these aspects have their own areas for improvement. The complexity of the structure of sustainability requires a basic common area to be focused, and in this study, quality has proven to be one. Quality and sustainability are in direct relation with each other. If we increase one the other one increases as well; for example, if no poverty goal is focused it will improve the quality of living and if the quality of living will be focused it will fulfil the goal – no poverty. The study begins with the question of if quality is an approach to achieving sustainability and in the end answer has been attained. The quality undoubtedly is an approach to achieving each aspect of sustainability. It prevails in the structure of TBL by showing which area quality can be increased to make sure this aspect stays stable. Further through the SDGs it can be derived that each goal had an area where quality needed to be worked on. The several zones of the quality are interlinked and quality of life will automatically improve the education, health water and sanitation services.

REFERENCES

Aswal, D. K. (2020). Quality infrastructure of India and its importance for inclusive national growth. *Mapan, 35*(2), 139–150.

Chan, S., Weitz, N., Persson, Å., & Trimmer, C. (2018). *SDG 12: Responsible consumption and produc-tion. A review of research needs.* Technical annex to the Formas report Forskning för agenda, 2030.

Chichilnisky, G. (1997). What is sustainable development? *Land Economics,* 467–491.

CSU, ISSC. (2015). *Review of the sustainable development goals: The science perspective.* International Council for Science (ICSU).

Devisscher, T., Konijnendijk, C., Nesbitt, L., Lenhart, J., Salbitano, F., Cheng, Z. C., Lwasa, S., & van den Bosch, M. (2019). SDG 11: Sustainable cities and communities – Impacts on forests and forest-based livelihoods. In *Sustainable development goals: Their impacts on forests and people* (pp. 349–385). Cambridge University Press.

Díaz, S., Settele, J., Brondízio, E. S., Ngo, H. T., Agard, J., Arneth, A., Balvanera, K. A., Butchart, S. H. M., Chan, K. M. A., Garibaldi, L. A., Ichii, K., Liu, J., Subramanian, S. M., Midgley, G. F., Miloslavich, P., Molnár, Z., Obura, D., Pfaff, A., & Zayas, C. N. (2019). Pervasive human-driven decline of life on Earth points to the need for transformative change. *Science, 366*(6471), eaax3100.

Eden, L., & Wagstaff, M. F. (2021). Evidence-based policymaking and the wicked problem of SDG 5 gender equality. *Journal of International Business Policy, 4,* 28–57.

Farooq, M. S., Riaz, S., Abid, A., Umer, T., & Zikria, Y. B. (2020). Role of IoT technology in agricul-ture: A systematic literature review. *Electronics, 9*(2), 319.

Feliciano, D. (2019). A review on the contribution of crop diversification to sustainable development goal 1 "No poverty" in different world regions. *Sustainable Development, 27*(4), 795–808.

Fraisl, D., Campbell, J., See, L., Wehn, U., Wardlaw, J., Gold, M., Moorthy, I., Arias, R., Piera, J., Oliver, J. L., Masó, J., Penker, M., & Fritz, S. (2020). Mapping citizen science contributions to the UN sustainable development goals. *Sustainability Science, 15,* 1735–1751.

González García, E., Colomo Magaña, E., & Cívico Ariza, A. (2020). Quality education as a sustain-able development goal in the context of 2030 agenda: Bibliometric approach. *Sustainability, 12*(15), 5884.

Goyal, A., Agrawal, R., & Saha, C. R. (2019). Quality management for sustainable manufacturing: Moving from number to impact of defects. *Journal of Cleaner Production, 241,* 118348.

Guégan, J. F., Suzán, G., Kati-Coulibaly, S., Bonpamgue, D. N., & Moatti, J. P. (2018). Sustainable Development Goal# 3, "health and well-being", and the need for more integrative thinking. *Veterinaria México OA, 5*(2), 0-0.

Gulseven, O. (2020). Measuring achievements towards SDG 14, life below water, in the United Arab Emirates. *Marine Policy, 117,* 103972.

Gupta, A. (2021). Focus on quality in higher education in India. *Indian Journal of Public Administration, 67*(1), 54–70.

Hope Sr, K. R. (2020). Peace, justice and inclusive institutions: Overcoming challenges to the imple-mentation of sustainable development goal 16. *Global Change, Peace & Security, 32*(1), 57–77.

Karaca, S., Dengiz, O., Turan, İ. D., Özkan, B., Dedeoğlu, M., Gülser, F., Sargin, B., Demirkaya, S., & Ay, A. (2021). An assessment of pasture soils quality based on multi-indicator weighting approaches in semi-arid ecosystem. *Ecological Indicators, 121,* 107001.

Kim, Y. K., & Trail, G. (2011). A conceptual framework for understanding relationships between sport consumers and sport organizations: A relationship quality approach. *Journal of Sport Management, 25*(1), 57–69.

Küfeoğlu, S. (2022). SDG-17: Partnerships for the Goals. In *Emerging technologies: Value creation for sustainable development* (pp. 497–504). Springer International Publishing.

Liao, C., Erbaugh, J. T., Kelly, A. C., & Agrawal, A. (2021). Clean energy transitions and human well-being outcomes in lower and middle income countries: A systematic review. *Renewable and Sustainable Energy Reviews, 145,* 111063.

Mensah, J. (2019). Sustainable development: Meaning, history, principles, pillars, and implications for human action: Literature review. *Cogent Social Sciences, 5*(1), 1653531.

Ministerio de Derechos Sociales y Agenda 2030. Objetivos de Desarrollo Sostenible. (2020). https://www.agenda2030.gob.es/objetivos

Mottaleb, K. A., Fatah, F. A., Kruseman, G., & Erenstein, O. (2021). Projecting food demand in 2030: Can Uganda attain the zero hunger goal? *Sustainable Production and Consumption, 28,* 1140–1163.

Oliveira-Duarte, L., Reis, D. A., Fleury, A. L., Vasques, R. A., Fonseca Filho, H., Koria, M., & Baruque-Ramos, J. (2021). Innovation ecosystem framework directed to sustainable development Goal# 17 partnerships implementation. *Sustainable Development, 29*(5), 1018–1036.

Pambreni, Y., Khatibi, A., Azam, S., & Tham, J. J. (2019). The influence of total quality management toward organization performance. *Management Science Letters, 9*(9), 1397–1406.

Pisoni, E., Christidis, P., Thunis, P., & Trombetti, M. (2019). Evaluating the impact of "Sustainable Urban Mobility Plans" on urban background air quality. *Journal of Environmental Management, 231*, 249–255.

Rai, S. M., Brown, B. D., & Ruwanpura, K. N. (2019). SDG 8: Decent work and economic growth–A gendered analysis. *World Development, 113*, 368–380.

Rao, N., Ranganathan, N., Kaur, R., & Mukhopadhayay, R. (2021). Fostering equitable access to quality preschool education in India: Challenges and opportunities. *International Journal of Child Care and Education Policy, 15*(1), 1–22.

Roy, P. (2018). Effects of poverty on education in India. *Journal of Emerging Technologies and Innovative Research, 5*(8), 331–336.

Quality-of-life indicators (UN 1993) include measures of the economy, social welfare, environment, health, and education.

Saiz, I., & Donald, K. (2017). Tackling inequality through the sustainable development goals: Human rights in practice. *The International Journal of Human Rights, 21*(8), 1029–1049.

Saner, R., Yiu, L., & Nguyen, M. (2020). Monitoring the SDGs: Digital and social technologies to ensure citizen participation, inclusiveness and transparency. *Development Policy Review, 38*(4), 483–500.

Smith, G. F. (1993). The meaning of quality. *Total Quality Management, 4*(3), 235–244.

Sumana, G., & Aswal, D. K. (2021). Importance of standards in biomedical device and its role in strengthening the healthcare sector. *Frontiers in Nanotechnology, 3*, 622804.

Sweis, R., Ismaeil, A., Obeidat, B., & Kanaan, R. K. (2019). Reviewing the literature on total quality management and organizational performance. *Journal of Business & Management (COES&RJ-JBM), 7*(3), 192–215.

Tang, T., Strokal, M., van Vliet, M. T., Seuntjens, P., Burek, P., Kroeze, C., Langan, S., & Wada, Y. (2019). Bridging global, basin and local-scale water quality modeling towards enhancing water quality management worldwide. *Current Opinion in Environmental Sustainability, 36*, 39–48.

Tomaselli, M. F., Timko, J., Kozak, R., Bull, J., Kearney, S., Saddler, J., & Zhu, X. (2019). SDG 9: Industry, innovation and infrastructure – anticipating the potential impacts on forests and forest-based livelihoods. In P. Katila, C. J. P. Colfer, W. de Jong, G. Galloway, P. Pacheco & G. Winkel (Eds.), *Sustainable development goals: Their impacts on forests and people* (pp. 279–314). Cambridge University Press.

Tortajada, C. (2020). Contributions of recycled wastewater to clean water and sanitation sustainable development goals. *NPJ Clean Water, 3*(1), 22.

United Nations Educational, Scientific and Cultural Organisation (UNESCO). (2017). *Unpacking Sustainable Development Goal 4 Education 2030.* Retrieved May 18, 2020, from http://unesdoc.unesco.org/images/0024/002463/246300E.pdf

Weststrate, J., Dijkstra, G., Eshuis, J., Gianoli, A., & Rusca, M. (2019). The sustainable development goal on water and sanitation: Learning from the millennium development goals. *Social Indicators Research, 143*, 795–810.

World Education Forum (WEF). (2016).Incheon Declaration and Framework for Action for the Implementation of Sustainable Development Goal 4. In *Towards Inclusive and Equitable Quality Education and Lifelong Learning Opportunities for All. Education 2030.*UNESCO. http://unesdoc.unesco.org/images/0024/002456/245656e.pdf

Zhang, J., Fu, B., Stafford-Smith, M., Wang, S., & Zhao, W. (2021). Improve forest restoration initiatives to meet Sustainable Development Goal 15. *Nature Ecology & Evolution, 5*(1), 10–13. http://unep.org/explore-topics/resource-efficiency/what-we-do/sustainable-consumption-and-production-policies

CHAPTER 12

FASHION VLOGGING FOR SUSTAINABLE COSMETICS: MODELLING THE RELATIONSHIP BETWEEN HEDONIC MOTIVATION AND IMPULSE BUYING INTENTION WITH PARASOCIAL INTERACTION AS A MEDIATOR

Parul Manchanda, Nupur Arora and Aanchal Aggarwal

Vivekananda Institute of Professional Studies-TC, New Delhi, India

ABSTRACT

Purpose: *This study analyses the mediating effect of parasocial interaction (PSI) in the link between hedonic motivation and impulsive buying intention (IBI) in fashion vlogging about sustainable cosmetics.*

Need for the Study: *Due to the mass popularity of YouTube, vlogging has led to an augmented level of PSI of vloggers with consumers, which strongly impacts a consumer's behavioural consequences and persuades consumers to indulge in impulsive buying. Thus, marketers need to comprehend the changing behavioural patterns, including sustainable products, as this new communication medium serves the future of promotion and advertising.*

Sustainable Development Goals: The Impact of Sustainability Measures on Wellbeing
Contemporary Studies in Economic and Financial Analysis, Volume 113B, 189–210
Copyright © 2024 by Parul Manchanda, Nupur Arora and Aanchal Aggarwal
Published under exclusive licence by Emerald Publishing Limited
ISSN: 1569-3759/doi:10.1108/S1569-37592024000113B012

Methodology: *Online questionnaires were administered to 349 Gen Z female fashion vlog followers. Structural equation modelling and Hayes Process macros were employed to test the model relationships.*

Findings: *Results indicate that PI with the fashion vlogger partially mediates between hedonic motivation and impulse buying intention for sustainable cosmetic products. Fashion consciousness (FC) was also established as a significant moderator between all the model relationships.*

Practical Implications: *The findings of the study would be helpful for fashion brands in the content development of visual marketing communications, which would tap the female Gen Z consumer. Improving the PSI between the follower and the fashion vlogger can be easily enhanced by delivering the right content through the vlogger's videos.*

Keywords: Parasocial interaction (PSI); hedonic motivation; fashion vlogger; impulse buying intention (IBI); sustainable cosmetics; process macros

INTRODUCTION

The recent exponential rise of social media platforms has considerably transformed our daily lives. Individuals spend an average of 147 minutes daily using social media, increasing their sensitivity to internet-supported marketing (Geyser, 2022). In an emerging economy like India, the situation is similar. The number of social network users in the United States is expected to reach 1.5 billion by 2040 (Basuroy, 2022). This massive increase in the penetration of the World Wide Web in the Indian market has further witnessed an upsurge of digital celebrities known as social media influencers (SMI) (Misra & Mukherjee, 2019). YouTube bloggers (referred to as vloggers from now on) are also a category of SMI who create and upload video content about various products, services, and sometimes personal lives (Lee & Watkins, 2016). This fresh mode of expression via vlogs has become increasingly popular since YouTube and Instagram have gained mass popularity (Ladhari et al., 2020). Moreover, a global survey conducted by Rakuten (2019) reveals some intriguing figures demonstrating a favourable consumer attitude towards video content (64%) compared to content types, such as photos (61%) or written media content (38%). They also can evoke positive and negative feelings amongst their followers and engage them (Liu et al., 2019). With the enormous popularity of vloggers and the growing importance of vlogs as an effective marketing instrument, marketers have thus started substituting traditional communication and diversified their ways of approaching customers mainly through these SMI (Lin et al., 2019). It has also been recommended that celebrities might stimulate strong PSI with their followers and viewers via social media platforms (Haobin et al., 2020; Stever & Lawson, 2013). As these proposed relations are suggested to progress to the stage where consumers commence to view this third-party connection as more influential than brands advertising them directly (Stern et al., 2007), this augmented level of PSI strongly impacts a consumer's behavioural consequences (Venus & Muqaddam, 2019) and persuades consumers to indulge in impulsive buying (Nuseir, 2020; Yu et al., 2019).

In this work, we have attempted to examine the concept of affective shopping motivation as a predictor of impulse buying intention (IBI). Though it is widely evident from the literature that impulse buying is an outcome of hedonic shopping motives (Dey & Srivastava, 2017), studies from the literature have helped us infer that social commerce platforms provide consumers with hedonic shopping value, which further imbibes in them an intention to indulge in impulsive buying (Badgaiyan et al., 2017; Chung et al., 2017). In the context of this paper, we explore the hedonic motivation of females to follow these fashion vloggers and their IBIs. Moreover, the literature suggests that more hedonically motivated consumers are relatively more involved in internet browsing over social media platforms (Zheng et al., 2019). They are more likely to form PSI relationships with other users. Therefore, this leads to an augmented interaction between the vlogger and the followers. Thus, this research tries to overcome one of the gaps by addressing how it can mediate the relationship between a critical antecedent of impulse buying and IBI, as the previous models have often emphasised the direct behavioural aspects of PSI (Dey et al., 2017; Vazquez et al., 2020).

Consequently, this academic research was undertaken in India's rising economy, which has a humongous active social media user base (Statista, 2022b). Additionally, this study has been conducted on Gen Z females (who follow fashion vloggers) and are considered the expanding new social influence and main customers in the global market. Gen Z is often called Digital Natives and comprises people born after 1997 or after that (Coughlin, 2018). These people are between 7 and 22 years of age (Dimock, 2019). This consumer segment grew up in a media-friendly atmosphere. They participate more actively in live streaming and chatting than other generations (Park, 2019) and are extensively influenced by the content provided by the vloggers (Mullen, 2019). Moreover, the present study employs fashion consciousness (FC) (here in sustainable cosmetic products) from the self-consciousness theory as a moderator to investigate its effect on the relationships mentioned above. Literature has previously supported the significance of gender in FC as a trait and established that females are more fashion-conscious than males (Gould & Stern, 1989). In addition, the literature suggests that hedonism influences the share of income spent on fashion products, with 'young fashion-conscious consumers' spending a more significant proportion (Gao et al., 2009). Additionally, fashion-conscious consumers often immerse themselves in parasocial intensive relationships and impulsive buying (Arviansyah et al., 2018; Wiranata & Hananto, 2020). Thus, the present scholarly work focuses on examining the following relationships:

- To explore the hedonic motivation of females to follow these fashion vloggers and their IBIs.

- To investigate the mediating role of parasocial interaction (PSI) (with the fashion vlogger) in the association between hedonic motivation and IBI.
- To examine the moderating role of FC (in sustainable cosmetic products) in the mediated relationship between hedonic motivation to watch fashion vloggers, PSI, and IBI.

Thus, the present work contributes to the existing body of knowledge and fills gaps in prior literature in many ways. The following objectives justify the gap:

(a) The paper examines the role of PSI as a mediator between hedonic motivation and IBI in the context of fashion vlogging, specifically in sustainable cosmetic products, which has yet to be addressed earlier.
(b) The paper employs FC as a significant moderator in a moderated mediation model (between the relationship between hedonic motivation, PSI and IBI).

THEORETICAL FRAMEWORK

Theory of Parasocial Interaction (PSI)

Horton and Wohl (1956) established PSI to define face-to-face contact in mass communication. According to Giles (2002, p. 279), 'Interaction between users of mass media and representations of humans appearing in the media (media figures such as presenters, actors, and celebrities) can establish a type of relationship to which the user responds as in a regular social relationship'. This concept of customers' connection to public or social figures in communication media was recognised decades before the invention of the Internet (Horton & Wohl, 1956). Traditional research related to PSI emphasised a viewer's affiliation with a personality in the domain of broadcast media (Dibble et al., 2016). Recent studies indicate that it may extend beyond these domains to celebrity endorsements, actors, social media personalities, and even YouTube bloggers (vloggers) (Hsu, 2020; Reinikainen et al., 2020). Research indicates celebrities may encourage PSI through social media platforms (Stever & Lawson, 2013). As these relationships are suggested to progress to the stage where consumers commence to view mediated personalities as 'real friends' (Stern et al., 2007), in the process, they develop better intimacy, liking, and credibility with their subscribers (Ledbetter & Redd, 2016).

Researchers have thus established strong predictors and outcomes of PSI (Daniel et al., 2018; Sokolova & Kefi, 2020). The current study employs this concept of PSI in the fashion vlogging industry. Prior literature on PSI (in the domain of communication) has already explained the (one-sided) partial interpersonal association that viewers tend to form with celebrities on television, radio, etc. (Rubin & McHugh, 1987). Even though the relationship mentioned above is one-sided, a celebrity has a strong potential to impact viewers' opinions and behaviour because of the presence of PSI (Brown & Basil, 2010; Rasmussen & Ewoldsen, 2016). The current work employs this notion in the relatively more interactive medium of YouTube. The authors argue that these fashion vloggers, 'virtual celebrities', develop a robust parasocial relationship with their followers (Ballantine & Martin, 2005). Horton and Wohl (1956) debate that once PSI is formed, the opinions, beliefs, and values maintained by the media personality commence to influence the individual to the point where the media character or personality becomes a role model for the viewer (Horton & Wohl, 1956). Additionally, since research reveals that PSI is also a factor influencing buying behaviour and impulse buying even in the context of social commerce platforms (Xiang et al., 2016), this theory is very relevant to the present study model.

Self-Consciousness Theory

The present paper employs the self-consciousness theory proposed by Buss and Craik (1980), a key concept for understanding self-concept. The key idea of this concept is the degree to which an individual focus on his or her inner or outer self: 'When self-awareness is turned inward, persons tend to have a high level of private self-awareness, being mindful of interior states such as feelings, moods, and beliefs' (Scheier, 1976, p. 628). However, when self-awareness is oriented outwards, public self-consciousness tends to increase. Thus, individuals with a high degree of public consciousness focus on themselves as a social entity (Buss & Craik, 1980; Buss, 1985). Therefore, individuals who score higher on the component of public self-consciousness are concerned about being witnessed and judged by others compared to those who score relatively less on the criteria of public self-consciousness (Buss & Craik, 1980).

Furthermore, Fenigstein et al. (1975) pioneered developing a scale for self-consciousness. Subsequently, Gould and Stern (1989) also stated that the conceptualisation of self-awareness proposed by Fenigstein et al. (1975) serves as the basis for the notion of 'fashion consciousness'. Furthermore, Gould and Stern (1989) emphasised the significance of gender in FC and established that females tend to be more fashion-conscious than males. According to them, females are inclined to emphasise their aesthetic appeal and are thus more self-conscious in public. Thus, we can assume from the above argument that (a) females are more fashion-conscious and (b) fashion-conscious consumers must be high on their 'public self-consciousness'. Thus, this work contributes to the current body of literature by investigating the role of public self-consciousness in sustainable cosmetic products. The paper incorporates the construct of 'FC' as a moderator, which was framed to conceptualise public self-consciousness within the context of fashion consumption (Gould & Barak, 1988; Gould & Stern, 1989).

LITERATURE REVIEW

Impulse Buying Intention and Hedonic Motivation

Shopping motivation has been one of the most fundamental concerns in consumer behaviour research. Scholars have classified it into two major types: cognitive motivation, which is called utilitarian, and affective motivation, which is called hedonic. Various studies have validated that consumers can be motivated to purchase products based on their utilitarian and hedonic values (Han et al., 2018; Holbrook & Hirschman, 1982; Lin et al., 2018; Ozkara et al., 2017).

In the context of the present study, we have selected only hedonic motivation as a predictor of IBI. This is because hedonic buyers exhibit a relatively higher level of impulsive shopping behaviour (Dey & Srivastava, 2017; Yu & Bastin, 2017). According to Holbrook & Hirschman (1982, p. 1), 'hedonic consumption designates those facets of consumer behaviour that relate to the multi-sensory, fantasy, and emotive aspects of one's experience with products'. Thus, a hedonic shopper frequently searches for fun, amusement, arousal, sensory stimulation, fantasy, novelty, surprise, and variety (Savelli et al., 2017). Furthermore, according to Rook and Fisher (1995), 'impulse buying can be described as having a strong and sudden desire to buy a product that one did not intend to purchase and doing so without much contemplation'. Recent research suggests that e-shoppers increasingly seek hedonic value online. They look for immersive opportunities while shopping, which gives them better satisfaction (Childers et al., 2001; Szymanski & Hise, 2000). Studies have also inferred that social commerce platforms provide consumers with hedonic shopping value/motivation, which further imbibes an intention to indulge in impulsive buying (Dey & Srivastava, 2017; Rezaei et al., 2016). One recent piece of prominent research in mobile commerce states that hedonic browsing is a direct predictor of consumers' urge to buy impulsively.

In contrast, utilitarian browsing is not a direct predictor but an indirect one (Zheng et al., 2019). The studies to date relating to hedonic motivation in the context of SMIs are minuscule. Only a few studies have been done in the context of studying the direct impact of hedonic motivation on social media platforms in the fashion context (Leverett, 2016). Thus, extrapolating from the above discussion, the following hypothesis is suggested:

> *H1.* A significant positive relation exists between hedonic motivation (to watch fashion vloggers) and impulse buying intention of sustainable cosmetic products.

Parasocial Interaction and Impulse Buying Intention

PSI has been defined as the 'illusion of a face-to-face relationship with a media personality' (Horton & Wohl, 1956, p. 188). The influence of PSI on consumer behaviour has been elaborated upon in prior literature within the offline context. Previous research on PSI suggests that enjoyment is a probable consequence of parasocial experience, and people tend to cultivate PSI relationships for entertainment (Klimmt et al., 2006; Levy & Windahl, 1984; Palmgreen et al., 1980). It has been highlighted in the literature that parasocial intensive relationships persuade consumers to make impulsive purchases (Nuseir, 2020; Yu et al., 2019). The authors argue that the increased interaction between the users and followers and the vloggers and experts lets users know their thoughts and lifestyles personally. Furthermore, the vlogger's expertise and personality encourage followers or viewers to develop and sustain PSI relations with them (Ladhari et al., 2020; Rasmussen, 2018).

Hence, these parasocial-intensive relationships may persuade consumers to make impulsive purchases. Therefore, based on the above argument, PSI substantially impacts consumers' impulse buying behaviour. The present work examines the influence of this PSI among fashion vloggers and women and their IBIs for sustainable cosmetic products. Thus, we propose the following hypothesis:

H2. A significant positive relationship exists between parasocial interaction and the impulse buying intention of sustainable cosmetic products.

Moreover, it has also been suggested that more hedonically motivated consumers are relatively more involved in internet browsing and interaction over social media platforms (Zheng et al., 2019). Thus, users are more likely to form PSI relationships with virtual celebrities. Literature also suggests that 'YouTube is a social network site conducive to developing parasocial relationships' (de Bérail et al., p. 1). Therefore, this would lead to increased activity between the blogger and the followers. Prior models on PSI are scarce in the social commerce context, and the prominent ones focus on its direct impact on behavioural aspects such as loyalty, eWOM (Labrecque, 2014), impulse buying (Vazquez et al., 2020) and attitude (Yuan et al., 2016). Only Chen et al. (2021) explored the mediating role of PSI in the relationship between YouTube celebrity characteristics and impulse behaviour. However, we wish to test how PSI can mediate the relationship between hedonic motivation and IBI. We propose this assumption due to two key reasons: (a) since a hedonically motivated shopper spends more time on social commerce platforms, they will develop a stronger PSI with the virtual celebrity; (b) only if the PSI is stronger one can indulge in impulse buying (Chen et al., 2021). We argue that prior to indulgently 'buying' impulsively, a consumer develops an IBI (Abbasi, 2017).

Furthermore, a few key reasons support the argument that PSI can be an effective mediator in the model. First, it has been argued in the above section that a superior magnitude of PSI impacts a consumer's IBI (Venus & Muqaddam, 2019; Xiang et al., 2016). Additionally, Arviansyah et al. (2018) suggest that vlogger-related factors affect the urge to buy impulsively in the presence of PSI as a mediating variable, applying the stimulus organism response model. Second, the literature has also suggested that individual consumer traits, such as hedonic motivations, influence impulse buying behaviour significantly (Xiang et al., 2016). Hence, for a hedonic shopper, forming a strong PSI with the fashion vlogger is a crucial step before there is an IBI to buy the products the vlogger recommends. The literature does not explore how hedonic shopping motivations might influence IBIs in the presence of PSI as a mediator. The current study attempts to fill this gap. Thus, extrapolating from the above argument, the authors of the paper suggest the following hypothesis:

H3. Parasocial interaction mediates the relation between hedonic motivation and impulse buying intention of sustainable cosmetic products.

Fashion Consciousness (FC) as a Moderator

FC is 'an individual's degree of involvement with the styles or fashion of clothing' (Nam et al., 2007, p. 103). The term also describes an individual's awareness of fashion and the skill to imitate and be responsive to the latest fashion trends (Milewski, 2005). The notion of FC has been studied in the literature, but most of the studies deal with apparel products (Hassan & Harun, 2016; Kautish & Sharma, 2018; Leung et al., 2015; Nam et al., 2007; Parker et al., 2004) or general FC (Kaur & Anand, 2018). Past literature establishes that hedonism is a crucial factor influencing the percentage of earnings splurged on fashion products, with a relatively higher fraction spent by young fashion-conscious consumers (Gao et al., 2009). Khuong and Tran (2015, p. 224) also suggest that 'customers with high novelty-FC always seek new fashions and fads with excitement and pleasure. These characteristics are similar to consumer hedonic purchase behaviour'.

Additionally, Sprotles and Kendall (1986) established a 'consumer decision-making style inventory' (CSI) that aids in defining and evaluating a consumer's eight key psychological characteristics in the decision-making process. Of these eight crucial characteristics, 'novelty-fashion awareness and impulsiveness' are cited as having the greatest impact on consumption. Hence, customers with a 'novelty and fashion consciousness' are predicted to experience more impulse purchases. The prominent literature adopts various models or a mediating variable in their models only (Kautish et al., 2018). However, the present paper argues that FC can also act as a significant moderator in the present model because individuals who are more FC are hedonic shoppers and thus might develop an IBI to buy the vlogger's recommended products sooner compared to those who are on the lower side of this dimension. Rather than focusing on the direct impact, this individual trait can work in the subconscious, and these consumers could build a strong association with fashion vloggers they admire. Thus, people with a higher level of this moderator (FC) would have a stronger relationship between hedonic motivation to purchase and IBI and vice versa for people on the weaker side of the moderator.

Furthermore, elaborating on hedonic motivation (or hedonism) and impulse buying, it has already been established that fashion-conscious consumers often indulge in impulse buying (Wiranata & Hananto, 2020). Also, the concept of 'fashion-oriented impulse buying' (Parks et al., 2005) is suggested to have a significant association with affective consumption factors such as fashion involvement or consciousness (Han et al., 1991) as well as hedonic consumption (Pentecost & Andrews, 2010). Finally, it is evident from the literature that consumers who are sensitive to fashion trends are relatively more specific to the aesthetic appeal of a product (Workman & Caldwell, 2007), and they tend to give more attention to fresh styles and trends in the market (Gehrt et al., 2007). SMI often have a robust positive influence on fashion consumers due to their product expertise in the field, thus developing a positive parasocial relationship with their followers (Quelhas-Brito et al., 2020). In this process, fashion consumers idealise vloggers as their friends and develop social intimacy (Bucy & Tao, 2007). Thus, it can be logically assumed that FC can act as a significant moderator in the relationship between

PSI and IBI as well because a highly FC consumer would be able to connect with the vloggers emotionally and view their content more often. This would aid in developing IBI of the products recommended by the vlogger. Thus, from the above argument, the authors try to fill the gap in the literature by conducting an in-depth examination of the moderating impact of this variable and not just the direct relationships with hedonic motivation, PSI or IBI.

H4a. FC (in sustainable cosmetic products) moderates the relationship between hedonic motivation and IBI. Specifically, higher levels of FC will strengthen the relationship between hedonic motivation and IBIs.

H4b. FC (in sustainable cosmetic products) moderates the relationship between hedonic motivation and parasocial interaction. Specifically, higher levels of FC will strengthen the relationship between hedonic motivation and parasocial interaction.

H4c. FC (in sustainable cosmetic products) moderates the relationship between parasocial interaction and IBI. Higher levels of FC will undeniably strengthen the relationship between parasocial interaction and IBIs.

After the above-detailed discussion and literature review, the paper proposes the following research model (depicted in Fig. 1).

DATA AND METHODOLOGY

Measurement Scales

To measure the study's variables, scales from the literature were adopted. PSI was gauged through a six-item scale adapted from the study of Labrecque (2014).

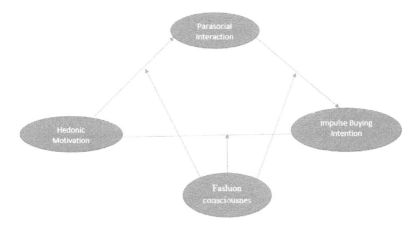

Fig. 1. Proposed Research Model. *Source*: Authors' Conceptualisation of the Research Model.

To measure hedonic motivation (to watch fashion vloggers), a four-item measurement scale was adapted from the work of Chen (2016) and Titze et al. (2008). The three-item scale proposed by Beatty and Ferrell (1998) was selected to measure the variable of IBI. All the statements were asked on a nine-point Likert scale, where 1 means 'strongly disagree' and 9 means 'strongly agree'. Finally, FC was measured using a four-item scale from Wells and Tigert (1971). We evaded the use of lengthy scales for measurement purposes in order to (a) curtail respondent monotony, exhaustion, and inattentiveness and (b) improve respondent contribution (Rosnow & Rosenthal, 1991).

Sample

The present study has selected Gen Z females as the sample. This is due to the following reasons:

(a) Gen Z consumers are the ones who participate more actively in live streaming and chatting in comparison to other generations (Park, 2019); (b) Gen Z is extensively influenced by the content provided by vloggers (Mullen, 2019); (c) Females are more fashion conscious as compared to men (Gould & Stern, 1989) and are impulsive buyers (Pentecost & Andrews, 2010); (d) Females spend significantly more money than men on fashion items (Pentecost & Andrews, 2010).

Questionnaire Administration and Data Collection

An online questionnaire was administered among female users of social networking platforms in India whose interest was fashion content. Those who marked 'yes' in the area of interest as fashion, only for those respondents, the form accepted responses. A sample of 374 Gen Z females aged between 18 and 25 participated in the survey. These females were pursuing their graduate and postgraduate courses and had been following famous fashion vloggers on YouTube and Instagram. A total of 349 usable responses were utilised for the study. The focus of the study was females, as they are more anxious and concerned with fashion advice than their male counterparts (Baron, 2020).

Statistical Tool

The present study employs AMOS 21 (structural equation modelling) and Hayes PROCESS MACROS to examine the moderated mediation model. According to Hayes (2015, p. 2), 'to claim mediation is moderated, one should (if not also must) have evidence that at least one of the paths in the mediated model' (X to M to Y) is moderated 42. Then, the moderated mediation model can be analysed using Hayes Process Macros.

Data Analysis and Empirical Results

In this study, the data are analysed in three steps. A confirmatory factor analysis was performed in the initial phase. In the second step, the structural model is analysed in AMOS to determine the link between variables (direct effects and mediating effects). The final step examines mediated moderation using Hayes Process Macros (2013). Since all variables were observable towards the end of phase two, PROCESS macros were an appropriate tool for testing the moderated mediation model (Hayes et al., 2017).

Common Method Variance (CMV)

CMV is one of the most widely accepted and employed methods. Harman's single-factor test was implemented to test the CMV among the study constructs (Podsakoff et al., 2003). The results explained 41% of the variance, signifying that the standard method variance is not present in the dataset. Another tool to verify the absence of the standard method is the latent factor method in AMOS (Podsakoff et al., 2003). The dataset of the present study was tested through this method, and the CMB value was again found to be less than 50%.

To gauge the internal consistency of the measurement items, Cronbach's alpha was calculated, and composite reliability was evaluated (Table 1).

Measurement Model

The discriminant validity results are depicted in Table 1, which signifies a high internal consistency. The average variance extracted (Table 2) was also higher than 0.5, which is adequate for convergent validity, according to Hair et al. (2014). The composite reliability was also satisfactory (Gefen et al., 2011). Table 3 mentions the measurement model fit indices, and all the fit indices appear to be within the limits.

Table 1. Reliability and Factor Loadings.

Construct	Adaptation	Item Code	Cronbach α
Hedonic motivation	Chen (2016) and Titze et al. (2008)	**Hed1**	0.893
		Hed2	
		Hed3	
		Hed4	
Fashion consciousness	Wells and Tigert (1971)	FC1	0.910
		FC2	
		FC3	
		FC4	
Parasocial interaction	Labrecque (2014)	**PSI1**	0.907
		PSI2	
		PSI3	
		PSI4	
		PSI5	
Impulse buying intention	Beatty and Ferrell (1998)	**IBI1**	0.830
		IBI2	
		IBI3	

Source: Authors' compilation from AMOS results.

Table 2. Discriminant Validity.

	CR	AVE	MSV	MaxR (H)	FC	Hedonic	PSI	IBI
INV	0.913	0.725	0.328	0.914	**0.852**			
Hedonic	0.899	0.690	0.295	0.908	0.543	**0.831**		
PSI	0.910	0.670	0.328	0.914	0.573	0.193	**0.818**	
IBI	0.840	0.637	0.251	0.854	0.475	0.301	0.501	**0.798**

Source: Authors' compilation from AMOS results.
Notes: The numbers in bold on the diagonal are the average variances extracted; the numbers below are the squared correlation coefficients between the constructs. PSI: parasocial interaction, IBI: impulse buying intention.

Table 3. Measurement Model-Model Fit.

Statistic	Value	Threshold
CMIN	1.415	Less than or equal to 5 (Byrne, 1998)
GFI	0.953	>0.90 (Byrne, 1998)
CFI	0.989	>0.9 (Byrne, 1998)
NFI	0.963	>0.95 (Hu & Bentler, 1999)
RMSEA	0.035	Up to 0.10 (MacCallum et al., 1996)

Source: Authors' compilation from literature.

Structural Model

Table 4 (Fig. 2) represents the structural model findings, which support our postulated hypotheses *H1*, *H2* and *H3* (*p*-value of 0.05). All the model fit indices were within the suggested and recommended statistical threshold values. The model fit indices were also found satisfactory. Table 5 states the values with the recommended threshold values. The R^2 for IBI was found to be 0.289 (28.9%), and for PSI, it was 0.041 (4.1%).

Furthermore, to support *H3*, apart from the significant relationship between the constructs, a mediation analysis was conducted in AMOS. One of the primary objectives of the present model is to examine the indirect effect of PSI in the relationship between hedonic values and the purchase intention of sustainable cosmetic products endorsed by the vlogger through *H3*. The results have also supported this hypothesis, confirming a partial mediation with an indirect effect

Table 4. Structural Model.

Hypothesis			Standardised Estimate	S.E.	C.R.	p	Decision
H1	IBI	← Hedonic	0.206	0.043	3.632	***	Supported
H2	IBI	← PSI	0.457	0.059	7.224	***	Supported
H3	PSI	← Hedonic	0.202	0.048	3.423	***	Supported

Source: Authors' compilation from AMOS results.
Note: ***$p \leq 0.05$; PSI: parasocial interaction, IBI: impulse buying intention.

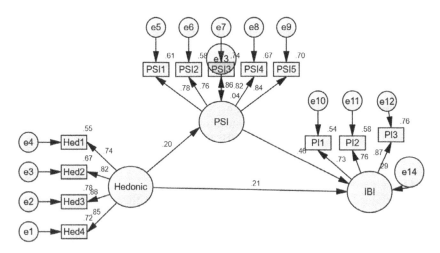

Fig. 2. Structural Model in AMOS. *Source*: Results retrieved from AMOS software.

Table 5. Model Fit Indices – Structural Model.

Statistic	Value	Acceptable Range
Chi square (CMIN)	1.417	Less than or equal to 5 (Byrne,1998)
GFI	0.967	>0.90 Byrne, 1998; Shevlin and Miles, 1998)
CFI	0.991	>0.9 (Byrne, 1998)
NFI	0.971	>0.95 (Hu & Bentler, 1999)
RMSEA	0.035	≤0.10 (MacCallum et al., 1996)

Source: Authors' compilation from literature.

value of 0.118 at $p < 0.05$ (refer to Table 6). The statistics of direct and indirect effects are mentioned in Table 6.

Moderated Mediation

After establishing the mediating role of PSI between hedonic values and IBI, the moderating role of FC was examined, as hypothesised in *H4a, H4b* and *H4c*.

Table 6. Standardised Direct and Indirect Effects.

	Total Effects			Direct Effects			Indirect Effects	
	Hedonic	PSI		Hedonic	PSI		Hedonic	PSI
PSI	0.331	0.000	PSI	0.331	0.000	PSI	0.000	0.000
IBI	0.666	0.357	IBI	0.548*	0.357	IBI	0.118*	0.000

Source: Authors' compilation from AMOS results.
Note: *p* < 0.05.

To test the hypotheses *H4a–H4c*, we employed Hayes's (2013, 2015) method to implement a moderated-mediation analysis with one-scale moderator as elaborated in Hayes (2013).

The output from PROCESS macros supports the hypotheses *H4a–H4c* that FC acts as a significant moderator between the relationship of hedonic values and PSI (model no. 59). Furthermore, the moderator was also found to be significant between the relationship of hedonic values and IBI of sustainable cosmetic products endorsed by the vlogger and also proved as a significant moderator between the relationship of PSI and IBI. Table 7 depicts the relevant statistics to support the argument, and the model summary is depicted in Table 8. Apart from the interaction effects, observing an inverse relationship between hedonic values and PSI ($\beta = 0.1898$, $p < 0.05$, Table 7) is interesting.

We attained two regression slopes to explain further the moderated effects of FC in the present model. The graphical presentation of the significant moderated mediation effects is depicted in Figs. 3 and 4. In the case of users with low FC, the moderation effect is insignificant. This explains that as FC rises, women followers of a vlogger show a weak relationship between PSI and hedonic values. As explained above in the results, rising hedonic values is causing low PSI; thus, at different levels of the moderator (low, medium and high), the exact relationship is depicted, and there is a significant moderation effect of FC. Furthermore, as depicted in Fig. 4, FC is a significant moderator of the relationship between

Table 7. PROCESS MACROS Output (Moderated Mediation).

PSI as the Outcome Variable					
Constructs	β Coefficient	*t*-Value	*p*-Value	LLCI	ULCI
Hedonic	−0.1309	−2.417	0.0161	−0.2375	−0.0244
FC	0.5638	9.795	0.000	0.5484	0.7760
Int_1	−0.0891	−2.570	0.000	−0.1118	−0.0149

Impulse buying intention (outcome variable).

Constructs	β Coefficient	*t*-Value	*p*-Value	LLCI	ULCI
Hedonic	0.3748	8.329	0.000	0.2863	0.4633
PSI	0.3150	7.002	0.000	0.2265	0.4035
FC	0.1743	3.255	0.001	0.0690	0.2796
Int_1 (Hedonic × FC)	−0.1100	−5.049	0.000	−0.1529	−0.0672
Int_2 (PSI × FC)	0.0804	3.674	0.000	0.373	0.123

Source: Authors' compilation from Hayes process macros results.

Table 8. Model Summary-Moderated Mediation.

Outcome variable	R	R^2	F	p
PSI	0.5688	0.3235	54.994	0.000
IBI	0.777	0.6043	104.76	0.000

Source: Authors' compilation from Hayes process macros results.

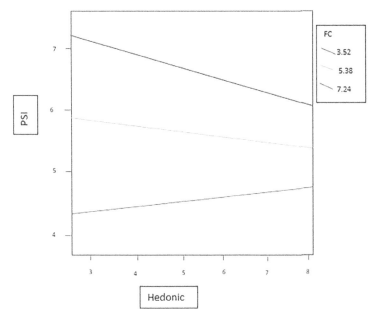

Fig. 3. Graph Representing Moderation Effect of Fashion Consciousness Between PSI and Hedonic Values. *Source*: Hayes process macros.

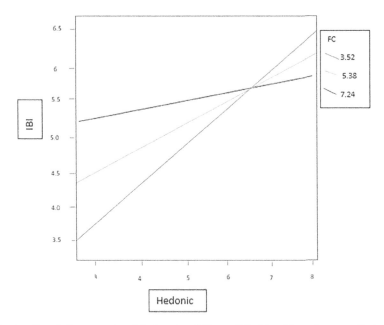

Fig. 4. Graph Representing Moderation Effect of Fashion Consciousness Between Impulse Buying Intention (IBI) and Hedonic Values. *Source*: Hayes process macros results.

hedonic values and IBI. There is a significant moderation effect for low, medium and high levels of FC. FC is also a significant moderator in the relationship between PSI and IBI (Fig. 5).

DISCUSSION

The study confirms a significant relationship between the hedonic motivation (to watch fashion vloggers) and the IBI of sustainable cosmetic products (*H1* supported; $\beta = 0.206$, $p < 0.05$). The relationship between the two key constructs – PSI and IBI – was also found to be significant (*H2* supported, $\beta = 0.457$, $p < 0.05$). These results agree with prior studies (Park & Lennon, 2006; Vazquez et al., 2020). Finally, hedonic motivation (to watch fashion vloggers) was also established to influence the formation of PSI (between the vlogger and the viewer) (*H3* supported, $\beta = 0.202$, $p < 0.05$). The results also illustrate a partial mediating role of PSI in the association between hedonic motivation and IBI of sustainable cosmetic products ($\beta = 0.118$, $p < 0.05$). It was also established that FC was a significant moderator in the present model on all three paths (*H4a*, *H4b* and *H4c* – all supported at $p < 0.05$) (Leeraphong & Sukrat, 2018; Xiang et al., 2016).

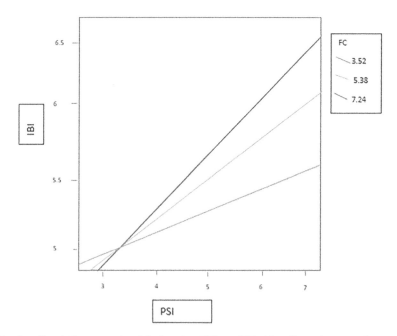

Fig. 5.   Graph Representing Moderation Effect of Fashion Consciousness Between Parasocial Interaction (PSI) and Impulse Buying Intention (IBI). *Source*: Hayes process macros results.

IMPLICATIONS

The present study contributes significantly to the extant literature on social media by bringing fresh insights into how vloggers can influence IBIs through a new communication medium. In the context of YouTube as a budding communication medium, this study highlights the importance of hedonic motivations and PSI in shaping IBI in the sustainable cosmetic industry through vloggers.

The results imply that creating an interactive relationship with female Gen Z consumers can help spur impulsive product purchases. Hedonic motivation has been suggested as a significant predictor of IBIs in prior literature (Chung et al., 2017; Rezaei et al., 2016). The present study confirms these findings in the fashion vlogging context. This would be helpful for fashion brands in the content development of their visual marketing communications, which would tap the female Gen Z consumer, who is high on hedonic motivation. Fun and enjoyment from watching a vlogger can be enhanced by improving the content delivered by the vlogger. Marketers should also consider whether the fashion vloggers they collaborate with can promote the product's hedonic value, which may be an essential phenomenon for the target consumers.

Furthermore, since Gen Z consumers are more involved in social media platforms, including YouTube, improving the PSI between the follower and the fashion vlogger can be easily enhanced by delivering the right content through the videos. Marketers in the fashion industry can select vloggers with similar profiles and target their viewers to strengthen PSI. Once the PSI is formed, triggering an impulse purchase when the consumer watches a video becomes easier. The vlogger can float a coupon code or a promotional offer with a link to purchase the product immediately when the video is over. This might aid in an impulse purchase reaction by the follower, and a transaction is made. Also, to trigger impulse purchases, passing information regarding new products or services through these vloggers to consumers regularly might help increase the sales of sustainable cosmetic product brands (Liu et al., 2013).

Finally, FC as a significant moderator can also be helpful for marketers and brands in the sustainable cosmetic industry. Females with higher FC depict stronger relationships between the model variables. Several innovative ways, such as organising online events that introduce the latest collections in the sustainable cosmetics market, would create excitement among female Gen Z fashion-conscious consumers who enjoy shopping for sustainable cosmetic products. Additionally, these special events can generate coupon codes for the first 100 registrations, which can be utilised in the next few hours to buy the products displayed in these online events. This would suffice a three-pronged objective, targeting impulse buyers in the sustainable cosmetic products market. Second, followers with strong PSI with the fashion vlogger would always try to participate in such events. Third, fashion-conscious consumers always want to add the newest collection to their wardrobes at an attractive price.

Further, technical tools like cookies or other online cues, frequently and effectively used in digital marketing on social media, could help identify YouTube users who are high on FC and create better-matched fashion vlog content. Finally, fast fashion brands can effectively target fashion-conscious, hedonic female buyers and indulge them in impulse purchases. FC has been suggested to be a significant consumer characteristic for fast-fashion brands. This individual characteristic inclines the customers towards the latest trends and makes them more interested in the latest fashion communications (Kaiser & Chandler, 1984; Kinley et al., 1999).

LIMITATIONS AND FUTURE SCOPE

The present research study considered only undergraduate students as we examined the behavioural aspects of Gen Z. Future studies can target a millennial sample or even baby boomers from the general population, adding further insights to the current body of knowledge. Further, although the sample size 349 was statistically sufficient to examine the proposed model, it may be enhanced for more generalised results. Additionally, the paper has considered Generation Z as the sample of respondents, which may have shown bias in their responses to portray socially and morally acceptable behaviour (Fischer et al., 2017). The present study does not emphasise any brand-specific behaviours in the context of PSI theory. Further examination focusing on specific brands of sustainable cosmetic products can provide exciting insights into the study topic. This work also attempts to elaborate on impulse buying behaviour in the context of sustainable cosmetic products only. Additional research can be conducted on varied product categories like entertainment, travel, food, etc., which are gaining popularity among YouTube users in the Indian market.

REFERENCES

Abbasi, A. Z., Ting, D. H., & Hlavacs, H. (2017). Engagement in games: developing an instrument to measure consumer videogame engagement and its validation. *International Journal of Computer Games Technology,* 2017.

Arviansyah, Dhaneswara, A. P., Hidayanto, A. N., & Zhu, Y. Q. (2018). Vlogging: Trigger to impulse buying behaviors. *PACIS, 3*(1), 249.

Badgaiyan, A. J., Dixit, S., & Verma, A. (2017). If brands are people, then people are impulsive – Assessing the connection between brand personality and impulsive buying behaviour. *Journal of Brand Management, 24*(6), 622–638.

Ballantine, D. S., White, R. M., & Martin, S. J. (2005). Tissue-Based. *Chemistry, 71*, 2205–2214.

Baron, J. (2020). The key to Gen Z is video content. *Forbes.* https://www.forbes.com/sites/jessicabaron/2019/07/03/the-key-to-gen-z-is-video content/#35c488d33484

Basuroy, T. (2022). Topic: Digital Advertising in India. *Statista.* Available: https://www.statista.com/topics/5831/digital-advertising-inindia/#topicOverview

Beatty, S. E., & Ferrell, M. E. (1998). Impulse buying: Modeling its precursors. *Journal of Retailing, 74*(2), 169–191.

de Bérail, P., Guillon, M., & Bungener, C. (2019). The relations between YouTube addiction, social anxiety and parasocial relationships with YouTubers: A moderated-mediation model based on a cognitive-behavioral framework. *Computers in Human Behavior, 99,*190–204.

Bucy, E. P., & Tao, C. C. (2007). The mediated moderation model of interactivity. *Media Psychology, 9*(3), 647–672.

Brown, W. J., & Basil, M. D. (2010). Parasocial interaction and identification: Social change processes for effective health interventions. *Health communication, 25*(6-7), 601–602.

Buss, D. M. (1985). Human mate selection: Opposites are sometimes said to attract, but in fact, we are likely to marry someone who is similar to us in almost every variable. *American Scientist*, *73*(1), 47–51.

Buss, D. M., & Craik, K. H. (1980). The frequency concept of disposition: Dominance and prototypically dominant acts 1. *Journal of Personality*, *48*(3), 379–392.

Byrne, B. M. (1998). *Structural equation modeling with LISREL, PRELIS, and SIMPLIS: Basic concepts, applications, and programming*. Lawrence Erlbaum Associates, Inc.

Chen, S. Y. (2016). Green helpfulness or fun? Influences of green perceived value on the green loyalty of users and non-users of public bikes. *Transport Policy*, *47*, 149–159.

Chen, T. Y., Yeh, T. L., & Lee, F. Y. (2021). The impact of Internet celebrity characteristics on followers' impulse purchase behavior: the mediation of attachment and parasocial interaction. *Journal of Research in Interactive Marketing*, *15*(3), 483–501.

Childers, T. L., Carr, C. L., Peck, J., & Carson, S. (2001). Hedonic and utilitarian motivations for online retail shopping behaviour. *Journal of Retailing*, *77*(4), 511–535.

Chung, N., Song, H. G., & Lee, H. (2017). Consumers' impulsive buying behavior of restaurant products in social commerce. *International Journal of Contemporary Hospitality Management*, *29*(2), 709–731.

Coughlin, J. (2018). Gen Z graduates into a new world of work, here is why you should care. Retrieved April 22, 2020, from https://www.forbes.com/sites/josephcoughlin/2018/05/27/gen-z-graduates-into-a-new-world-of-work-here-is-why-should-you-should-care/#372206804ab7

Daniel, E. S., Jr, Crawford Jackson, E. C., & Westerman, D. K. (2018). The influence of social media influencers: Understanding online vaping communities and parasocial interaction through the lens of Taylor's six-segment strategy wheel. *Journal of Interactive Advertising*, *18*(2), 96–109.

Dey, D. K., & Srivastava, A. (2017). Impulse buying intentions of young consumers from a hedonic shopping perspective.*Journal of Indian Business Research*, *9*(4), 266–282.

Dibble, J. L., Hartmann, T., & Rosaen, S. F. (2016). Parasocial interaction and parasocial relationship: Conceptual clarification and a critical assessment of measures. *Human Communication Research*, *42*(1), 21–44.

Dimock, M. (2019). Defining generations: Where millennials end, and generation Z begins. *Pew Research Center*, *17*(1), 1–7.

Fenigstein, A., Scheier, M. F., & Buss, A. H. (1975). Public and private self-consciousness: Assessment and theory. *Journal of Consulting and Clinical Psychology*, *43*(4), 522.

Fischer, D., Böhme, T., & Geiger, S. M. (2017). Measuring young consumers' sustainable consumption behavior: Development and validation of the YCSCB scale. *Young Consumers*, *18*(3), 312–326.

Gao, L., Norton, M. J., Zhang, Z. M., & Kin-man To, C. (2009). Potential niche markets for luxury fashion goods in China. *Journal of Fashion Marketing and Management: An International Journal*, *13*(4), 514–526.

Gefen, D., Rigdon, E. E., & Straub, D. (2011). Editor's comments: an update and extension to SEM guidelines for administrative and social science research. *MIS quarterly*, iii–xiv.

Gehrt, K. C., Onzo, N., Fujita, K., & Rajan, M. N. (2007). The emergence of Internet shopping in Japan: Identification of shopping orientation-defined segments. *Journal of Marketing Theory and Practice*, *15*(2), 167–177.

Geyser, W. (2022). The State of Influencer Marketing 2022: Benchmark Report. *Influencer Marketing Hub*. Retrived from: https://influencermarketinghub.com/influencer-marketing-benchmark-report/ on January 2021.

Giles, D. C. (2002). Parasocial interaction: A review of the literature and a model for future research. *Media Psychology*, *4*(3), 279–305.

Gould, S. J., & Stern, B. B. (1989). Gender schema and fashion consciousness. *Psychology & Marketing*, *6*(2), 129–145.

Han, H., Lee, M. J., & Kim, W. (2018). Role of shopping quality, hedonic/utilitarian shopping experiences, trust, satisfaction and perceived barriers in triggering customer post-purchase intentions at airports. *International Journal of Contemporary Hospitality Management*, *30*(10), 3059–3082.

Haobin Ye, B., Fong, L. H. N., & Luo, J. M. (2021). Parasocial interaction on tourism companies' social media sites: Antecedents and consequences. *Current Issues in Tourism*, *24*(8), 1093–1108.

Hassan, S. H., & Harun, H. (2016). Factors influencing fashion consciousness in hijab fashion consumption among hijabistas. *Journal of Islamic Marketing*, *7*(4), 476–494.

Hayes, J. R. (2013). *The complete problem solver*. Routledge.

Hayes, A. F. (2015). An index and test of linear moderated mediation. *Multivariate Behavioural Research*, *50*(1), 1–22.

Hayes, A. F., Montoya, A. K., & Rockwood, N. J. (2017). The analysis of mechanisms and their contingencies: PROCESS versus structural equation modelling. *Australasian Marketing Journal*, *25*(1), 76–81.

Holbrook, M. B., & Hirschman, E. C. (1982). The experiential aspects of consumption: Consumer fantasies, feelings, and fun. *Journal of Consumer Research*, *9*(2), 132–140.

Horton, D., & Richard Wohl, R. (1956). Mass communication and parasocial interaction: Observations on intimacy at a distance. *Psychiatry*, *19*(3), 215–229.

Hsu, C. L. (2020). How vloggers embrace their viewers: Focusing on the roles of para-social interactions and flow experience. *Telematics and Informatics*, *49*(4), 101364.

Kaiser, S. B., & Chandler, J. L. (1984). Fashion alienation: Older adults and the mass media. *International Journal of Aging & Human Development*, *19*(3), 203–221.

Kaur, H., & Anand, S. (2018). Segmenting generation Y using the Big Five personality traits: understanding differences in fashion consciousness, status consumption and materialism. *Young Consumers*, *19*(4), 382–401.

Kautish, P., & Sharma, R. (2018). Consumer values, fashion consciousness and behavioural intentions in the online fashion retail sector. *International Journal of Retail & Distribution Management*, *46*(10), 894–914.

Khuong, M. N., & Tran, T. B. (2015). Factors affecting impulse buying toward fashion products in Ho Chi Minh City – A mediation analysis of hedonic purchase. *International Journal of Trade, Economics and Finance*, *6*(4), 223–229.

Kinley, T. L., Conrad, C. A., & Brown, G. (1999). Internal and external promotional references: An examination of gender and product involvement effects in the retail apparel setting. *Journal of Retailing and Consumer Services*, *6*(1), 39–44.

Klimmt, C., Schmid, H., Nosper, A., Hartmann, T., & Vorderer, P. (2006). How players manage moral concerns to make video game violence enjoyable. *Communications*, *309*–328.

Labrecque, L. I. (2014). Fostering consumer–brand relationships in social media environments: The role of parasocial interaction. *Journal of Interactive Marketing*, *28*(2), 134–148.

Ladhari, R., Massa, E., & Skandrani, H. (2020). YouTube vloggers' popularity and influence: The roles of homophily, emotional attachment, and expertise. *Journal of Retailing and Consumer Services*, *54(3)*, 102027.

Ledbetter, A. M., & Redd, S. M. (2016). Celebrity credibility on social media: A conditional process analysis of online self-disclosure attitude as a moderator of posting frequency and parasocial interaction. *Western Journal of Communication*, *80*(5), 601–618.

Lee, J. E., & Watkins, B. (2016). YouTube vloggers' influence on consumer luxury brand perceptions and intentions. *Journal of Business Research*, *69*(12), 5753–5760.

Leeraphong, A., & Sukrat, S. (2018, August). How Facebook live urges S.N.S. users to buy impulsively on C2C social commerce? In *Proceedings of the 2nd international conference on E-society, E-education and E-technology* (pp. 68–72).

Leung, A. C., Yee, R. W., & Lo, E. S. (2015). Psychological and social factors of fashion consciousness: An empirical study in the luxury fashion market. *Research Journal of Textile and Apparel*, *19*(3), 58–69.

Leverett, A. K. (2016). Impacts Of Visual Aesthetics And Hedonic Experience On Intent To Purchase Sustainable Beauty Products. Unpublished thesis. Texas State University, San Marcos, Texas.

Levy, M. R., & Windahl, S. (1984). Audience activity and gratifications: A conceptual clarification and exploration. *Communication Research*, *11*(1), 51–78.

Lin, H. C., Bruning, P. F., & Swarna, H. (2018). Using online opinion leaders to promote the hedonic and utilitarian value of products and services. *Business Horizons*, *61*(3), 431–442.

Lin, M. H., Vijayalakshmi, A., & Laczniak, R. (2019). Toward an understanding of parental views and actions on social media influencers targeted at adolescents: The roles of parents' social media use and empowerment. *Frontiers in Psychology*, *10*, 2664.

Liu, Y., Li, H., & Hu, F. (2013). Website attributes in urging online impulse purchase: An empirical investigation on consumer perceptions. *Decision Support Systems*, *55*(3), 829–837.

Liu, M. T., Liu, Y., & Zhang, L. L. (2019). Vlog and brand evaluations: The influence of parasocial interaction. *Asia Pacific Journal of Marketing and Logistics, 31*(2), 419–436.

MacCallum, R. C., Browne, M. W., & Sugawara, H. M. (1996). Power analysis and determination of sample size for covariance structure modeling. *Psychological Methods, 1*(2), 130.

Milewski, J. A. (2005). *Fashion and the culture of consumption: Perceptions of fashion trends among college students* [Doctoral dissertation]. State University of New York at Buffalo.

Misra, P., & Mukherjee, A. (2019). YouTuber icons: An analysis of the impact on buying behaviour of young consumers. *International Journal of Business Competition and Growth, 6*(4), 330–345.

Mullen, C. Almost 1 in 4 Gen Z women typically learn about new products via influencers. *Bizjournals. Com.* https://www.bizjournals.com/bizwomen/news/latest-news/2019/11/almost-1-in-4-gen-z-women-typically-learn-about.html?page=all

Nam, J., Hamlin, R., Gam, H. J., Kang, J. H., Kim, J., Kumphai, P., Starr, C., & Richards, L. (2007). The fashion-conscious behaviours of mature female consumers. *International Journal of Consumer Studies, 31*(1), 102–108.

Nuseir, M. T. (2020). The extent of the influences of social media in creating impulse buying tendencies. *International Journal of Business Innovation and Research, 21*(3), 324–335.

Ozkara, B. Y., Ozmen, M., & Kim, J. W. (2017). Examining the effect of flow experience on online purchase: A novel approach to the flow theory based on hedonic and utilitarian value. *Journal of Retailing and Consumer Services, 37*, 119–131.

Palmgreen, P., Wenner, L. A., & Rayburn, J. D. (1980). Relations between gratifications sought and obtained: A study of television news. *Communication Research, 7*(2), 161–192.

Park, E. J. (2005). Analysis of structural equation model on impulse buying behavior for fashion products. *Journal of the Korean Society of Clothing and Textiles, 29*(9), 1306-1315.

Park, J. H. (2019). A study on mobile video usage of Generation Z in the Republic of Korea based on the grounded theory-focused on YouTube. *Journal of Communication Design, 67*, 313–329.

Park, J. H., & Lennon, S. J. (2004). Television apparel shopping: Impulse buying and parasocial interaction. *Clothing and Textiles Research Journal, 22*(3), 135–144.

Park, J., & Lennon, S. J. (2006). Psychological and environmental antecedents of impulse buying tendency in the multichannel shopping context. *Journal of Consumer Marketing, 23*(2), 56–66.

Parker, R. S., Hermans, C. M., & Schaefer, A. D. (2004). Fashion consciousness of Chinese, Japanese and American teenagers. *Journal of Fashion Marketing and Management: An International Journal, 8*(2), 176–186.

Pentecost, R., & Andrews, L. (2010). Fashion retailing and the bottom line: The effects of generational cohorts, gender, fashion fanship, attitudes and impulse buying on fashion expenditure. *Journal of Retailing and Consumer Services, 17*(1), 43–52.

Podsakoff, P. M., MacKenzie, S. B., Lee, J. Y., & Podsakoff, N. P. (2003). Common method biases in behavioural research: A critical review of the literature and recommended remedies. *Journal of Applied Psychology, 88*(5), 879.

Quelhas-Brito, P., Brandão, A., Gadekar, M., & Castelo-Branco, S. (2020). Diffusing fashion information by social media fashion influencers: Understanding antecedents and consequences. *Journal of Fashion Marketing and Management: An International Journal, 24*(2), 137–152.

Rasmussen, L. (2018). Parasocial interaction in the digital age: An examination of relationship building and the effectiveness of YouTube celebrities. *The Journal of Social Media in Society, 7*(1), 280–294.

Rasmussen, E. E., & Ewoldsen, D. R. (2016). Treatment via television: The relation between watching Dr. Phil and viewers' intentions to seek mental health treatment. *Journal of health communication, 21*(6), 611–619.

Reinikainen, H., Munnukka, J., Maity, D., & Luoma-aho, V. (2020). 'You are a great big sister' – Parasocial relationships, credibility, and the moderating role of audience comments in influencer marketing. *Journal of Marketing Management, 36*(3–4), 279–298.

Rezaei, S., Ali, F., Amin, M., & Jayashree, S. (2016). Online impulse buying of tourism products. *Journal of Hospitality and Tourism Technology, 7*(1), 60–83.

Rook, D. W., & Fisher, R. J. (1995). Normative influences on impulsive buying behavior. *Journal of Consumer Research, 22*(3), 305–313.

Rosnow, R. L., & Rosenthal, R. (1991). If you're looking at the cell means, you're not looking at *only* the interaction (unless all main effects are zero). *Psychological Bulletin, 110*(3), 574–576.

Rubin, R. B., & McHugh, M. P. (1987). Development of parasocial interaction relationship. *Journal of Broadcasting & Electronic Media,31,*279.

Savelli, E., Cioppi, M., & Tombari, F. (2017). Web atmospherics as drivers of shopping centres' customer loyalty. *International Journal of Retail & Distribution Management, 45*(11), 1213–1240.

Scheier, M. F. (1976). Self-awareness, self-consciousness, and angry aggression 1. *Journal of Personality, 44*(4), 627–644.

Song, H. G., Chung, N., & Koo, C. (2015). Impulsive buying behavior of restaurant products in social commerce: A role of serendipity and scarcity message. In A. Kankanhalli, A. B. Jones & T. Teo (Eds.), *PACIS 2015 proceedings* (p. 113). http://aisel.aisnet.org/pacis2015/113

Sprotles, G. B., & Kendall, E. L. (1986). A methodology for profiling consumers' decision-making styles. *Journal of Consumer Affairs, 20*(2), 267–279.

Statista. (2022b). Number of Smartphone Subscriptions Worldwide from 2016 to 2027. Accessed April 24. https://www.statista.com/statistics/330695/number-of-smartphone-users-worldwide/.

Stern, B. B., Russell, C. A., & Russell, D. W. (2007). Hidden persuasions in soap operas: Damaged heroines and negative consumer effects. *International Journal of Advertising, 26*(1), 9–36.

Stever, G. S., & Lawson, K. (2013). Twitter as a way for celebrities to communicate with fans: Implications for the study of parasocial interaction. *North American Journal of Psychology, 15*(2), 339–354.

Szymanski, D. M., & Hise, R. T. (2000). E-satisfaction: An initial examination. *Journal of Retailing, 76*(3), 309–322.

Titze, S., Stronegger, W. J., Janschitz, S., & Oja, P. (2008). Association of built-environment, social-environment and personal factors with bicycling as a mode of transportation among Austrian city dwellers. *Preventive Medicine, 47*(3), 252–259.

Vazquez, D., Wu, X., Nguyen, B., Kent, A., Gutierrez, A., & Chen, T. (2020). Investigating narrative involvement, parasocial interactions, and impulse buying behaviours within a second screen social commerce context. *International Journal of Information Management, 53*(4), 102135.

Wells, W. D., & Tigert, D. J. (1971). Activities, interests and opinions. *Journal of Advertising Research, 11*(4), 27–35.

Wiranata, A. T., & Hananto, A. (2020). Do website quality, fashion consciousness, and sales promotion increase the impulse buying behavior of e-commerce buyers? *Indonesian Journal of Business and Entrepreneurship, 6*(1), 74–74.

Workman, J. E., & Caldwell, L. F. (2007). Centrality of visual product aesthetics, tactile and uniqueness needs of fashion consumers. *International Journal of consumer studies, 31*(6), 589–596.

Xiang, L., Zheng, X., Lee, M. K., & Zhao, D. (2016). Exploring consumers' impulse buying behavior on social commerce platform: The role of parasocial interaction. *International Journal of Information Management, 36*(3), 333–347.

Yu, C., & Bastin, M. (2017). Hedonic shopping value and impulse buying behaviour in transitional economies: A symbiosis in the Mainland China marketplace. In *Advances in Chinese brand management* (pp. 316–330). Palgrave Macmillan.

Yu, X., Kim, K., & Wang, S. (2019, July). The influence of live streaming service of web celebrity on consumer impulsive buying behavior. In *2019 Global fashion management conference, Paris* (p. 700).

Yuan, C. L., Kim, J., & Kim, S. J. (2016). Parasocial relationship effects on customer equity in the social media context. *Journal of Business Research, 69*(9), 3795–3803.

Zheng, X., Men, J., Yang, F., & Gong, X. (2019). Understanding impulse buying in mobile commerce: An investigation into hedonic and utilitarian browsing. *International Journal of Information Management, 48*, 151–160.

INDEX

Printed and bound by CPI Group (UK) Ltd, Croydon, CR0 4YY

07/05/2024

14498921-0001